Marina Lebedeva

RUSSIAN STUDIES OF INTERNATIONAL RELATIONS

From the Soviet Past to the Post-Cold-War Present

With a foreword by Andrei P. Tsygankov

ibidem-Verlag
Stuttgart

Bibliografische Information der Deutschen Nationalbibliothek
Die Deutsche Nationalbibliothek verzeichnet diese Publikation in der Deutschen Nationalbibliografie; detaillierte bibliografische Daten sind im Internet über http://dnb.d-nb.de abrufbar.

Bibliographic information published by the Deutsche Nationalbibliothek
Die Deutsche Nationalbibliothek lists this publication in the Deutsche Nationalbibliografie; detailed bibliographic data are available in the Internet at http://dnb.d-nb.de.

Cover picture: MGIMO Building, Moscow. © copyright 2011 by Igor Lileev. Printed with kind permission.

Gedruckt auf alterungsbeständigem, säurefreien Papier
Printed on acid-free paper

ISSN: 1614-3515

ISBN-13: 978-3-8382-0851-0

© *ibidem*-Verlag
Stuttgart 2018

Alle Rechte vorbehalten

Das Werk einschließlich aller seiner Teile ist urheberrechtlich geschützt. Jede Verwertung außerhalb der engen Grenzen des Urheberrechtsgesetzes ist ohne Zustimmung des Verlages unzulässig und strafbar. Dies gilt insbesondere für Vervielfältigungen, Übersetzungen, Mikroverfilmungen und elektronische Speicherformen sowie die Einspeicherung und Verarbeitung in elektronischen Systemen.

All rights part of this publication may be reproduced, stored in or introduced into a retrieval system, or transmitted, in any form, or by any means (electronical, mechanical, photocopying, recording or otherwise) without the prior written permission of the publisher. Any person who does any unauthorized act in relation to this publication may be liable to criminal prosecution and civil claims for damages.

Printed in the EU

Soviet and Post-Soviet Politics and Society (SPPS) Vol. 187
ISSN 1614-3515

General Editor: Andreas Umland,
Institute for Euro-Atlantic Cooperation, Kyiv, umland@stanfordalumni.org

Commissioning Editor: Max Jakob Horstmann,
London, mjh@ibidem.eu

EDITORIAL COMMITTEE*

DOMESTIC & COMPARATIVE POLITICS
Prof. **Ellen Bos**, *Andrássy University of Budapest*
Dr. **Ingmar Bredies**, *FH Bund, Brühl*
Dr. **Andrey Kazantsev**, *MGIMO (U) MID RF, Moscow*
Prof. **Heiko Pleines**, *University of Bremen*
Prof. **Richard Sakwa**, *University of Kent at Canterbury*
Dr. **Sarah Whitmore**, *Oxford Brookes University*
Dr. **Harald Wydra**, *University of Cambridge*

SOCIETY, CLASS & ETHNICITY
Col. **David Glantz**, *"Journal of Slavic Military Studies"*
Dr. **Marlène Laruelle**, *George Washington University*
Dr. **Stephen Shulman**, *Southern Illinois University*
Prof. **Stefan Troebst**, *University of Leipzig*

POLITICAL ECONOMY & PUBLIC POLICY
Prof. em. **Marshall Goldman**, *Wellesley College, Mass.*
Dr. **Andreas Goldthau**, *Central European University*
Dr. **Robert Kravchuk**, *University of North Carolina*
Dr. **David Lane**, *University of Cambridge*
Dr. **Carol Leonard**, *Higher School of Economics, Moscow*
Dr. **Maria Popova**, *McGill University, Montreal*

FOREIGN POLICY & INTERNATIONAL AFFAIRS
Dr. **Peter Duncan**, *University College London*
Prof. **Andreas Heinemann-Grüder**, *University of Bonn*
Dr. **Taras Kuzio**, *Johns Hopkins University*
Prof. **Gerhard Mangott**, *University of Innsbruck*
Dr. **Diana Schmidt-Pfister**, *University of Konstanz*
Dr. **Lisbeth Tarlow**, *Harvard University, Cambridge*
Dr. **Christian Wipperfürth**, *N-Ost Network, Berlin*
Dr. **William Zimmerman**, *University of Michigan*

HISTORY, CULTURE & THOUGHT
Dr. **Catherine Andreyev**, *University of Oxford*
Prof. **Mark Bassin**, *Södertörn University*
Prof. **Karsten Brüggemann**, *Tallinn University*
Dr. **Alexander Etkind**, *University of Cambridge*
Dr. **Gasan Gusejnov**, *Moscow State University*
Prof. em. **Walter Laqueur**, *Georgetown University*
Prof. **Leonid Luks**, *Catholic University of Eichstaett*
Dr. **Olga Malinova**, *Russian Academy of Sciences*
Prof. **Andrei Rogatchevski**, *University of Tromsø*
Dr. **Mark Tauger**, *West Virginia University*

ADVISORY BOARD*

Prof. **Dominique Arel**, *University of Ottawa*
Prof. **Jörg Baberowski**, *Humboldt University of Berlin*
Prof. **Margarita Balmaceda**, *Seton Hall University*
Dr. **John Barber**, *University of Cambridge*
Prof. **Timm Beichelt**, *European University Viadrina*
Dr. **Katrin Boeckh**, *University of Munich*
Prof. em. **Archie Brown**, *University of Oxford*
Dr. **Vyacheslav Bryukhovetsky**, *Kyiv-Mohyla Academy*
Prof. **Timothy Colton**, *Harvard University, Cambridge*
Prof. **Paul D'Anieri**, *University of Florida*
Dr. **Heike Dörrenbächer**, *Friedrich Naumann Foundation*
Dr. **John Dunlop**, *Hoover Institution, Stanford, California*
Dr. **Sabine Fischer**, *SWP, Berlin*
Dr. **Geir Flikke**, *NUPI, Oslo*
Prof. **David Galbreath**, *University of Aberdeen*
Prof. **Alexander Galkin**, *Russian Academy of Sciences*
Prof. **Frank Golczewski**, *University of Hamburg*
Dr. **Nikolas Gvosdev**, *Naval War College, Newport, RI*
Prof. **Mark von Hagen**, *Arizona State University*
Dr. **Guido Hausmann**, *University of Munich*
Prof. **Dale Herspring**, *Kansas State University*
Dr. **Stefani Hoffman**, *Hebrew University of Jerusalem*
Prof. **Mikhail Ilyin**, *MGIMO (U) MID RF, Moscow*
Prof. **Vladimir Kantor**, *Higher School of Economics*
Dr. **Ivan Katchanovski**, *University of Ottawa*
Prof. em. **Andrzej Korbonski**, *University of California*
Dr. **Iris Kempe**, *"Caucasus Analytical Digest"*
Prof. **Herbert Küpper**, *Institut für Ostrecht Regensburg*
Dr. **Rainer Lindner**, *CEEER, Berlin*
Dr. **Vladimir Malakhov**, *Russian Academy of Sciences*

Dr. **Luke March**, *University of Edinburgh*
Prof. **Michael McFaul**, *Stanford University, Palo Alto*
Prof. **Birgit Menzel**, *University of Mainz-Germersheim*
Prof. **Valery Mikhailenko**, *The Urals State University*
Prof. **Emil Pain**, *Higher School of Economics, Moscow*
Dr. **Oleg Podvintsev**, *Russian Academy of Sciences*
Prof. **Olga Popova**, *St. Petersburg State University*
Dr. **Alex Pravda**, *University of Oxford*
Dr. **Erik van Ree**, *University of Amsterdam*
Dr. **Joachim Rogall**, *Robert Bosch Foundation Stuttgart*
Prof. **Peter Rutland**, *Wesleyan University, Middletown*
Prof. **Marat Salikov**, *The Urals State Law Academy*
Dr. **Gwendolyn Sasse**, *University of Oxford*
Prof. **Jutta Scherrer**, *EHESS, Paris*
Prof. **Robert Service**, *University of Oxford*
Mr. **James Sherr**, *RIIA Chatham House London*
Dr. **Oxana Shevel**, *Tufts University, Medford*
Prof. **Eberhard Schneider**, *University of Siegen*
Prof. **Olexander Shnyrkov**, *Shevchenko University, Kyiv*
Prof. **Hans-Henning Schröder**, *SWP, Berlin*
Prof. **Yuri Shapoval**, *Ukrainian Academy of Sciences*
Prof. **Viktor Shnirelman**, *Russian Academy of Sciences*
Dr. **Lisa Sundstrom**, *University of British Columbia*
Dr. **Philip Walters**, *"Religion, State and Society"*, *Oxford*
Prof. **Zenon Wasyliw**, *Ithaca College, New York State*
Dr. **Lucan Way**, *University of Toronto*
Dr. **Markus Wehner**, *"Frankfurter Allgemeine Zeitung"*
Dr. **Andrew Wilson**, *University College London*
Prof. **Jan Zielonka**, *University of Oxford*
Prof. **Andrei Zorin**, *University of Oxford*

* While the Editorial Committee and Advisory Board support the General Editor in the choice and improvement of manuscripts for publication, responsibility for remaining errors and misinterpretations in the series' volumes lies with the books' authors.

Soviet and Post-Soviet Politics and Society (SPPS)
ISSN 1614-3515

Founded in 2004 and refereed since 2007, SPPS makes available affordable English-, German-, and Russian-language studies on the history of the countries of the former Soviet bloc from the late Tsarist period to today. It publishes between 5 and 20 volumes per year and focuses on issues in transitions to and from democracy such as economic crisis, identity formation, civil society development, and constitutional reform in CEE and the NIS. SPPS also aims to highlight so far understudied themes in East European studies such as right-wing radicalism, religious life, higher education, or human rights protection. The authors and titles of all previously published volumes are listed at the end of this book. For a full description of the series and reviews of its books, see www.ibidem-verlag.de/red/spps. **Editorial correspondence & manuscripts** should be sent to: Dr. Andreas Umland, Institute for Euro-Atlantic Cooperation, vul. Volodymyrska 42, off. 21, UA-01030 Kyiv, Ukraine **Business correspondence & review copy requests** should be sent to: *ibidem* Press, Leuschnerstr. 40, 30457 Hannover, Germany; tel.: +49 511 2622200; fax: +49 511 2622201; spps@ibidem.eu. **Authors, reviewers, referees, and editors** for (as well as all other persons sympathetic to) SPPS are invited to join its networks at www.facebook.com/group.php?gid=52638198614 www.linkedin.com/groups?about=&gid=103012 www.xing.com/net/spps-ibidem-verlag/	**Recent Volumes** 179 Mikhail Minakov Development and Dystopia Studies in Post-Soviet Ukraine and Eastern Europe With a foreword by Alexander Etkind ISBN 978-3-8382-1112-1 180 Aijan Sharshenova The European Union's Democracy Promotion in Central Asia A Study of Political Interests, Influence, and Development in Kazakhstan and Kyrgyzstan in 2007–2013 With a foreword by Gordon Crawford ISBN 978-3-8382-1151-0 181 Andrey Makarychev, Alexandra Yatsyk (eds.) Boris Nemtsov and Russian Politics Power and Resistance With a foreword by Zhanna Nemtsova ISBN 978-3-8382-1122-0 182 Sophie Falsini The Euromaidan's Effect on Civil Society Why and How Ukrainian Social Capital Increased after the Revolution of Dignity With a foreword by Susann Worschech ISBN 978-3-8382-1131-2 183 Andreas Umland (ed.) Ukraine's Decentralization Challenges and Implications of the Local Governance Reform after the Euromaidan Revolution ISBN 978-3-8382-1162-6 184 Leonid Luks A Fateful Triangle Essays on Contemporary Russian, German and Polish History ISBN 978-3-8382-1143-5 185 John B. Dunlop The February 2015 Assassination of Boris Nemtsov and the Flawed Trial of his Alleged Killers An Exploration of Russia's "Crime of the 21st Century" With a foreword by Vladimir Kara-Murza ISBN 978-3-8382-1188-6 186 Vasile Rotaru Russia, the EU, and the Eastern Partnership Building Bridges or Digging Trenches? ISBN 978-3-8382-1134-3 187 Marina Lebedeva Russian Studies of International Relations From the Soviet Past to the Post-Cold-War Present With a foreword by Andrei P. Tsygankov ISBN 978-3-8382-0851-0

Contents

Foreword 9

Introduction 13

Part 1
Background of the Development of Russian IR Studies

Chapter 1
Why Is It Important to Understand the Development of Russian IR Studies? 17

    1.1 Political Organization of the World: IR Studies at the Crossroads 17

    1.2 The Place of Russia in the Political Transformation of the World 27

Chapter 2
The Soviet Period in the Development of IR Studies: The Influence of the Past 31

    2.1 Formation of IR Studies in the USSR 31

        2.1.1 Establishment of the First Centers of IR Studies . 31

        2.1.2 Historical and Oriental Schools: Contribution to IR Studies 34

    2.2 The Development of IR Studies in the USSR after World War II 36

        2.2.1 Development of Organizational Forms of Studying International Relations 36

        2.2.2 Shifts in Theoretical Foundations and IR Issues . 39

        2.2.3 The Main Characteristics of Soviet Research in the Field of International Relations 48

Chapter 3
The Establishment of IR Studies in Contemporary Russia 53
 3.1 Trends in Russian IR Studies in the Late 1980s 53
   3.1.1 The "New Political Thinking" and Its Impact on International Relations 53
   3.1.2 A Change in the Content of International Studies in the Years of *Perestroika* 57
 3.2 Institutional Changes in IR Studies (1990s and Later) 60
   3.2.1 Research Centers, IR Association, and New Journals 60
   3.2.2 Regional Dimensions of IR Studies in Russia 67

Chapter 4
Education in the Field of International Relations 73
 4.1 The Teaching of International Relations in the Soviet Union 73
 4.2 Teaching International Relations in the Post-Soviet Period 79
 4.3 Contemporary Issues and Challenges in Teaching International Relations 87

Part 2
The Current State of IR Studies in Russia

Chapter 5
Theoretical Research in the Field of International Relations 95
 5.1 The Place of Theoretical Research in Russian IR Studies 95
 5.2 Theoretical Foundations of Russian IR Studies 97
 5.3 Theoretical Attitudes Toward International Relations in Russia 104

Chapter 6
Security Issues in Russian IR Studies 113

    6.1 New Aspects of International Security in Russian IR Studies After the End of the Cold War 113

    6.2 Relations Between Russia and NATO, the Issue of Nonproliferation and Arms Control 116

    6.3 Conflicts and Peacemaking 121

    6.4 Terrorism and the Problems of Countering Terrorism. 126

    6.5 Studies of Information (Cyber) Security in Russia 131

Chapter 7
The Economic Component of Russian IR Studies 135

    7.1 Directions of Russian Studies in the Field of International Political Economy 135

    7.2 Economic Crises and Their Impact on World Politics .. 142

    7.3 Energy Issues in Russian IR Studies 147

Chapter 8
Development of Social and Humanitarian Issues in Russian IR Studies 151

    8.1 The Growth of Social and Humanitarian Components in World Politics 151

    8.2 Russian Attention to Social and Humanitarian Issues . 154

    8.3 Soft Power and Public Diplomacy in Russian IR Studies 156

    8.4 Analysis of Human Capital in Russian IR Studies 162

Conclusion 165

Bibliography 169

Annex 207

    Main abbreviations 207

    Titles of Russian journals 209

Foreword

Studying international relations (IR) requires understanding several principal points. First, any IR study aims to contribute to a rationally developed worldview with clearly established relationships among its various dimensions and components. Every scholar seeks to understand the object of his attention in its utmost wholeness and completeness. An IR scholar, whichever his subject of interest may be, must be interested in uncovering larger layers and implications behind his or her research. This is even more applicable to IR theory, which is concerned with understanding issues of global significance, such as structure of the international system, causes of war, and rules of world order.

The second key point is that studying IR is rooted in national and sociocultural conditions. Any science, including the science of IR, is based on certain historical and cultural assumptions about the world that are common for a particular region from which such science originates. From this perspective, any search for objectivity and rationality, however important, takes place within socially and politically determined boundaries. For example, the intellectual dominance of the Western IR has been possible to the extent acceptable by non-Western cultures. The more the world experiences the rise of non-Western cultures and traditions, the more likely we are to observe challenges posed to the Western idea of rationality.

Finally, as an inherently cultural phenomenon, successful IR research involves a critical dialogue among scholars in national and global contexts. As the search for rationality and objectivity is culturally contested, it is essential to constantly compare various locally developed worldviews. It is only in the process of such dialogue that genuinely global insights, ideas, and theories can emerge, thereby empowering humanity with broadly shared practical solutions for preventing the world from crises and wars.

Russian IR studies develop with these points in mind. Russian scholars commonly test their theoretical and empirical analyses of global issues in various international and domestic settings. Out of its historical interaction with the outside world, Russia has developed three distinct schools of thinking—Westernist, Statist, and Civilizationist. Westernizers view the West and its institutions as the most viable and progressive in the world by calling Russia to emulate Western nations and by placing emphasis on Russia's similarity with them. Statists stress values of a strong independent state, the state's ability to govern and preserve the social and political order. While not inherently anti-Western, Statists value Russia's sovereignty and power and seek their recognition by the outside world. Finally, Civilizationists make sense of the world in terms of relations among different cultures and civilizations viewing Russia as principally distinct from the West. Members of these intellectual schools debate their positions with each other and abroad, thereby contributing to development of IR in Russia and overcoming dangers associated with the so-called "clash of civilizations."

The book by Marina M. Lebedeva, a leading Western-minded IR scholar in Russia, is important in at least two respects. First, the book helps to fill a large gap by systematically describing and generalizing from the rich and diverse experience of Russian IR development over the last century. This is indeed the first book of such genre and it should stimulate the discussion about shortcomings and achievements of international studies in Russia. Lebedeva traces developments of Russian IR since the Soviet era, considering and analyzing its various contexts and complexities. The author takes a historiographic approach assessing various scientific directions and research programs in appropriate intellectual and historical settings. In particular, Lebedeva provides a detailed analysis of the social and political origins of IR in the Soviet period, and she devotes considerable room to describing various developments by contemporary Russian scholars in the areas of theory, international security, political economy, sociohumanitarian issues, and regional studies.

The second reason why this book should be read by scholars of Russia and IR in general is that the book invites us to continue the discussion and dialogue over some, in principle, important issues of the development of IR. Striving to be objective in her analysis, Lebedeva does not shy away from expressing her own positions as she does with respect to geopolitics, the Russian official worldview, principles of producing scholarly knowledge, and the prospects of national schools in IR theory. Lebedeva's position is that of a Westernizer who believes in IR theories' universal appeal, and she remains critical of geopolitics and national theoretical schools as largely incompatible with modern conditions and the principles of globalization.

It is important to continue the discussion of these issues. Scholars, including myself, have had opportunities to argue a differing viewpoint. Globalization should not be viewed as impeding pluralistic developments within and outside of the Western world. The problem is partly related to the fact that globalization is in the process of unravelling as the world order is being currently challenged and transformed. The more important point is that the globalization we know has been largely shaped and defined by America and American IR scholars who have sought to present their theories as universally applicable. Searching for universality and objectivity, many IR scholars – including grand theorists – nevertheless have developed world views that are consistent with their country's needs and interests. From this perspective, Lebedeva's selection of Russian IR as the subject of investigation contributes to our understanding of knowledge boundaries in her own country, for Russian approaches to understanding global issues will ultimately bear a national imprint.

The desire to build "universal" theories is common today not only for American and European IR, but for those of China, India, and other rising powers. This is only natural for any large culture and national state tends to produce its knowledge as "objective" when it reaches a certain level of development and ambition to define the outside world. In this respect, every large culture has an "imperial" intellectual ambition. Post-Soviet Russia, too, is likely to eventually move from producing narrow and specialized knowledge to the one that is more general and theoretical and therefore helpful in positioning the country in the increasingly multipolar and multicultural world.

One can hope that Russia is getting closer to the stage of debating the mentioned theoretical issues. Reaching clarity with respect to goals and tasks of Russian IR and its national boundaries is necessary for developing an active and fruitful dialogue with foreign colleagues. In the world of coexisting world orders and socio-mental systems, comparing and reconciling diverse world views remains a constant challenge. Each such system is rooted in its own cultural and epistemological context and therefore possesses certain boundaries of knowledge. These boundaries, while sometimes invisible, are nevertheless real and demand to be recognized. A major task of IR scholars is not only to study different mental systems and worldviews, but to compare and juxtapose these for the purpose of discovering points of their compatibility in the interests of a greater stability and peace in the global world.

Andrei P. Tsygankov
July 2018

Introduction

The task of writing a book about the development and current state of international studies in Russia is not only difficult, but also — to some extent — it is impossible, at least for one person, because material that is too extensive and heterogeneous must be covered, and to be an expert on all issues of international relations is certainly unrealistic. An analysis of Russian international studies would be more accurate if it were done by a team of authors, where each is a specialist in a particular area. Undoubtedly, in that scenario, there would be more facts, names, publications, different estimates, and so on. At the same time, in such a scenario, it would be much more difficult to present a single picture of international research in the country; it would be very diverse. Obviously, both options — collective and individual study of international relations in Russia — have their advantages and disadvantages. There will probably be many more books and articles to come on the development of international research in Russia. In some ways, their authors will agree with the ideas, which are expressed in the book, and in some ways not. It is important that such studies continue in future.

It is especially difficult to write about Russian international relations because, primarily, at present there are very few studies reflecting on the formation and development of international research even in Russia. One of the preliminary studies was undertaken by Ivan G. Tyulin (Tyulin 1997). Later, other attempts were made (see Tsygankov, Tsygankov 2005d; Lebedeva 2013), but in general, an analysis of trends in the development of Russian international research has not been undertaken. This is partly because Russian IR studies have started rather recently, since the formation of the current Russian state.

Upon writing this book, I realized that I am offering my vision of the development of international studies in Russia, limited by my experience, communication with colleagues, and the processes that I observed. Certainly, some important facts and aspects can fall out of the scope of my attention and, therefore, are not reflected in the book. In the future, I hope these facts and aspects will be fulfilled by other scholars or by me.

The book consists of two parts. The first part is devoted to the origins of the development of IR studies in the Soviet Union, and then in the new Russia: how they began and the reasons for their development. In my opinion, understanding the current state of science in any country is impossible without an appeal to its formation. Therefore, the first part discusses the formation of international studies in the USSR, as well as the specificity of education in the field of international relations in the country during the Soviet time. Two periods are clearly distinguished here: (1) before World War II, when the Soviet Union found itself on the periphery of the world arena, and (2) after the end of World War II, when the Soviet Union became a superpower. The change in the position of the Soviet Union in the world had a significant impact on IR studies and education; they intensified, and their development took place in institutional terms. Research institutes appeared in the Academy of Sciences of the USSR and engaged in the study of international relations, and scientific journals began to be published. The next stage in the development of international studies in the country is associated with *perestroika*—the development of openness in science and education.

The second part of the book examines the current state of IR studies in Russia with regard to the main issues of international relations and world politics. This part is the most provocative. It is obvious that international relations in Russia are diverse. Most of them cover the study of countries and regions that relate to area studies and so are not considered in this book. This book focuses on theoretical research, as it allows us to assess the general direction of thought in the field of IR studies, and on the three largest fields of international relations: (1) security, (2) international political economy, and (3) humanitarian issues.

Part 1
Background of the Development of Russian IR Studies

Part 1

Chapter 1
Why Is It Important to Understand the Development of Russian IR Studies?

1.1 Political Organization of the World: IR Studies at the Crossroads

Every country has its own peculiarities in the research of international relations, which reflects the specifics of its traditions in the study of social relations, foreign policy, and, in general, perceptions of the world. Russia is not an exception here. What are the main features of Russian international research?

Russian IR authors write relatively little in English; they publish even less in leading international journals on international relations. They are "poorly integrated into international discussions about the main directions of political, economic, and social aspects of global development, and, consequently, are deprived of the opportunity to influence the intellectual 'frame' of the international environment" (Istomin, Baykov 2013). As a result, Russian research in the field of international relations is in many ways a *terra incognita* for world science. However, this situation is typical for many non-English-speaking countries. Many years ago, this was the basis upon which Stanley Hoffman called the study of international relations an American social science (Hoffmann 1977). However, in recent years, European scholars, probably largely influenced by processes of European integration as well as globalization, have become much more intensively involved in English-language researching of international relations. Chinese scholars, for other reasons which are mainly related to general attitudes regarding the development of Chinese science, also increasingly publish in English. At the same time, interest in Chinese studies, at least until recently, fueled attention on the fast-growing Chinese economy.

This cannot be said about Russian IR studies. In general, Russian research remains at the periphery of the global process in the field of international studies (Tsygankov, Tsygankov 2014). This is despite the fact that the task of deeper integration of Russian science was set into the world at an official level. Moreover, a few studies on the analysis of the development of international studies in Russia appeared (see Tsygankov, Tsygankov 2005d; Sergunin 2000; Lebedeva 2004a). Prior to this, foreign authors analyzed IR studies of the Soviet Union (see Light 1988). Currently, the interest of Western authors in Russian research is at a minimum, and this can be illustrated by the fact that Russian studies are not available in *International Relations in Europe: Traditions, Perspectives and Destinations*, which introduces the development of IR studies in various European countries (Jorgensen, Knudsen 2006). Another illustrating example concerns not only the lack of research by Russian authors, but also the lack of interest in a Russian understanding of certain aspects of international relations. Thus, in the book *Many Globalizations: Cultural Diversity in the Contemporary World*, authors from different countries analyze the development of globalization in their respective country based on preselected parameters. The book presents an analysis of how the process of globalization covers different countries located in Europe, North and South America, Africa, and Asia. The following ten countries were selected for analysis: The United States, China, Germany, Chile, South Africa, Hungary, India, Taiwan, Japan, and Turkey (Berger, Huntington 2002). Russia was not among them. Apparently, the authors could not attribute Russia to one of the four categories on which they gave an analysis of countries: (1) globalization and alternative modernities, (2) globalization and regional subglobalization, (3) globalization on the periphery, and (4) the American vortex. Russia could hardly fit into any of these categories. In any case, the Russian mode of globalization is not represented in the book.

More examples could be given. What are the reasons for such negligible interest in Russia, its place in the system of international relations, as well as Russian IR studies? First, there is the fact that in the 1990s Russian influence on world politics significantly decreased. Consequently, the scientific interest of Western scholars also disappeared. Researchers "switched" to other regions such as China and the Greater Middle East. In addition, the social science of international relations, unlike that in China, passively integrated into world science to a great extent, although significant steps were taken in this area. Finally, Russian IR studies were influenced by the fact that in the past, Soviet studies of international relations were to a large extent ideologized. There are other reasons mentioned by A. Korobkov, some of which include the level of English proficiency of Russian researchers, which is insufficient for publication in leading English-language journals, as well as a lack of understanding of Western models of scientific writing, and the presence of a journalistic genre in scientific works (Korobkov 2012).

Meanwhile, it took little more than 25 years for Russian science and education in the field of international relations to develop on a fundamentally different basis. What happened during these years? What did Russia achieve in this period? What kind of research in the field of international relations is the most relevant now, and how are IR experts trained in contemporary Russia? What if Russian science in the field of international studies is included or not in global science? The answers to these questions depend not only on the development of Russian science, but also on an understanding of Russian international relations by researchers from other countries. As noted by A.P. Tsygankov and P.A. Tsygankov: "Western scholars can improve their understanding of the world by studying international relations as a discipline outside the West" (Tsygankov, Tsygankov 2007a). In addition, Russian studies in the field of international relations, like any national school, are important components of global research. Finally, knowledge of research in the field of international relations is one of the keys to understanding the foreign policy of a particular state. Of course, there is no direct connection between international research and the foreign policy of any state. Russia in this respect is no exception. Nevertheless, the identification of this indirect link will make it possible to better understand and foresee Russia's foreign policy steps in the international arena.

In recent years, the importance of research in the field of international relations, which is being conducted in various countries, has become well understood. It is not a matter of coincidence that one hears calls for careful study of the theoretical foundations of various national schools of international research more often (see, for example, Acharya, B. Buzan 2010; Makarychev, Morozov). There are several reasons for this interest. First, the development of globalization, understood in this case as the process of the transnationalization of the world, and the strengthening of the process of border transparency, forces researchers and practitioners to turn to an analysis of how international reality is perceived in various regions and countries of the world. For IR studies, globalization has a dual significance. On the one hand, globalization creates conditions for closer international cooperation (modern information technologies greatly simplify this process) and simultaneously stimulates international interactions as well as creates conflicts. On the other hand, globalization is the object of research, the focus of the field of IR studies. Moreover, most importantly, globalization is only one of the manifestations of a profound transformation of the contemporary political organization of the world, which seems to cover the following three levels:

Political system of the world (Westphalian systems)
The system of international (interstate) relations and its part — the regional subsystem
Political systems of states

Graphically, this can be represented in the form of a pyramid based on the Westphalian system with its idea of sovereignty. Through the idea of sovereignty, this system largely determines the other two systems: the system of interstate relations and the political system of a state (Fig. 1.1).

Fig. 1.1 Political organization of the world: three levels

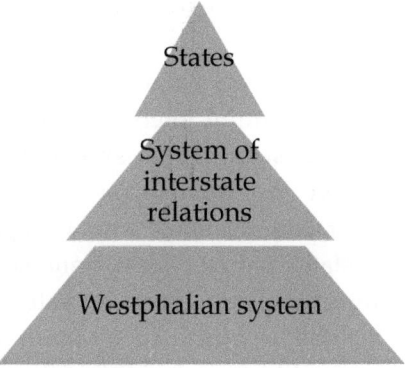

At the end of the twentieth century and the beginning of the twenty-first century, all three levels of political organization of the world underwent transformation, which generated a fundamentally different magnitude of crisis, forming a kind of "perfect storm", or synergy, when processes at each of the levels intensify the processes of the other two levels (Lebedeva 2016a).

As part of the transformation of the Westphalian system, not only were non-state actors activated on the international level, something which was shown by J. Nye and R. Keohane more than 40 years ago (Keohane, Nye 1971), but also the important event was the collapse of the colonial system and the accession of former colonies to the United Nations. As a result, Westphalian principles, one of the keys to which is sovereignty, have become global, like the system itself. At the same time, within the Westphalian system, three groups of states began to form, differently related to the system itself. The first group consists of the Westphalian states, or the states of modernity, which are characterized by the orientation to sovereignty, territorial integrity, and so on. The second group includes post-Westphalian states (postmodern states). For them it is typical to build supranational bodies, blurring the lines between domestic and foreign policy and mutual control. Finally, the third group is represented by pre-Western states (premodern states) and is characterized by an orientation toward clan and/or religious relations in domestic politics (Lebedeva 2008; Kharkevich 2010;

Poggi 2007). All these groups of states today coexist simultaneously and all have features of each type of group. However, defining features of a group dominate.

Russian studies of international relations mostly focus on the second level, on the structure of interstate relations. Indeed, the disintegration of the interstate bipolar system at the end of the twentieth century gave rise to another crisis related to the configuration of interstate relations. The Westphalian system, having emerged as a state-centrist system, from the very beginning assumed the formation of relations between states. These relations are described as theoretical constructions (multipolar, unipolar, and bipolar systems), and historical realities ("European concert", interwar system, postwar system, etc.). There is nothing unusual in changing the systems of international relations. However, as a rule, one system of international relations succeeded another system as a result of postwar agreements. Hence, Russian authors sometimes remark that after the end of the Cold War, no agreements were concluded, and "rules of behavior" were not fixed. But there are also points of view that the restructuring of the system of international relations need not necessarily go through wars. Thus, V.G. Baranovskiy writes that the system of interstate relations can progress via gradual evolutionary changes (Baranovskiy 2017a), and A. Kortunov points to the possible further development of a liberal world order (Kortunov 2016).

In general, the problem of interstate relations today is much more complicated, because in contemporary conditions we can hardly confine ourselves to the configuration of the world's leading powers, as it was before. First, the process of transformation of the Westphalian system, of course, has an impact on interstate relations. In particular, the influence of state leaders is "blurred" by the action of non-state actors. Second, the single resource complex, which was previously concentrated in the hands of the leading states, is now splitting up. Only the United States continues to be a leader in main spheres to a certain extent: military, political, economic, and in many respects humanitarian (including mass culture) (Nye 2002). Other states focus on one or two kinds of resources. For example, Australia and New Zealand became leaders of the social-humanitarian sphere, acting as the leading countries for providing services in the field of higher education for the entire Asia-Pacific region (Lebedeva 2014). The world, indeed, becomes polycentric, and that is why the definition of the system of interstate relations as a configuration of the interaction of the leading powers is unlikely to be adequate to reality. In connection with the growing complexity in Russian studies, the term "multipolar world" increasingly replaces the term "polycentricity of the world". Thus, A.A. Dynkin emphasizes that the emerging polycentricity of the contemporary world differs significantly from the various types of "polarity" of the past. Polycentricity is characterized, according to A.A. Dynkin, by the following features:

> Firstly, the leading centers of the world are represented not only by Western ones, but also by centers of other civilizations. Unlike previous times, the current model has a multi-civilization basis;
> Secondly, polycentricity develops under the conditions of a new stage of globalization, in which not only states participate, but also numerous interstate entities, non-state actors, including transnational corporations, nongovernmental organizations, etc.;
> Thirdly, in the emerging polycentricity common "rules of the game" (norms and institutions that could effectively regulate the interaction of actors — both cooperation and rivalry) are not developed yet;
> Fourthly, the differences in the parameters of the power of the various centers of power are leveled by nuclear weapons. At present, everything, and in the future most likely all centers of force will possess nuclear weapons for deterrence. (Dynkin 2012, 654)

One can agree with the majority of points mentioned above. However, the fourth point, according to which all centers of power will possess nuclear weapons, remains very challenging. In addition, the centers in this case are understood as power centers but not as educational, economic, cultural, and so on. In general, the main problem with such a description of the polycentric world is that two political systems — the Westphalian system and the system of interstate relations — are not differentiated. This is typical of Russian researchers.

Despite the fact that the majority of Russian researchers recognize the collapse of the bipolar system, there are also other points of view. A.V. Fenenko (responding to the article by I. Timofeev (Timofeev 2017)) believes that we continue to live in the system based on the agreements of the Yalta Conference in February 1945 and the Potsdam Conference in August 1945, which laid the foundation for the bipolar system. Arguments of A.V. Fenenko are as follows:

1) Up to the present time, the following are the rules developed by the victorious powers:
- Recognition of the formal equality of all peoples and races;
- Restriction of the right of states to conduct war. According to the UN Charter, declaration of the state of war is possible only in the order of self-defense
- Recognition of the UN as an international institution for global governance
- The existence of special rights among the five "victorious powers" in the Second World War within the framework of the UN Security Council
- The existence of a legal monopoly of the five permanent members of the UN Security Council for the possession of nuclear weapons, as recorded in the Treaty on the Non-Proliferation of Nuclear Weapons (NPT)
- 2) The ratio of power capabilities among states has not fundamentally changed. In mid-2010 the world from the point of view of distribution of power capabilities is divided into the following:
- "Nuclear superpowers" (the United States and Russia) that retain nuclear missile–nuclear parity, as well as the quantitative and qualitative separation of their nuclear forces from the rest of the members of the "nuclear club"
- Regional nuclear powers (France, Great Britain, and People's Republic of China), which do not possess a full-fledged strategic nuclear weapon
- Illegal nuclear powers (India, Pakistan, Israel, and North Korea)

- Nonnuclear countries that have conventional weapons and are included in the military–political blocs
- Nonnuclear countries that have conventional weapons and are not part of the military–political blocs
- Nonnuclear countries, where the development of military capabilities are limited by international legal framework (Germany, Japan). (Fenenko 2017)

Even if we take the arguments presented by A.V. Fenenko into account, it is difficult to agree that the structure of interstate relations in the world at the end of the twentieth century and at the beginning of twenty-first century did not change at all. Today, there is no strict separation between a states' resources in three dimensions (ideological, political, and economic), which there has been in the past. Moreover, it is possible to detect significant changes in all the parameters listed by Fenenko. In other words, the changes in the configuration of interstate relations that occur at present compared with the period after the end of World War II are clearly traced.

Political systems of states (mainly premodern states) certainly changed more often in the course of history compared to systems of international relations. Taking democratization, one of the most important parameters of this transformation, as a basis, Samuel Huntington has shown that the process of development comes in waves: after the increase in the number of states that have embarked on the democratic path of development, a rollback follows. At the same time, the general vector for increasing the number of democratic states in the world remains (Huntington 1991). The following question arises: Does this "rollback" always go along the path of authoritarianism? Recent events in the Greater Middle East show that a rollback can occur in the direction of the disintegration of all state structures and their relations replaced with tribal or religious principles. That is, a kind of archaization of the state (Lebedeva, Kharkevich, Zinovieva, Koposova 2017). It is possible, of course, to argue that the states of the region were not democratic, so one cannot properly discuss a rollback. However, after attempts to undertake democratic reforms, or at least evidencing a desire to see these transformations, at least in a number of cases, changes have led to the archaization of the country.

The end of the twentieth century gave birth to another wave of transformation of the political systems of states in Central and Eastern Europe: the emergence of new states in the territory of the former Soviet Union. At the same time, the political system of South Africa changed. Relatedly, the statehood of Namibia was being formed. There were changes in several other regions of the world. These processes are well described in the literature. Important factors in the development of this wave of transformation of the political systems of states were both internal processes and, in many ways, external processes, which were caused by the collapse of the bipolar system and the erosion of the Westphalian system.

Almost all researchers of international relations in Russia (but also in other states) point out the political transformation of the world either by reference to the erosion of the Westphalian system or — more often — to the disintegration of the bipolar system of interstate relations. Meanwhile, the complete process of restructuring all three levels of political organization of the world with their mutually reinforcing influence on each other is not indicated. However, such radical transformation affecting all levels has occured for the first time in the world. To a certain extent, a similar situation developed after World War II, and especially after World War I. But in both cases the Westphalian system did not undergo significant changes, despite systems of interstate relations being restructured, and the political systems of states having changed.

After the Russian Revolution and the end of World War I, a socialist state emerged which "dropped out" of the Westphalian system because it declared *class* as the main structural unit of political organization, not the state. The Genoa conference of 1922 was the first step in "embedding" Soviet Russia in the Westphalian system. Georgy Chicherin, speaking at the conference, proclaimed the principle of peaceful coexistence of states with different political systems. Thus, he "justified" the possibility of combining the Westphalian system with different political systems. Later, the idea of peaceful coexistence was repeatedly used by Soviet politicians and researchers (see Tomashevskiy 1972; Chubaryan 1976). The Westphalian system combines very different states (including socialist ones) in terms of their political systems. The Westphalian system combines very differently in terms of political organization of states, including socialist ones. This was possible because the Westphalian system assumed that a state that enters the system can be organized in different ways. This kind of "tolerance" of the Westphalian system allowed this system to survive for over 350 years.

Gradually, the process of including the Soviet Union into the Westphalian system moved on, although Soviet Russia, and then the USSR, operated with a kind of "dualism": on the one hand, orientation toward the workers and communist parties and understanding the principle of peaceful coexistence as a process of class struggle, with the indispensable victory of the proletariat (the class approach); on the other hand, a simultaneous orientation of interstate relations within the Westphalian system. Therefore, after World War II, despite the fact that several socialist states were formed at once, the experience of embedding a socialist state into Westphalian relations was already present. In this sense, the situation was less complicated than it was at the beginning of the twentieth century.

1.2 The Place of Russia in the Political Transformation of the World

The study of international relations in Russia is influenced by the situation in the world, the place that Russia occupies in the political organization of the world, and how Russia perceives itself and others. As for the situation in the wider political organization of the world, throughout the twentieth century Russia was at the "epicenter" of transformations of the political organization of the world. Russia challenged the Westphalian system in 1917. In addition, it became one of the central links in the breakdown of the two systems of interstate relations: at the beginning of the twentieth century after the end of World War I and at the end of the twentieth century when the bipolar system disintegrated.

At the beginning of the twentieth century, as a result of the October Revolution of 1917, Russia actually initiated the implementation of another system of political organization, which was not based on a national state with its sovereignty (the Westphalian system), but on class relations. The extent to which this new system was utopian can be debated. Russia began to implement an alternative project of political organization, the contours of which were developed by Karl Marx and Friedrich Engels. After the October Revolution, Lev Trotsky tried to develop this project on a worldwide scale. He used the thesis, which was put forward by Marx and Engels in the *Communist Manifesto*, of a permanent revolution (Marx, Engels 1955-1974). According to Trotsky, because the proletariat in Russia was small, the final victory of a socialist revolution in Russia could be possible only if it was supported by revolutions in other countries; that is, the revolution must be permanent (Trotsky 2005). In this case, according to Trotsky, the Russian proletariat would receive the support of the proletariat of the European countries.

Using the framework of this model, Vladimir Lenin developed the idea of the withering away of the state. Lenin based this on Engels' *Anti-Dühring*. Engels wrote that in the past all states reflected the position of the dominant class, and in the future the state will act as the representative of the whole of society and in this sense the state will wither away (Engels 1955-1974). Lenin believed that the withering away of the state will occur in a communist society. Continuing this logic further, it is necessary to recognize that the main structural element of the Westphalian system — a state — will disappear. It is noteworthy that before the collapse of the USSR, The Academy of Sciences hosted a discussion on the topic "The place and role of the USSR in global civilization process". Speaking to this, the USSR academic and Director of the Institute of USA and Canadian Studies, G. Arbatov, said the following: "In 1917, we undertook an unprecedented attempt to escape from contemporary civilization and to realize a fundamentally new model of global development in a particular country" (Mesto i rol SSSR ... 1991: 5 [The place and the role of the USSR... 1991: 5]).

Initially, in 1917, it was obvious that the national states of the Westphalian system could not agree with other principles of political organization. As a result, for several years Russia found itself in international isolation, becoming a kind of outcast from the Westphalian system. Russia did not participate in the Versailles (1919) and Washington (1921–1922) conferences following World War I, which formed the postwar system of international relations.

After the Genoa Conference, despite the fact that Russia gradually began to integrate into the existing political organization of the world based on the principles of Westphalian relations, it did not play a leading role in the world until World War II. After the end of World War II, the USSR became the leader around which one of the poles of the bipolar system was formed. Over a number of decades, the USSR largely determined developing trends in the world arena.

The USSR, and then Russia, following the earlier classification of states which was formed in the second half of the twentieth century as mainly the Westphalian states, despite the fact that the idea of class struggle and the victory of communism on a world scale persisted until the disappearance of the Soviet Union.

The disintegration of the bipolar system painfully affected Russia's self-perception. In addition, the reference to the "loss" of Russia in the Cold War, repeatedly sounded both from a number of foreign politicians and from some researchers, ignoring the interests of Russia on a number of issues, etc., has led to a response. In the 1990s, the United States as the leader of the world was perceived negatively in Russia. Events in the 2000s have led to the isolation of Russia not only in economic and political areas but also partly in IR studies. After a surge of interest in Russian IR studies in the late 1980s–1990s, in the 2000s there has been a decline in such interest. In the West the number of people who were studying Russian international relations or the Russian language declined. In turn, a number of Russian authors also largely "turned" in the direction of focusing on the development of Russia's own approaches to the analysis of international issues.

Thus, at the beginning of the twentieth century, and at its end, Russia experienced a transformation at all the three levels of political organization of the world. In both cases, the state was formed on new principles. Moreover, in 1917, the political system of the Russian state underwent transformation twice. The February Revolution of 1917 overthrew the monarchy and abolished the old institutions of power, and a provisional government was formed. As a result of the October Revolution of 1917, the ministers of the provisional government were arrested, and the state began to be rebuilt on different principles.

In 1991, after the collapse of the Soviet Union, Russia also abandoned previous principles and guidelines. Once again, the task of state-building arose, and with it a revision of the political picture of the world.

In the twentieth century, as well as in the early twenty-first century Russia was in the center of turbulence of the political organization of the world. It is hard to say how well this is realized in Russia. At least on an intuitive level, many people felt this special position of Russia in the world. In particular, it manifests itself in a special demand, including at the level of mass consciousness (which follows from almost all public opinion polls) of Russia's active position in the international arena. One of the explanations for this phenomenon can be the feeling of being at the center of the political changes of political organization of the world that directly affected Russia and the desire to influence the processes which are taking place.

All this could affect the development of IR studies in Russia. Understanding it will help to identify those priorities and problems that are in the focus of current Russian international relations.

Chapter 2
The Soviet Period in the Development of IR Studies: The Influence of the Past

2.1 Formation of IR Studies in the USSR

2.1.1 Establishment of the First Centers of IR Studies

Contemporary IR studies in Russia, despite the drastic changes experienced by the country, are influenced by what has been done in previous periods of its development. First, the past to some extent always has an impact in any state and on any field of research. Therefore, it would be wrong to ignore the past. Second, as discussed in the previous chapter, in the twentieth century Russia not only experienced sharp turns in its history but also found itself at the center of changes in the political organization of the wider world, which also affected Russia's self-perception and its IR studies. Moreover, this position of Russia in relation to the broader political transformation of the world appears to be significant not only for Russian IR studies but also for IR studies conducted outside Russia. Understanding the development of research ideas leads to understanding what was/is happening in the world. Finally, it is impossible to assess Russian international relations without considering the baseline and the parameters with regard to which it has developed.

Speaking about the Soviet period in studies of international relations, one should keep in mind that the sphere of international activity in the USSR before World War II was small. The point here is not so much that the Soviet Union was not recognized immediately after the revolution, but that despite recognition before World War II, the Soviet Union was not included in interstate interaction and international institutions. In addition, the Soviet system as a whole was largely centralized; international contacts, especially since the 1930s, were strictly controlled and regulated, and the scope of international activity was limited.

There are different arguments about when international relations was formed as a research field. The most common point of view connects the process with the end of World War I and the appearance of the Department of International Politics at the University of Wales (now Aberystwyth University) in the United Kingdom. Another argument relates this process deeply into history, seeing, for example, the "Melos Dialogue" of Thucydides as the first essay on international relations (see Hoffmann 1977).

It appears that the argument according to which the era of international research begins from the twentieth century deserves more support. Otherwise, it is difficult to distinguish the history of international relations (and Thucydides is the historian) and research in the field of international relations. If we do not draw a distinction between history and proper IR studies, we deprive IR studies of its own subject of study. In addition, the opening of the Department of International Politics at the University of Wales (Aberystwyth University) marked not just a definite point that records the beginning of research in this field, but also the institutionalization of international relations as a scientific and educational discipline.

Thus, if we proceed from thinking of the formation of international studies as being at the beginning of the twentieth century, Russia was one of the first among states to discover this field of studies. In Russia at that time, the external world was studied mainly in the context of the institutions and structures formed by the Comintern (Mesto i rol SSSR… 1991 [The place and the role of the USSR… 1991]). The Institute of World Economy and World Politics, established in 1925 (shortly after the international recognition of the socialist Russia), played a special role in these structures. Formed under the Communist Academy, the Institute of World Economy and World Politics, headed by its first director F.A. Rothstein, was intended to become a scientific center which would establish approaches to the study of foreign policy and economic relations between the USSR and other countries (Cherkasov 2004).

In 1927, Eugene Varga, a Hungarian social democrat and an active leader of Communist International, became the director of the institute. Stalin trusted and supported Varga, especially after he opposed the opinion of most economists and correctly estimated the collapse of the New York Stock Exchange as the beginning of the deepest economic crisis in the history of capitalism. Later in 1933, again, contrary to the opinion of the majority in Communist International, Varga convinced Stalin that the crisis was waning, and that the West was entering a period of economic depression (Cherkasov 2004).

The Institute of World Economy and World Politics focused primarily on the world economy, based on the Marxist understanding that economics determines politics. Varga was an economist and he shared these views. In addition to economics, the institute engaged in the study of the world revolutionary movement, the position of the proletariat in capitalist countries, as well as other issues.

In the 1930s, the Central Committee of the Communist Party of the Soviet Union (CPSU) instructed the institute to concentrate its efforts on analyzing the following issues:

- "General problems of imperialism and the world economic crisis
- The situation and problems of the working class and labor movement in capitalist countries
- International imperialist contradictions, the preparation of war, and intervention against the USSR
- Colonial problems and colonial revolutions
- Agrarian relations and agrarian problems in capitalist countries
- World industry and measures of the USSR to master the experience of advanced capitalist technology
- International markets and foreign trade of the USSR". (Cherkasov 2004: 28)

The Institute of World Economy and World Politics was closed in 1947 and resumed its work in 1956.

The initial theoretical orientation of this period in the development of international studies in the USSR was Marxism-Leninism. Marxism-Leninism saw classes, not states, as the main actors of world politics. Moreover, Marxism-Leninism was based on ideas about the opposite motivations of participants in the international arena: the bourgeoisie (respectively, the bourgeois state) is striving for profit and the proletariat (socialist state) for socialist revolution leading to the liberation of the working people (Tsygankov 2003: 113-115). Marxism-Leninism assumed proletarian solidarity and in this respect it manifested some kind of transnationalism, the idea of which in world IR studies appears much later and is usually associated with the development of neoliberalism. At the same time, there was a messianic orientation of the USSR, expressed in an effort to free the whole world from "bourgeois domination". In practice, this manifested itself in the development of contacts and ties with workers and communist parties, in supporting their activities, and in manifesting class solidarity with the proletariat of other countries. When interpreting the results of the analysis of international relations, the class basis of any action of the participants has always been considered.

2.1.2 Historical and Oriental Schools: Contribution to IR Studies

IR studies were developing in the USSR mainly within the framework of history (Torkunov 2012a), although international law and economics also had some influence. During this time, studies were published by leading scholars such as L.N. Ivanov (Ivanov 1927; Ivanov 1928; Ivanov 1929), E.V. Tarle (Tarle 1936; Tarle 1941-1944), V.S. Sergeev (Sergeev 1938), and V.M. Khvostov (Khvostov 1940). A collective three-volume work on the history of diplomacy was published in the 1940s. Well-known historians such as S.V. Bakhrushin, A.V. Efimov, E.A. Kosminsky, A.L. Narochnitsky, V.P. Potemkin, V.S. Sergeev, and S.D. Skazkin took part in the writing (Potemkin 1941-1945). This volume has been translated into a number of European languages. Many of the historical studies of those days (in particular, Potemkin 1941-1955) are still good examples of historical analysis. In principle, a historical essay in international relations was typical for many European countries, and not only for the Soviet school of IR studies. P.A. Tsygankov noted that "only after 1945, international relations theory began to break free from the 'strangulation' of history and 'crushing' by law" (Tsygankov 1996: 11).

In the USSR, close to the historical school, although somewhat apart from it, was the oriental school of studies. It was formed largely on historical grounds, but cultural, linguistic, and ethnographic knowledge occupied a significant place in oriental studies. The roots of Russian oriental studies go deep into tsarist Russia. Most of Russia's territory is located in Asia; therefore, Russia has long been interested in studying the countries of this region. Studies of oriental languages began in Russia during the time of Peter the Great. However, the intensive development of oriental studies in the country occured at the beginning of the nineteenth century, when a number of institutions of this school were created. Thus, in November 1818, Count S. Uvarov wrote to the board of the Russian Academy of Sciences requesting that a separate room be set aside; the result was the establishment of the Asiatic Museum. It had a large collection of manuscripts in eastern languages, as well as books on the culture and history of Asian countries. The Asiatic Museum conducted scientific works. These studies were also published in European countries. Gaining popularity, in 1876, the Asiatic Museum became the organizer of the Third International Congress of Orientalists in St. Petersburg.

In the mid-nineteenth century, on the basis of Imperial decree, the Faculty of Oriental Studies was opened in St. Petersburg State University. It later became one of the leading world oriental centers. In 1930, as a result of the unification of a number of scientific orientalist institutions in Leningrad, the Institute for Oriental Studies was formed.[1] It was transferred to Moscow in 1950, although a large part of its funds remained in Leningrad.

---

1   Institute for Oriental Studies: http://ivran.ru

At the very beginning of the nineteenth century, oriental institutions were also being formed in Moscow. One among them was the Lazarevsky Institute of Oriental Languages, where they began to teach and study Arabic, Armenian, Persian, and Turkish languages. In 1921, several oriental faculties united with the Lazarevsky Institute (which by that time had another name) in a single institution, the Moscow Institute of Oriental Studies.

During the Soviet period, orientalists were assigned tasks aimed at determining ways of exerting a strong influence on developing countries in order to direct them towards socialist development. Therefore, from a political point of view, it was important to study the countries of the East in their struggles against colonial domination. At the same time, the realities of the countries of Asia and Africa were not always well aligned with Marxism-Leninism. This gave orientalists a certain freedom in interpreting what was happening in this region.

2.2 The Development of IR Studies in the USSR after World War II

2.2.1 Development of Organizational Forms of Studying International Relations

After victory in World War II, the position of the USSR in the international arena changed radically. The Soviet Union had become a leading state, which started to form a new system of interstate relations. At the same time, international contacts and the international activities of the Soviet Union were dramatically expanded: the USSR became a permanent member of the UN Security Council, joined a number of international organizations, and initiated the establishment of intergovernmental organizations. To realize all these functions, a fundamentally different scale of IR studies was required.

The change in the Soviet Union's position in the system of interstate relations led to changes in two main parameters: (1) the rapid development of research centers, as well as the appearance of academic journals on international relations in the Soviet Union, and (2) shifts in theoretical approaches and in the themes of research. The USSR increasingly needed to analyze the positions of various states in the international arena, so the focus in IR studies shifted from analysis of the international communist and workers' movement (although this remained a priority issue) to study of the behavior of states in the international arena.

Significant organizational changes occurred after the Twentieth Congress of the CPSU (February 1956), which gave impetus to IR studies in the Soviet Union. G.A. Arbatov noted:

> Twentieth Congress changed the situation. We took a step towards a realistic understanding of the world. There was a need to create a new institution and such was the Institute of World Economy and International Relations. A new stage in the development of our political thought has begun. Institutes increased quantitatively. Several institutions have been established in order to study the world. (Mesto i rol SSSR...: 4 [The place and the role of the USSR... 1991: 4]).

Indeed, during this period a number of institutes of the Academy of Sciences were being created which have since focused on the study of international relations. So, after the closure in 1947, the activity of the Institute of World Economy and World Politics was resumed in 1956 under a different name—the Institute of World Economy and International Relations.[2] A number of other institutes were also created within the framework of the Academy of Sciences of the USSR: in 1959 the Institute for African Studies,[3] in 1966 the Institute of the Far East,[4] in 1967 the Institute of the USA and Canada,[5] and in 1969 the Institute of Latin America.[6] Later, the development of European integration, as well as the importance of Europe for the Soviet Union, led to the fact that in 1987 the Institute of Europe was also founded under the Academy of Sciences.[7] The

---

2   Now Primakov National Research Institute of World Economy and International Relations RAS: https://www.imemo.ru/
3   Institute of Africa RAS: https://inafran.ru/en/
4   Institute of the Far East RAS: http://www.ifes-ras.ru/about-ifes-ras
5   Institute of the USA and Canada RAS: http://www.iskran.ru
6   Institute of Latin America RAS: www.ilaran.ru (in Russian); http://www.ilaran.ru/?n=8&r=4942 (in Spanish)
7   Institute of Europe RAS: http://en.instituteofeurope.ru/

creation of the Institute of Europe was also influenced by the process of perestroika and the strengthening of contacts with European countries as well as by the process of integration within Europe.

Studies on the international communist and workers' movement issues, as well as on the socialist countries, were conducted mainly in two other institutes of the Academy of Sciences of the USSR: the Institute of the International Communist and Workers' Movement (founded in 1966) and the Institute of the World Socialist System (established in 1960). Both of these institutes were later transformed. The Institute of Scientific Information on Social Sciences (INION) of the Academy of Sciences, created in 1968, along with its library, has become a good information base for research on international relations. From 1972 to 2015, INION was headed by two graduates of Moscow State Institute of International Relations (MGIMO): academicians V.A. Vinogradov and Yu.S. Pivovarov. Both paid much attention to the selection of books, articles, and other materials on international relations. The institute conducted abstracting of this literature.

Studies were also conducted in two educational institutions in which personnel were trained in the field of international relations— Moscow State Institute of International Relations (MGIMO) and the Diplomatic Academy. Both structures belonged to the Ministry of Foreign Affairs. The study of some aspects of international relations was held at the Lomonosov Moscow State University, the Leningrad State University, and the Kiev State University. With the development of institutions and research on international relations, new scientific journals were also published in the USSR: *Mirovaya ekonomika i mezhdunarodnye otnosheniya* [World Economy and International Relations]; *SShA i Kanada: ekonomika, politika, ideologiya* [USA and Canada: Economy, Policy, Ideology]; *Azya i Afrika segodnya* [Asia and Africa Today]; *Problemy Dalnego Vostoka* [The Far East Issues]; and *Sovetskoye vostokovedenie* [Soviet Oriental Studies],[8] as well as other journals. Since the 1960s,

---

8   The journal was published under different names: *Problemy vostokovedeniya* [Oriental Studies Issues] (1959–1961), *Narody Azii i Afriki* [Peoples of Asia and

the Soviet Union formed IR studies with its institutions and its own circle of experts (Tyulin 1997).

2.2.2 Shifts in Theoretical Foundations and IR Issues

In the Soviet Union, despite official recognition of only one methodological direction — Marxism-Leninism — in fact, IR studies were influenced by two paradigms: (1) Marxism-Leninism and (2) realism. After World War II, Marxism-Leninism, while remaining in foreign policy rhetoric, was increasingly replaced by intuitive realism. In fact, it was realism. However, intuitive realism was not related to theoretical studies of classical realism.

In IR studies of the postwar period, realism was manifested by considering the state as virtually the only actor in international relations (despite the fact that international inter-party ties continued to develop). However, when analyzing the state, its class nature was noted — bourgeois or socialist. National interests in research were the leading category of analysis. It was pointed out that there were contradictions in the interests of bourgeois states, which lead to conflicts and wars between them. The starting point was that the socialist state, in order to protect its interests, must be strengthened and should be able to protect itself.

At the same time, realism as a theory was not represented in the USSR until its disintegration. Classic studies of realism such as by E. H. Carr, H. Morgenthau, and others were not introduced into scientific circulation. For this reason, this theoretical approach in the Soviet Union can be defined as "intuitive realism". During the Soviet period, theories of international relations as they developed in the broader world were not taught or studied at all in the Soviet Union. Moreover, most of the foreign theoretical studies on international relations were in libraries with limited access to readers. However, classic works on diplomacy were translated into Russian and were published, particularly in books by Harold Nicolson (Nicolson 1941; Nicolson 1945; Nicolson 1965), Ernest

---

Africa] (1961–1990). Currently, it is published as "*Vostok. Afro-Aziatskiye obshchestva; istoriya i sovremennost*" [East. Afro-Asian societies: history and modernity]. Shortened name is "*Oriens*".

Satou (Satou 1961), Kikujiro Isii (Isii 1942), Richard Zalett (Zalett 1956), Zhules Cambon (Cambon 1946), and others.

Marxism-Leninism remained as the main framework for the analysis of international relations, but intuitive realism was increasingly introduced into the practice of research. One of the most significant manifestations of the ideological prevalence of intuitive realism over Marxism-Leninism was the closure of the Institute of World Economy and World Politics in 1947. It was believed that the cause of disgrace of E.S. Varga were his studies of the capitalist economy, which testified to the erroneousness of the widespread in the USSR thesis about the decay of capitalism. His personal relationships with other people were also mentioned. In particular, G.A. Arbatov pointed out that the initiator of the closure of the Institute was the economist N.A. Voznesensky (Mesto i rol SSSR... 1991 [The place and the role of the USSR... 1991]). In part, this is probably true, but there was another side to the matter, which is clarified in connection with the publication of Varga's letters 25 years after his death, where he accuses Stalin of retreating from the principle of proletarian internationalism (Varga 1991a; Varga 1991b). In other words, in this case, proletarian internationalism (as a part of Marxism-Leninism), or the peculiar "transnationalism" of Varga, went against the intuitive realist views of Stalin on the power of the state.

With the strengthening of the state and the transformation of the USSR into a superpower, the realistic orientation in international studies has become increasingly stronger. As a result, a rather original and surprising symbiosis arose between these two approaches of (1) intuitive realism and (2) proletarian internationalism. The leading place in this pair was owned by realism, and the influence of Marxism-Leninism, in fact, was limited to the sphere of rhetoric and cooperation with communist and workers' parties. It is noteworthy that the emphasis on intuitive realism, combined with Marxism-Leninism, was reflected in the party hierarchy. Thus, the Minister of Foreign Affairs, A.A. Gromyko, who was responsible for interstate relations in 1973, became a member of the Politburo of the CPSU Central Committee, while his colleague B.N. Ponomarev, who was involved in international party relations, remained a candidate member of the Politburo of the CPSU Central Committee.

At the same time, Marxism-Leninism (more precisely, Marxism) proved to be a good basis for the development of a systematic approach in the field of international relations in the Soviet Union, since it made it possible to present international relations as an integral system with structural elements. It is clear that in the framework of Marxism these structural elements, first of all, were classes. However, in the study of countries, researchers pointed out other structural units; that is, in fact, they followed the realistic tradition of studying international relations.

It should be noted that, in general, one of the founders of the systematic approach was the Russian researcher and participant in the revolutionary movement in tsarist Russia, A.A. Bogdanov. Bogdanov formulated an idea according to which all the developing objects of nature and society are integral entities or systems consisting of many elements (Bogdanov 1922).

Later, the ideas of system analysis were accepted by the Soviet specialist in the theory of management, deputy chairman of the State Planning Commission and an academician, D.M. Gvishiani (Gvishiani 1972), who was one of the most active proponents of the creation of the International Institute for Applied System Analysis in Austria. The USSR and the United States became the organizers of this institute in 1972. Later, other countries joined the activities of this institute. The Institute for System Studies was founded in 1976 in the USSR as a branch of Austria's Institute. System analysis has become widespread in the USSR in the social sciences, including international relations. As noted by I.G. Tyulin, between 1970 and 1980 in the Soviet Union the idea of a systematic approach and the view of international relations as a dynamic integrity were actively defended and developed (Tyulin 1997).

Ideas of integrity, as well as international relations and sociology, can be traced in the work of F.M. Burlatskiy and A.A. Galkin in the early 1970s (Burlatskiy, Galkin 1974). At the same time, it should be kept in mind that sociology, which formed in

Russia in the nineteenth century, was revived in the USSR only in the 1960s. A little later, E.A. Pozdnyakov made an attempt to apply a systematic approach to international relations. He proceeded from the fact that it is not enough to analyze only the foreign policy of states on which Soviet researchers concentrated. He wrote about the need to see an integral system of international interaction, according to which states form a system (Pozdnyakov 1976). M.A. Khrustalev (Khrustalev 1987), as well as scholars under the leadership of V.I. Gantman (see Gantman 1984), started to develop further theoretical aspects of system analysis applicable to international relations. Later, N.A. Kosolapov and a number of other authors continued this tradition.

It should be noted that neo-Marxism, like realism, was not generally represented in Soviet IR studies of the postwar period. Complicated relations with the communist parties of a number of European countries led to the fact that Soviet scholars tried to distance themselves from any other directions in Marxism, except Marxism-Leninism.

At the same time, theoretical issues were discussed in Soviet IR studies. In this regard, there were several significant events. In 1969, for example, a discussion took place on the pages of the journal *World Economy and International Relations* on the interdisciplinarity of IR studies (Problemy teorii... 1969 [Theories's issues... 1969]). This discussion stimulated the development of IR studies in the USSR, as far as it expanded the understanding of the subject, which previously was largely reduced to historical description. Later, however, international issues began to be described more in terms of a multidisciplinary rather than an interdisciplinary approach. This situation was typical not only of Soviet science but also of IR studies in other countries. In general, interdisciplinarity has many positive aspects in IR education. However, in conducting interdisciplinary research, problems arise, because in this case the subject of the study might be lost. In IR studies, there is a possibility to miss the political perspective (which is the key point for IR studies), dissolving it in a multidisciplinary way.

In the 1970s, a group headed by V.I. Gantman started to work at the Institute of World Economy and International Relations (IMEMO). The result of this work was the publication of the book *Modern Bourgeois Theories of International Relations: A Critical Analysis* (Gantman 1976), which introduced to Russian authors the directions of IR studies conducted abroad. At approximately the same time, a study of American foreign policy was published by V.F. Petrovskiy, one of the leading members of the USSR's Ministry of Foreign Affairs (Petrovskiy 1976). Somewhat later, I.G. Tyulin published a book on the theoretical directions of research on international relations in France (Tyulin 1988). In fact, all these studies were about theoretical directions being developed abroad. In addition, in the USSR interest was also shown in theoretical studies on international relations which were published in the socialist countries. The studies of Professors Jozef Wiatr and Yuzef Kukulka of Warsaw University were translated into Russian (Wiatr 1979; Kukulka 1980).

All this became a significant stimulus for the development of theoretical work in the field of international relations in the USSR. Theoretical research had begun to develop in Moscow State Institute of International Relations since the late 1960s, as the practice required adequate assessments of international political reality. D.V. Ermolenko and Yu.A. Zamoshkin played a major role in the development of theoretical aspects of Soviet international relations during this period. Ermolenko drew attention to the sociological aspects of international relations (Ermolenko 1975), as well as to the importance of technological developments for international relations (Akhtamzyan, 2013). Zamoshkin's studies focused on a person and those processes that occur with the person in a capitalist society (see Zamoshkin 1966). Later, the study of the human factor in international relations was continued by E. Ya. Batalov (Batalov 2005).

One of the first studies in which the question of the need to develop the theoretical aspects of international relations in the USSR was posed became a small book by some professors of MGIMO (V.I. Antyukhina-Moskovchenko, A.A. Zlobin, and M.A.

Khrustalev) published in 1980 (Antyukhina-Moskovchenko, V.I., Zlobin, A.A., Khrustalev 1980). In those days the very assumption that Marxism-Leninism might not fully describe the theoretical foundations of international reality was truly revolutionary. I.G. Tyulin has described the process of theoretical research in the field of international relations in the Soviet Union in some detail (Tyulin 1997).

Issues of theory and methodology of international studies in the Soviet Union were in close relation to an applied task. This task was an attempt to forecast the development of international relations. Several publications on these issues were published in the USSR (Kokoshin 1975; Gvishiani 1977).

In the second half of the 1970s, the Problem Research Laboratory (PRONIL) was established at MGIMO to conduct applied research. The laboratory was headed by Professor V.B. Tikhomirov. Research using quantitative methods of analysis of international relations began to be developed in the PRONIL. Soon after, Tyulin became the head of the Problem Research Laboratory. He paid much attention to the selection of cadres. Representatives of different disciplines began to work in PRONIL. These were specialists in the field of international relations, economists, lawyers, psychologists, and mathematicians. A similar laboratory was founded at the Diplomatic Academy. This laboratory was more focused on creating databases on international relations.

In the late 1970s and early 1980s, the use of quantitative methods for applied analysis of international relations began to attract the attention of Soviet researchers. Studies using quantitative methods of analysis in political science in the United States were published (see Melikhov 1979). But the most important step was conducting research with quantitative methods. Soviet scholars began to use methods such as cognitive mapping and content analysis in international relations (see, for example, Lukov, Sergeev 1982; Vasilev, Lebedeva 1988). This happened against the background of the rejection of quantitative measurements and an attempt to apply objective methods in the Soviet Union. For the first time, the description of quantitative methods in international studies was provided in the studies of the group under the leadership of V.I. Gantman (Institute of World Economy and International Relations). In MGIMO, these methods were used to study international relations. Quantitative methods in the studies of international relations did not develop widely in the Soviet Union and later in Russia. However, the experience of such studies was undoubtedly positive as an attempt to eliminate subjectivism and ideological attitudes.

In the 1970s and 1980s, the themes of IR studies conducted in the USSR expanded somewhat. The study of countries and regions, foreign policies, and bilateral relations remained central in research. The focus of attention of researchers was also Soviet-American relations, and other bilateral relations of the leading states of the world (see, for example, Kokoshin 1984; Kremenyuk 1982; Ivanov 1982). Studies of socialist countries and developing countries were also developed. A number of institutes of the Academy of Sciences of the USSR began to work in these areas.

In addition, great attention was paid to the historical issues of the development of international relations (see, for example, Gromyko, Ponomarev 1982) as well as diplomacy (see, for example, Dmitrichev 1981; Zorin 1977; Israelyan 1990). Among the literature on diplomacy was the work of the Deputy Minister of Foreign Affairs A.G. Kovalev, *The ABC of Diplomacy*, which had several editions. It developed theoretical questions of diplomacy and gave historical examples (see Kovalev 1988). Military and political matters were one of the key issues in Soviet studies of international relations, although publications on these issues remained exclusively within the framework of the official position of the USSR (see, for example, Petrovskiy 1982; Primakov 1983; Usachev 1974, Arbatov 1984).

Along with these trends, new areas of research appeared and they remain relevant to the present. Thus, the development of integration processes has stimulated, among other things, theoretical studies of integration (see Baranovskiy 1983). There were studies on emerging global problems and the interdependence of the world (see Bogomolov 1983; Gvishiani 1979;

Gvishiani 1981; Inozemtsev 1981; Zagladin, Frolov 1976; Maksimova 1982; Frolov 1980; Shakh 1981; Shmelev 1983); the impact of the scientific and technological revolution on international relations (see Bykov 1979; Gauzner 1972); environmental issues (see Budyko 1977; Gorizontov 1982; Zhiritskiy 1979; Maklyarskiy 1980) and resources (see Sitnikov 1979; Studenetskiy, Parin 1980; *Problemy okruzhayushchey sredy* ... 1974 [Environmental issues... 1974]), including food resources (see Knyazhinskaya 1979; Shishkov, Mirovitskaya 1983).

The analysis of conflicts held a special place in IR studies in the Soviet Union in 1970s–1980s. Examination of both specific conflicts and general theoretical issues of conflicts are the focus of a number of studies. In particular, studies on conflicts written by E.M. Primakov, V.V. Zhurkin, V.A. Kremenyuk, N.I. Doronina and other authors were published (Zhurkin, Primakov 1972; Primakov 1978; Kremenyuk 1977; Kremenyuk 1979; Zhurkin 1975; Doronina 1081). The Institute for Scientific Information in Social Sciences (INION) published a reference book on the study of international conflicts (Vneshnepoliticheskie konflikty... 1979 [International conflicts... 1979]). The book on the study of conflicts abroad was published by IMEMO under the editorship of V.I. Gantman (Gantman 1983).

Primakov and Zhurkin developed a method of analysis of conflict which received the name of situational analysis. Situational analysis was aimed at comprehensively analyzing a conflict situation and forecasting possible scenarios for its development. In 1980, for this work, they (among other authors) were awarded the State Prize, which was awarded annually in the USSR for outstanding achievements in science and technology, literature, and art. The success of situational analysis largely depends on its organizers, whose tasks include preparing a scenario for discussing the issue. It is important to formulate the questions accurately and select experts who will participate in the discussion (for details, see Primakov 2006).

New to Soviet IR studies was the appeal to the problems of negotiation and mediation as a means of conflict management.

Previously, these issues in the USSR were slightly touched upon only in the field of law (see Pushmin 1970; Pushmin 1974; Ladyzhenskiy, Blishchenko 1963). Undoubtedly, the process of detente set by the Helsinki process, as well as the emergence of global problems in the world, which can be resolved only through joint efforts of various countries through negotiation mechanisms, have become a significant impetus for addressing the problems of negotiation. In the USSR the focus of research was not only on historical aspects of negotiations, which was generally characteristic of IR studies in the Soviet Union, but also on methodological issues of the studying of negotiation processes (see Tyulin, Khrustalev 1981; *Voprosy teorii i praktiki...* 1981 [Theory and practice issues... 1981]). Scholars from Problem Research Laboratory (PRONIL, MGIMO), V.B. Lukov and V.M. Sergeev, developed a computer model for assessing the positions of negotiating parties (Lukov, Sergeev 1981). The model contained the basic position of parties of the Conference on Security and Cooperation in Europe (CSCE) and allowed researchers to trace the evolution of these positions, as well as areas of overlap or divergence in their positions. This study was highly appreciated by foreign scholars (Frei 1984). To some extent, Soviet IR studies of the 1970s shifted from confrontational rhetoric to analyzing international relations and to searching for possible zones of cooperation. Of course, the opposition of the two systems, capitalist and socialist, did not disappear from publications. During this period a number of studies were conducted; these studies aimed at understanding interaction and cooperation in the world arena. This was especially evident after the Helsinki Final Act, when more attention was paid to the study of international cooperation and negotiation processes. However, these studies went into decline in the early 1980s due to a "cooling" in international relations between East and West. They resumed with the announcement of perestroika.

2.2.3 The Main Characteristics of Soviet Research in the Field of International Relations

In general, the following points were typical for IR studies of the Soviet period. Perhaps no other direction of the scientific and educational sphere had such a capital "centricity" as international relations. Moreover, the government of the Soviet Union set tasks for the development of science and higher education in Siberia and the Far East in order to create appropriate departments of the Academy of Sciences, universities, academic towns, and so on. However, this was not related to international relations. The fact that the study of international relations was held only in Moscow was not accidental. External relations in the Soviet Union were highly centralized and limited. In fact, practically, only Moscow was interested in scientific and educational products on international relations.

Another limitation of the research and teaching of international relations in the Soviet Union was the ideological and methodological framework. Unlike the previous feature, this feature was not specific just to the sphere of international relations. Such a methodological base led to the isolation of Soviet scholars on international relations from research conducted in other countries, which was another characteristic of IR study in the USSR undertaken after World War II. In the 1920s, there were attempts to establish contacts between Russian and European scholars of this field. Thus, in 1926, with the active participation of the Soviet academician Yevgeniy Tarle, a scientific committee on relations with scientists of the USSR was established in Paris. However, later such initiatives were curtailed. Of course, cooperation with foreign colleagues was in existence, but it was limited and was represented from the Soviet side only by leading scholars. Young scholars usually did not have such an opportunity to communicate. However, this isolation was not unique. Although to a much lesser degree, this isolation was exposed, for example, in French political science and French IR studies (Favre 1996). Of course, one can speak of isolating national schools of international research only in relative terms, since even "the Soviet science of international relations could not develop in absolute isolation from world thought" (Tsygankov 1994, 23–24).

The next feature of Russian studies on international relations was that they were largely oriented toward the study of countries, but not issues. Academic institutions such as the Institute of the USA and Canada, the Institute of Oriental Studies, the Institute for African Studies, and the Institute of Europe studied their respective regions and countries, although there were some exceptions. Primarily, it is necessary to name the Institute of World Economy and International Relations. The very name of the institute suggested a departure from a particular region or country. However, in general, in the Soviet Union, region and country not only dominated in the fields of study and education but also actually subordinated everything to itself. Some shifts, however, occurred at the end of the 1970s and 1980s, when research on problems of conflict, negotiation, and so on appeared. But such studies were still a clear minority.

Soviet science, as well as education in the field of international relations, was based mostly on historical knowledge. Despite the fact that I.G. Tyulin writes about the formation of actual research on international relations in the country in the 1960s–1980s, which separated from the complex of historical, legal, and economic disciplines (Tyulin 1997), history remained as the dominant one. The historical roots of IR studies were to some extent typical of international relations in many countries. However, in western universities and research centers, political science developed simultaneously. In the USSR, political science began to receive wide recognition only in the late 1980s.

It should be noted that the relationship between political science and international relations in the world generally developed uneasily. Political science initially began to focus on the study of the political systems of states, while international relations began to focus on interstate interaction. As a consequence of the separation of subject areas, political science and research in the field of international relations began to develop in parallel. This led to the formation of largely separate structures such as associations, research centers, and scientific journals.

Somewhat closer to international relations (more precisely, to area studies) was a comparative political science (Lebedeva, Melvil 1999a). However, the complexity of the interaction between the two disciplines was due to differences in the conceptual apparatus and methods of research. In the second half of the twentieth century, a certain convergence of the two disciplines was beginning to take place owing to a number of studies. Thus, G. Allison in analysis of the Cuban missile crisis showed that the foreign policy of a state depends on groups of influence within the state, the interaction of which produces some compromise (Allison 1971). In turn, R. Putnam proposed to consider interstate negotiations as a double interaction (two-level games): on the one hand, between the states conducting negotiations, and on the other, within each state to develop a position (Putnam). Later, similar work began to appear more widely and, although gradually a certain convergence of disciplines occurred, political science and IR studies have continued to be "neighbors", having some intersection with each other.

In the Soviet Union, these studies were little known. In addition, the peculiarity of the Soviet Union was that international relations as an academic discipline began to develop before political science. Departments of political science appeared in the country in the late 1980s and early 1990s. At the same time, articles on political science, particularly with reference to international relations, began to be published in the country (see, for example, Muradyan 1990). Prior to that time, there was the Soviet Association of Political Sciences, and in 1979 the Eleventh Congress of the International Political Sciences Association was held in Moscow. However, there were no professional political science journals and no education in the field of political science in the Soviet Union before the end of 1980s.

International relations, unlike political science in the USSR, developed for many decades, although its development was limited by ideological and political reasons, of course. Having its own specifics throughout the Soviet period, IR studies, nevertheless, developed both in terms of organization and content.

At the end of the twentieth century, a lot of countries voiced their opinions to create a unified political science, which had to include IR studies (see Milner 1998; Werner, S., de Mosquita 2003). The question of a unified political science also began to rise in Russian publications (Lebedeva, M.M., Melvil 1999a; Melvil 2004; Ilin 2004).

Chapter 3
The Establishment of IR Studies in Contemporary Russia

3.1 Trends in Russian IR Studies in the Late 1980s

3.1.1 The "New Political Thinking" and Its Impact on International Relations

The study of international relations was significantly revived during the second half of the 1980s and the early 1990s. Of course, this applies not only to research in the field of international relations, but all social sciences were influenced by changes occurring in the country. Primarily, *perestroika* had affected the internal political sphere. The problems of domestic policy were at the center of both the research perspective and the broader public discussion in the Soviet Union.

As for research in international relations, there have also been significant changes that could not be overlooked: the end of the Cold War and the expansion of contact with the West had been the focus of attention. Usually, the international sphere in all countries is more conservative than domestic policy. However, it was not so in this case. The process of opening up to the outside world was directly connected with the changes inside the Soviet Union. In general, the trends that were laid during this period continued to operate throughout almost the entire 1990s.

Since the second half of the 1980s, significant changes have taken place in IR studies in the Soviet Union. Primarily, publications by foreign scholars became available to a wide circle of Soviet researchers. Previously, if these publications were in the USSR, they were in the departments of libraries with limited access to readers; these access restrictions were lifted. Moreover, the new most significant publications of foreign authors were immediately translated into Russian and intensively discussed in leading journals, as well as at scientific seminars. In 1990, there was a discussion on F. Fukuyama's article "The End of History?" in the *USA and Canada: Economy, Policy, Ideology* (*Konets istorii*... 1990 [The End of History...1990]). The discussion was reduced to criticism of Fukuyama's position, and this was partly because the author's position really raised many questions such as, in particular, what does "the end of history" mean, how should further historical development go, and so on. Incidentally, in other countries this article also caused a flurry of criticism. Soviet traditions, which were connected with criticism of bourgeois approaches, were also affected. However, the very fact of discussion in leading Russian journals of the problems of international relations almost immediately after the publication of this article was very noteworthy. In the same year, a translation of this article into Russian was published in *Voprosy filosofii* (*Russian Studies in Philosophy*) (Fukuyama 1990). A little later, "The Clash of Civilizations" by S. Huntington was translated and published in Russia a year after its original publication (Huntington 1994).

In the 1990s, many books and articles by foreign authors were translated. P.A. Tsygankov and A.P. Tsygankov defined this period as a mastering of world intellectual experience by Russian researchers in the field of social sciences and in particular in international relations (Tsygankov, Tsygankov 2005a). Russian experts in the field of international relations, including those from regions far from Moscow and St. Petersburg, quickly began to orient themselves well in foreign directions and approaches to the study of international relations. This was especially true for young researchers. This was facilitated by compulsory studying of foreign languages in the training of specialists in the field of international relations. At the same time, as A.D. Bogaturov noted, sometimes Russian scholars produced an artificial connection between knowledge of foreign ideas and their own studies (Bogaturov 2000). However, familiarity with the research of foreign authors contributed to changes in the methodological foundations of Russian IR studies. Russian scholars moved away from Marxism-Leninism, but they did not come across a "great" post-Soviet idea, as noted by A.P. Tsygankov and P.A. Tsygankov (Tsygankov,

Tsygankov 2005b, 15). As the great idea, they understood a kind of "mainstream" Russian international studies, such as "democratic peace," "international society," or Chinese "great harmony". Indeed, Russian scholars did not create a "great idea" in the field of IR studies. At the same time, it is not entirely clear if researchers from different countries put forward together the "great idea" in the field of international relations (it is often observed in the natural sciences that it is enough to look at the list of Nobel Prize laureates). If so, the meaning of the "national idea" is lost.

What came to replace Marxism-Leninism? The answer is not so well defined. Owing to several reasons, it is quite difficult to classify approaches to the study of international relations in Russia in this period. There is an overlay of political views of scientists on their research positions. In this respect, the field of international relations is one of the most politicized in Russia. However, in Russia, owing to political changes, both within the country and connected with the disintegration of the bipolar system of international relations, politicization was felt most acutely.

In April 1985, in the Soviet Union, Mikhail Gorbachev declared a foreign policy called the "new political thinking"[9]. Its essence was that relations between the USSR and the West should cease to be viewed as an indispensable confrontation with the prospect of a victory of the Communist idea. The priority of universal values over class was declared. V.V. Sogrin noted that in practice universal values have to be turned into socialist ones (Sogrin 1992). However, the Soviet Union made moves toward the West on a number of topical international issues, including the reunification of Germany and the withdrawal of troops from Afghanistan. The Soviet-American dialogue on disarmament issues resumed, and the unblocking of regional conflicts began. An interesting point was the proclamation of a balance of interests, instead of the traditional balance of powers within the framework of realism (see Rogov 1989; Udalov 1990). In other words, at the

---

9   Beseda M.S. Gorbacheva s redaktorom gazety «Pravda». *Pravda*, 8 aprelya 1985 goda [Interview the editor of newspaper "Pravda" with M.S. Gorbachev. April 8, 1985]

official foreign policy level, there was clearly a departure not only from Marxism-Leninism but also from the intuitive realism that prevailed in the Soviet period of the past.

Many scholars and politicians supported and developed the idea of the "new political thinking" (see, for example, Timofeev 1989). The very fact of its official distribution, of course, played a role. At the same time, in the era of Gorbachev, publications with sharp criticism of the foreign policy course associated with the end of the Cold War and the "new political thinking" appeared (see, for example, Froyanov 1999). The existence of different foreign policy course assessments became a new phenomenon in the USSR.

A.P. Tsygankov and P.A. Tsygankov wrote about a growing diversity of views in Russia (pluralization) and identified two tendencies in IR studies during this period: (1) westernization and (2) isolationism. Westernization refers to the dependence of Russian research on Western theories and approaches, while isolation refers to the rejection of Western approaches (Tsygankov, Tsygankov 2005b).

These two trends began to operate from the late 1980s and are present even today. The trend associated with attempts to build Russian approaches to international relations was more or less homogeneous, and it has been reduced to the search for Russia's special path. However, the same could not be said of "westernization", which has been rather heterogeneous.

Nevertheless, theoretical approaches to international relations that were being used at the end of the twentieth century and those that are being used now are Western ones. *Perestroika*, in the field of foreign policy, is "new political thinking" about openness. All these gave a significant boost to liberal ideas for Russian IR studies. During the period of *perestroika*, discussion amongst Soviet and foreign researchers on the problems of international relations were to some extent within a framework of a liberal paradigm (see Gromyko, Hellman 1998; Allison, Ury, Allyn 1989). Later, in the 1990s, a number of Russian studies were carried out in the liberal tradition, particularly concerning issues on negotiation and globalization.

In the late 1980s a realistic tradition rooted in the intuitive realism of the past continued to develop. There were many studies that were primarily devoted to relations between the USSR and the United States, as well as bilateral relations with other states. In turn, the Marxist tradition at the end of the Soviet era also continued in a number of studies, mostly concerning issues of socialist and developing countries. Overall, the theoretical basis of Russian IR studies in the late 1980s had not formed, although all the directions of so-called classical approaches—realism, liberalism, and neo-Marxism—emerged. In addition, we should agree with A.A. Sergunin that "Russian international studies have experienced a very quick and dramatic transformation from a discipline dominated by Marxist ideology to a multiparadigmatic discourse" (Sergunin 2005a, 54). It appears that such a rapid development of various paradigmatic orientation of research in Russia was largely facilitated by the fact that not only was the Marxist paradigm presented in the Soviet period, but also intuitive realism was the process of *perestoika* that stimulated the development of the liberal approach.

3.1.2 A Change in the Content of International Studies in the Years of *Perestroika*

In the course of *perestroika*, IR studies in Russia in terms of content increased considerably. The issues of conflicts and their settlement became relevant because of the needs to unlock regional conflicts and to seek solutions to conflict situations that emerged in relation to the Soviet Union (Nagorny Karabakh, Alma-Ata, and then in other places).

These processes gave impetus to new studies in the field of conflicts. It became obvious that in the past insufficient attention was paid to the study of conflicts. In earlier studies of conflicts, emphasis was not so much on resolving conflicts but on identifying the reasons for their development. In part, this emphasis on development of conflicts, and not on the process of their settlement, was due to the scientific tradition in Russia. Unlike, for example, American science, where there is a strong focus on pragmatism and much attention is paid to the technology of negotiation and conflict resolution, in Russia the factors that generate conflict were studied to a greater extent.

The tradition of studying the emergence and development of conflicts continued in a number of studies during the period of *perestroika*, including those of V.A. Kremenyuk (Kremenyuk 1990), E.V. Yegorova (Yegorova 1988), and others. The work of Yegorova largely continued the tradition of the previous Soviet period regarding analysis of American studies of conflicts. However, she made a fundamentally new step for Soviet IR studies. For the first time in the study of conflicts in the USSR, Yegorova paid close attention to the psychological aspects of conflict. In turn, Kremenyuk Began to study the process of settling international conflicts. This aspect was not previously dominant in the Soviet research.

As a part of conflict studies in the late 1980s, negotiating issues began to develop vigorously. Specific negotiations and general issues related to the negotiation process, including regarding technology behind the negotiation process, began to be analyzed. The principle of solving the problem based on a balance of interests, unlike the previously dominant principle of maximizing winnings, developed (Tyulin 2005).

Studies of international negotiations were held at MGIMO, at the Institute of the USA and Canada, and began to develop in other centers also. An.V. Zagorskiy, M.M. Lebedeva (Zagorskiy, Lebedeva 1989), V.L. Israelyan (Israelyan 1988), V.A. Kremenyuk (Kremenyuk 1991; Kremenyuk 1991), V.B. Lukov, and V.M. Sergeev (Lukov1988; Lukov, Sergeev 1981), as well as other authors published studies on negotiations. Thus, An. Zagorskiy developed a model for assessing the positions of parties in negotiations, previously proposed by V.B. Lukov and V.M. Sergeev. He introduced the notion of the "negotiation concept", which includes basic objectives, a list of priorities, and a number of other components. According to Zagorskiy, an essential element in the preparation of the negotiation concept is an analysis of possible solutions that are not equivalent to the negotiators: one option may be more acceptable for one party, but for the other one, the opposite. He also introduced an element in the study of a negotiation process: conditions for the acceptability of the variant of decisions. Conditions for acceptability are compensation for the costs of any option.

Another area of negotiation research, developed at this time in MGIMO Problem Research Laboratory, was connected with analysis of negotiating tactics. Structural elements were singled out in negotiating, such as ways of submitting a position, the stages of negotiating, and tactical methods. It was proposed to monitor the progress of negotiations on the basis of structural elements (Kovaleva, O.M., Lebedeva 1981). This direction of the study of negotiations had received a high estimation of American researchers. Thus, Bennett noted that in the field of study of tactical techniques, Soviet researchers were even more advanced than American scholars (Bennett 1997).

In the late 1980s, in addition to problems of international conflicts and the conducting of negotiations, security studies went through significant changes. Security studies during the Cold War was one of the most important issues, and at the same time it was very sensitive. In fact, researchers supported the official position without using special data and facts, because a significant amount of information was classified. With the processes of *perestroika*, security issues became more open. In addition, a number of Soviet scholars, in particular, A.G. Arbatov, V.V. Zhurkin, A.V. Kortunov, and S.A. Karaganov (Arbatov 1988; Arbatov 1990; Zhurkin, Karaganov, Kortunov, 1989) departed from a focus on the military power of national security, which was actually based on the idea of the military superiority of the USSR. In contrast, a concept of reasonable defense sufficiency was developed (Tyulin 1997).

The processes of *perestroika* significantly influenced not only IR studies in the USSR, but they also introduced some practices that were elaborated by Soviet scholars from the field of IR issues into the domestic sphere. This concerns the problems of conflict resolution and negotiation, since negotiation and mediation procedures were not used earlier in the Soviet Union. Conflicts in the USSR were usually handled by administrative methods "from above", In addition to this, conciliation procedures between and within a party's structures and administration's structures were used. But there were no talks inside the country. The emergence of the first serious conflicts in the Soviet Union on ethnic grounds – as well as in social relations – required appropriate technologies. In 1990, *Getting to Yes* (by R. Fisher and W. Ury), with a foreword by V.A. Kremenyuk, the Deputy Director of the Institute of the USA and Canadian Studies, was translated into Russian and published in the USSR (Fisher, Ury 1990). Moreover, studies by Russian researchers were published on issues of negotiation technology prepared by experts in the field of international relations and which focused on domestic political problems (Israelyan, Lebedeva 1991). A similar situation developed in other areas. For example, the rapid development of business in the country, its access to the international arena, led to the demand for books on protocol and etiquette, which were also originally published by specialists in the field of international relations.

3.2 Institutional Changes in IR Studies (1990s and Later)

3.2.1 Research Centers, IR Association, and New Journals

The change in the content of international research was accompanied by significant organizational transformations. On the one hand, it was caused by the logic of the political development of the world (in particular, the integration processes), and on the other hand, by the transformations that took place in Russia itself. Obviously, domestic changes have proved to have a more significant impact.

As for the changes that have taken place in the wider world, the development of European integration became the basis for the organization of the Institute of Europe under the Academy of Sciences, which was established in 1987.[10] Its first director was the

---

10 Institute of Europe RAS: http://en.instituteofeurope.ru/

academician V.V. Zhurkin. Since January 2000, the institute began to publish the quarterly journal *Contemporary Europe*.[11]

Security issues, despite the proclaimed "end of history", continued to be a significant theme in international relations. As a result, in 1999 the Russian Academy of Sciences established the Institute of International Security Problems.[12] However, the Institute of International Security Problems has not launched its activity in full. One of the reasons, apparently, is financial, and as a consequence is personnel-based.

In the late 1980s and early 1990s, Russia faced a financially difficult situation, which affected science and education to a large extent. Insufficient funding of science forced qualified researchers to leave academic structures for the first time and to create business structures such as banks and corporations (Tyulin 2005). Nevertheless, the institutes of the Academy of Sciences continued to work. Moreover, as was noted, new institutions were being created. At the same time, a number of institutes of the Russian Academy of Sciences, which were not directly related with IR studies (e.g. the Institute of Slavic Studies, the Institute of Comparative Political Science, the Institute of Sociology, the Institute of Ethnology and Anthropology, and the Institute of General History) started to pay more attention to international issues. Attention to international issues to a great extent was due to Russia's increased involvement in global issues.

In February 1992 the Russian Institute for Strategic Studies (RISI) was established by the Decree of the President of the Russian Federation.[13] Its tasks were to provide analytical materials, expert assessments, and recommendations for Russian state structures, national security issues, and issues of strategic importance for Russia. In 1992-2009, the institute focused on analytical issues of the most complex international situations.

---

11 'Contemporary Europe': http://www.sov-europe.ru/english/index.htm
12 Institut Problem mezhdunarodnoy bezopasnosti [Internatational secirity institute]: http://www.ipmb.ru/
13 Rossiyskiy institut strategicheskikh issledovaniy [Russian Institute of Strategic Studies]: http://riss.ru/

The Ministry of Foreign Affairs played a significant role in the reorganization of scientific research in the country in the field of international relations. First, in the previous period, at two educational institutions of the Ministry of Foreign Affairs —

MGIMO and the Diplomatic Academy — scientific research laboratories were established which expanded and intensified their activities during the years of *perestroika*. Second, as one of the divisions of the Ministry of Foreign Affairs, the Scientific-Coordination Center was created; its task was to interact with academic structures of the country (Pokhlebkin 1992). Under the Ministry of Foreign Affairs of the USSR, the Scientific Council was also formed, which brought together specialists from various fields, including space, medicine, energy, ecology, and, of course, international relations. In 1990, the Minister of Foreign Affairs of the USSR, E.A. Shevardnadze, speaking at a meeting of the Scientific Council, formulated three main levels of its activity: (1) the development of conceptual foundations for the analysis of current international relations; (2) discussion and decisions on specific international issues; and (3) development of a theoretical framework of foreign policy (Shevardnadze 1990). The scope of the Ministry of Foreign Affairs became broader and involved experts for consultation, participation in negotiations, and analysis of foreign policy situations. In the early 1990s, non-state centers for the analysis of international relations appeared in Russia for the first time. In 1992, the Council for Foreign and Defense Policy (CFDP / SVOP) was formed, uniting politicians, researchers, businessmen, and journalists. It was headed by S.A. Karaganov. The CFDP identified tasks for itself such as facilitating the development of, and implementing strategic concepts for the development of, Russia, its foreign and defense policy, and forming the Russian state and civil society in the country.[14]

One of the first nongovernmental research centers in Russia was the PIR-Center (Center for Political Studies), founded in 1994. The PIR-Center began to specialize in the study of security issues,

---

14 Sovet po vneshney i oboronnoy politike [Council for Foreign and Defense Policy]: http://svop.ru/about/

nuclear nonproliferation, and international information security,[15] that is, on some of the most sensitive issues of international relations for any state-security apparatus. The PIR-Center began to publish a scientific journal, which until 2007 was under the title *Nuclear Control*, and then was changed to *Security Index*.[16] The PIR-Center laid the foundation for the formation of the Center for Analysis of Strategies and Technologies (CAST), a nongovernmental organization founded in 1997, which began to study issues of the defense industry and military-technical cooperation.[17] CAST publishes the journal *Eksport vooruzheniy* [Arms exports],[18] which is dedicated to issues of military-technical cooperation and the defense industry complex, as well as other periodicals, including in English, on security and arms issues: *Moscow Defense Brief* (trends in Russia's rolling policy and industry),[19] and *Periscope* (daily reviews of events in the field of military-technical cooperation and the military-industrial complex).[20]

Later, other nongovernmental organizations engaged themselves in analysis of international relations, and consulting services began to emerge in Russia, but they were often represented by only a few researchers who appeared in the media as experts and consultants.

A significant factor for IR studies in the country was the development of political science. Despite the fact that political science in the USSR began to evolve in the 1950s, and in 1960 the Soviet Political Science Association was established, which joined the International Political Science Association (IPSA) and began publishing yearbooks (see, for example, *Mezhdunarodnye otnosheniya*... 1976 [International relations... 1976]; *Vzaimosvyaz i vzaimovliyanie*... 1982 [Relationship and mutual influence... 1982ъ),

---

15 PIR-Center: http://www.pircenter.org/en/
16 Security Index: http://www.pircenter.org/en/security-index
17 Centr analiza strategiy i tekhnologiy (AST) [Center for strategies and technologies analisys]: http://www.cast.ru/
18 Eksport vooruzheniy [Arms exports]: http://www.cast.ru/eng/journal/
19 Moscow Defense Brief: http://mdb.cast.ru/
20 Periskop: http://periscope2.ru/

the association's activities were limited to a small group of people, mostly experts in law. Political science in the country was firmly established in the late 1980s. At first, political science was designed to be a university discipline at Leningrad State University[21] in the late 1980s, but later it quickly developed in Russia. In December 1991, the Russian Political Science Association (RPSA)[22] was created, which became the successor of the Soviet Political Science Association in IPSA.

The development of political science contributed to the growth of organizational forms of IR studies in Russia. Following the creation of the RPSA, the Russian International Studies Association (RISA)[23] was formed in 1999. The initiator of its creation was MGIMO, which became its headquarters. RISA came to be a member of the World International Studies Committee (WISC). In the 1990s, there were new associations of researchers involved in the study of international relations, including the Association of European Studies,[24] which was established in 1992. Since 1994, the association has been a member of the European Community Study Association (ECSA-World).[25]

In the 1990s, the first Russian and foreign foundations began to operate in Russia, which started to provide grants, including for research in the field of international relations. Among national funds, the Moscow Public Science Foundation (MPSF) was founded in 1991 for organizing scientific conferences and research in the field of social sciences on the basis of grants. It operated until the middle of the 2000s. The founder and president of the MPSF was A.V. Kortunov. The MPSF helped publish the work of many Russian researchers in the field of international relations, and IR studies in Russia began to develop.

Later, state foundations were created: the Russian Humanitarian Science Foundation (RHF)[26] and the Russian Science

---

21 Now it is called St Petersburg State University: http://english.spbu.ru/
22 Russian Political Science Association: http://rapn.ru/
23 Russian International Studies Association (RISA): http://risa.ru
24 Association of European Studies (AES): http://www.aevis.ru/
25 European Community Study Association (ECSA): http://www.ecsaworld.eu/
26 Russian Humanitarian Science Foundation: http://www.rfh.ru/index.php/ru

Foundation (RSF).[27] In 2016, RHF merged with another Russian foundation—the Russian Foundation for Basic Research (RFBR).[28] Their activities were aimed at providing grant support to researchers, including those in the field of international relations. In 2000, the Academic Educational Forum on International Relations was established among the non-state foundations for international relations. It was "more concerned with network-building among individuals"[29]. According to A.P. Tsygankov and P.A. Tsygankov, the development of IR studies in the Russian regions had become possible largely due to grant support (Tsygankov, Tsygankov 2005a).

Russia had also established research foundations that have become technologically advanced, or at least touched on issues of international relations, particularly the Gorbachev Foundation,[30] where V.B. Kuvaldin helped address challenges in international relations.

The Russian International Affairs Council (RIAC)[31] is a nonprofit organization that is still active in the field of international relations. It was established in 2010 by order of the president of the Russian Federation. The mission of RIAC is as follows: "The RIAC mission is to facilitate Russia's peaceful integration into the global community, partly by organizing greater cooperation between Russian academic institutions and foreign centers."[32] Established in 2004, the Valdai Discussion Club also aims "to operate the relationship between Russian and international intellectual elite, and to make an independent, unbiased scientific analysis of political, economic, and social events in Russia and the rest of the world."[33]

---

27 Russian Science Foundation: http://рнф.рф/en
28 Russian Foundation for Basic Research (RFBR): http://www.rfbr.ru/rffi/eng
29 Academic Educational Forum on International Relations: http://www.obraforum.ru/
30 The International Foundation for Socio-Economic and Political Studies (Gorbachev Foundation): http://www.gorby.ru/en/
31 Russian International Affairs Council (RIAC): http://russiancouncil.ru/en/
32 RIAC: http://russiancouncil.ru/en/about-us/what_is_riac/
33 Valdai Discussion Club: http://valdaiclub.com/about/valdai/

The Izborsk Club, established in 2012, views its tasks in the opposite way. The tasks of the club include facilitating the formation of a powerful political-ideological coalition of patriotic statesmen, an imperial front that opposes manipulation carried out in Russian politics by foreign centers of influence and the "fifth column" from within the country.[34] It cannot be said that such a view is mainstream in contemporary IR studies in Russia, although it is fairly common.

Since the 1990s, the number of Russian journals aimed at publishing research on international relations significantly increased: *Polis. Politicheskie issledovaniya Polis* [Polis. Political Studies], Kosmopolis [*Cosmopolis*] (also published two numbers: *Kosmopolis* and *Kosmopolis. Almanakh*), *Mezdunarodnye protsessy* [International Trends], *Politiya* [Politia], *Sovremennaya Evropa* [Contemporary Europe], *Vestnik MGIMO – Universiteta* [MGIMO Review of International Relations], *Rossiya v globalnoy politike* [Russia in Global Politics], *Sravnitelnaya politika* [Comparative Politics], Pro et Contra, and a number of others including journals in Russian regions. The content of IR journals that were published during the Soviet time changed substantially (Tyilin 2005).

In 2016 the journals Polis. Political Studies, Contemporary Europe, International Trends, and World Economy and International Relations were included in the Scopus database, and the journal MGIMO Review of International Relations in the databases "The European Reference Index for the Humanities and the Social Sciences (ERIH PLUS)" and "Web of Science". This list has expanded considerably. The inclusion of Russian journals (including those related to international relations) in international databases strengthened publication activity of the authors; this was set as one of the objectives at the federal level. At the same time, as I. Istomin and A. Baykov noted, almost all journals, with a few exceptions, have an institutional affiliation: they are published either by universities or by institutes of the Russian Academy of

---

34 Izborskiy klub [Izborsk club]: http://www.izborsk-club.ru/opr/izborsk-c.php

Sciences. That is, they are not really all-Russian venues for discussion (Istomin, Baykov 2013).

In recent years in Russia, considerable attention has been paid to various scientometric indicators. A science index database was created based on the Russian index of scientific citations. Data on researchers involved in IR studies are included in the general database on political sciences, indicating the number of published research findings, h-index, and other indicators.[35] Despite the problem of science-based indicators, these are a stimulus for the intensification of scientific research, including in the field of international relations in Russia.

Finally, in terms of organizational issues, the important point was the intensification of ties between Russian researchers and their international colleagues, the participation of Russian specialists in international relations in international conferences, the holding of international conferences in Russian territory, and joint grants held by Russian and foreign researchers on IR studies.

3.2.2 Regional Dimensions of IR Studies in Russia

One of the most important events since the 1990s was that international studies in Russia for the first time went beyond the boundaries of Moscow. IR studies were being developed in the territory of the former USSR, in the regions of Russia (primarily at universities' centers), as well as in the CIS and Baltic countries. By the end of the 1990s, their number in Russia had become significant. There was even a reference book on the centers of international research in the CIS (Bogaturov, Kortunov 1999).

Initially IR studies began to develop in St. Petersburg State University (the dean was K.K. Khudoley) and in Nizhny Novgorod State University (the dean was O.A. Kolobov), a little later in Kazan State University, Far Eastern Federal University (Vladivostok), and Ural Federal University named after the first President of Russia B.N. Yeltsin (Yekaterinburg). IR studies have begun to be taught at universities in a number of other Russian cities. As a rule, at

---

35 Russian Index of scientific citations E-library: http://elibrary.ru/authors.asp

universities international relations were studied by scholars who graduated in the field of history. Faculties of international relations were separated from faculties of history. This is a common characteristic of almost all universities in the country: IR faculties were mainly based on historical faculties.

St. Petersburg State University was one of the first universities to declare itself as a center for IR studies outside of Moscow. The geographical position of the university influenced the choice of the leading issues in its research, of course. To a large extent it became a center for European studies. K.K. Khudoley, the first dean of the Faculty of International Relations at St. Petersburg State University and the head of the Department of European Studies, had contributed a lot to the development of these issues from an organizational and scientific points of view (see Khudoley 2002a; Khudoley 2003; Khudoley 2002b). As the Faculty of International Relations at St. Petersburg State University evolved, the research topics expanded. Thus, research on Russia-EU relations began to take shape, including in the energy sector (see Romanova 2002; Romanova 2013; Shirin 2007), as well as study of the Baltic region (see Barygin, Lanko, Fofanova 2005; Katsy 2003), American studies (see Golubev 2010; Bogdanov 2010; Kubyshkin, Tsvetkova 2013; Shiryaev 2011), analysis of global problems (see Yagya 2011; Alimov 2003), the study of the activities of international nongovernmental organizations (see Stetsko 2015), social and humanitarian issues (see Bogolyubova, Nikolaeva 2013), problems of the Arctic (see Konyshev, Sergunin 2011), and theoretical aspects of IR (see Konyshev, Sergunin 2013). In fact, now the Faculty of International Relations presents all the main issues of international relations.

The Faculty of International Relations at St. Petersburg State University began to recruit scholars from other Russian regions. In particular, several professors from Nizhny Novgorod, also from Volgograd, moved to work there. Such a practice of internal mobility of scholars in the field of international relations is still a rarity in Russia.

Now in St. Petersburg, international relations are also being studied in the North-West Institute of Management of the Russian Presidential Academy of National Economy and Public Administration.[36] They focus on Eurasian integration, as well as on international activity in the North-West regions of Russia (see Kosov 2013; Shamakhov 2003; Kosov 2013).

In Nizhny Novgorod State University in the 1990s-early 2000s, a group of young researchers under the leadership of O.A. Kolobov began to develop issues around historical aspects of the development of conflicts, focusing on the Arab-Israeli conflict (see Kolobov, Kornilov, Sergunin 1991; Kolobov, Kornilov, Makarychev, Sergunin 1992b) and the history and theory of international relations (see Kolobov 2001; Safronova 2001; Sergunin, Makarychev 1999). The university paid a lot of attention to security issues (see Kolobov, Kornilov, Makarychev, Sergunin. 1992b; Kolobov, Baluev 1997 i grugie 1997; Kokhlysheva 2000; Kolobov 2005). It also prepared work on a comparative analysis of foreign policy decision-making in different countries of the world (see Kolobov, Kornilov, Makarychev, Sergunin 1992a). Until now, this work remains in demand in Russia. In recent years, Nizhny Novgorod State University has been reorganized and the Institute of International Relations and World History has been founded, with M.I. Rykhtik as its director. Scholars of this institute are increasingly turning to analysis of new issues of international relations, such as biopolitics, international crime, and social networks (see Rykhtik, Kvashnin 2009; Rykhtik 2012; Baluev, Kaminchenko 2012).

International studies and education have also been developed in Nizhny Novgorod State Linguistic University. At the beginning of the twenty-first century, the university produced a series of publications on international relations (see *Mezhdunarodnye otnosheniya v XXI veke...* 2000 [International relations in the XXI century... 2000]; *Rossiyskie regiony...* 2000 [Russian regions... 2000],

---

36 North-West Institute of Management Russian Presidential Academy of National Economy and Public Administration: http://www.sziu.ru/staticheskie-stranitsyi/747/north-west-institute-of-management/

Rossiya pered globalnymi vyzovami 2002 [Russia facing global challenges 2002]).

Significant centers for IR studies and education in Russia became the universities of Kazan, Vladivostok, Yekaterinburg, and Volgograd. At the Higher School of International Relations and Oriental Studies at the Kazan Federal University, much attention was paid to oriental issues (see Shagalov, Grishin, Akhmetova 2015). Asian issues with an orientation mainly on the Asia-Pacific region, were also presented in studies of the Institute of Oriental Studies and the School of Regional and International Studies (SRIS) of Far Eastern Federal University. (see Azizian, Lukin 2012; Sevastyanov 2005).

The Department of International Relations of Institute of Humanities of Ural Federal University deals with a wide range of subjects. In terms of regional specifics, studies are conducted both on European and Asian issues, reflecting the fact that the university is located on the border of Europe and Asia (see *Uralskoe vostokovedenie...*[37]; Mikhaylenko 1998). A.S. Burnasov, associate professor, developed an interesting direction of research about the role of logistics companies in world politics. His article, published in the journal *Vestnik MGIMO-Universiteta*, became one of the most widely read of this journal (Burnasov 2013).

The Faculty of History of Tomsk State University has been conducting studies on current asymmetric conflicts (see Deriglazova 2009), and Volgograd State University has been developing American studies and work on the international activities of Russian regions (see Kurilla, Zhuravleva 2007; Kurilla 2016). Balkan studies, the analysis of the regions of Europe, the study of international consultations, and other research projects are being conducted at Ivanovo State University (see Polyvyanniy 2015; Budanova 2013; Zobnin 2015).

Moscow is a subject of the Russian Federation and so in this sense it is a Russian region. In the capital, in addition to the

---

[37] *Uralskoe vostokovedenie: Mezhdunarodniy almanakh* [Ural Oriental Studies. International Almanac]. Yekaterinburg: Izdatelstvo Uralskogo Federalnogo Universiteta

previously mentioned institutes of the Academy of Sciences, MGIMO and the Diplomatic Academy, IR studies are conducted at the RUDN University,[38] the Russian Presidential Academy of National Economy and Public Administration,[39] Lomonosov Moscow State University,[40] National Research University Higher School of Economics,[41] and at a number of other Moscow universities and centers. The range of issues in IR studies in Moscow is the broadest, reflecting all directions and approaches.

In general, speaking about the development of IR studies in Russia, it should be noted that this process was long and it evolved both during the Soviet period and *perestroika* and during the formation of new Russia. As a result, Russian IR studies have ceased to be limited to Moscow. In this sense, they have indeed ceased to be elitist (Sergunin 2005a).

---

38 RUDN University: http://www.rudn.ru/en_new/
39 The Russian Presidential Academy of National Economy and Public Administration: http://www.ranepa.ru/eng/
40 Lomonosov Moscow State University: https://www.msu.ru/en/
41 National Research University Higher School of Economics (HSE) https://we.hse.ru/en

Chapter 4
Education in the Field of International Relations

4.1 The Teaching of International Relations in the Soviet Union

There was quite a significant distinction between academic and universities' sciences in the USSR. Studies were conducted in the research institutes of the Academy of Sciences or in specialized scientific research centers (institutes) under various ministries. Teaching was carried out in educational institutions and universities. The difference between educational institutions and universities usually consisted in the fact that universities had a larger number of faculties, which were diverse (mathematics, science, and humanities), while educational institutes trained students in a specific profile (medicine or physics), although leading universities and institutes in the country also carried out research, of course.

Initially, in the USSR specialized training in international relations was not conducted. On the one hand, this was not necessary because of the USSR's limited contacts with the outside world at the beginning of the twentieth century. On the other hand, authorities feared the appearance of an uncontrolled interest in knowledge in the field of international relations, which could have contributed to the erosion of the socialist system in the Soviet Union. Until the mid-1930s, there were no faculties or departments specializing in international relations in the USSR.

In 1934, the Institute of Diplomatic and Consular Staff was established for training diplomatic personnel. The duration of study was two years.[42] This was the model for today's Russian

---

42 Istoriya Diplomaticheskoy akademii MID Rossii [The history of Diplomatic Academy MFA of Russia]. Diplomatic Academy: http://www.dipacademy.ru/about/history/

Diplomatic Academy. The institute was renamed several times: first as the Higher Diplomatic School, and then as the Diplomatic Academy[43]

The Russian Diplomatic Academy was built largely on the same principles as many diplomatic academies in the world. It gave specialized knowledge to those who, having already obtained a higher education, switched to work at the Ministry of Foreign Affairs or, after working there for several years, went to the Diplomatic Academy for retraining. However, there were differences. First, at that time in the Soviet Union, there was no place to acquire basic education in the field of international relations or political science. And this is despite the fact that in 1804 the Faculty of Moral and Political Sciences was established at Moscow Imperial University. However, later, this department was almost forgotten.[44] Second, to be enrolled in the Diplomatic Academy, approval of a party organization was necessary.

By the end of World War II it became evident that the scale of Soviet involvement in international affairs, as well as its role in the international arena, was dramatically increasing. This necessitated more focused training of personnel for practical work in the field of international relations. In 1943, at Moscow State University (MSU) named after M.V. Lomonosov, the faculty of international relations was established. A year later, this faculty was transformed into Moscow State Institute of International Relations (MGIMO).[45]

Like the Diplomatic Academy, MGIMO became an educational institution of the Ministry of Foreign Affairs, but at the same time it was subordinate to the Ministry of Education. However, unlike the Diplomatic Academy, which is engaged in retraining, MGIMO provided a complete higher education. At that time in the USSR, there was no division into bachelor's and master's degrees, and it took four years to receive higher education in

---

43   Diplomatic Academy: http://www.dipacademy.ru/
44   Zorin V. Politologiya dlya sovremennoy Rossii [Political science for contemporary Russia]. *REX Information Agency*: http://www.iarex.ru/articles/48583.html
45   Moscow State Institute of International Relations (MGIMO): http://mgimo.ru/

international relations. Soon this term was increased to five years (Torkunov 2014).

Both the Diplomatic Academy and MGIMO provided training for social science candidates. This degree was analogous to the Ph.D.. However, requirements for obtaining a "candidate of science" degree were somewhat different to those required for obtaining the analogous Ph.D. For example, to obtain the degree of "candidate of science" it was necessary to pass examinations in international relations, foreign languages, and philosophy in order to publish academic articles (usually at least three), or to write a dissertation (about 200 pages). A wide range of topics was discussed at the department, and then before the dissertation council of MGIMO or the Diplomatic Academy. This was the usual procedure for this degree for all fields of science, not only for international relations. The decision of the dissertational council was made based on a secret ballot, and it was then approved by the Higher Attestation Commission (VAK) of the USSR, formed under the Ministry of Higher Education.

In the USSR, there was one more degree, which was doctor of science. To obtain it one needed to possess a much larger number of scientific publications, including a monograph. The volume of the doctoral dissertation was usually twice that of the candidate's thesis. The procedure for defending a doctoral dissertation was the same as for a Ph.D. thesis. The presence of two degrees (candidate and doctor of science) and the procedure for obtaining them with subsequent approval of the decision of dissertational councils by VAK have been preserved largely to the present day. However, now there are a few exceptions; some universities (including MSU, St. Petersburg University, MGIMO, RUDN, and some others) have the right to make independent decisions on awarding a degree without subsequent approval by VAK.

The activities of MGIMO began in 1944 with the enrollment of 250 students.[46] Many students of the first sets were participants in

---

46 Istoriya fakulteta Mezhdunarodnye otnosheniya [The history of International Relations faculty]. *MGIMO*: http://mgimo.ru/study/faculty/mo/docs/istori ya-fakulteta/

the war. Training in international relations has focused largely on the study of foreign languages: initially it was English, German, and French (Torkunov 2014) (usually a student during the training had to master at least two foreign languages) and the history of international relations. Significant subjects were economics and law. In this regard, education in international relations in the USSR was not much different from a similar education provided in Western universities, although in other countries less attention was paid to the study of foreign languages during the education in international relations. At the same time, despite the fact that Marxism assumed considerable attention to economic issues, it cannot be said that economic courses were highly distinguished from others. In general, they were smaller than the historical courses.

At the same time, neither political science nor theory of international relations was taught in the Soviet Union, as these disciplines did not exist in the USSR. It was only in the late 1980s that courses on political science and the theory of international relations were beginning to be introduced into the educational process. However, it was necessary to not simply "add" political science to the curricula of training. A political perspective needed to be organically incorporated into international political issues, by creating new curricula and textbooks (Torkunov 2016).

Training in the USSR was largely ideologized: books on the classics of Marxism, documents of party congresses and conferences, and materials relating to the international communist and workers' movement were studied. As a result, training programs in international relations in the Soviet period were intricately intertwined with practical orientation and ideological attitudes.

MGIMO delivered the absolute majority of specialists in the Ministry of Foreign Affairs of the USSR and paid much attention to providing students a good educational basis, primarily in history and in foreign languages. As a practically oriented field, international relations was one of the few exceptions in social and the humanities in the USSR, which tried to minimize the differences between academic education and future practical activity, believing that a good knowledge provides for better focus on practice.

Many high-ranking officials of the Ministry of Foreign Affairs taught at MGIMO from the very beginning (when it was established). Many of them had academic degrees and academic titles. Among them were the following: academician S.L. Tikhvinsky, a sinologist, who worked in various positions in the Ministry of Foreign Affairs of the USSR and had the rank of Ambassador Extraordinary and Plenipotentiary; academician V.G. Trukhanovsky, who worked as Consul General in the city of Kermanshakh (Iran), as head of the UN division at the MFA of the USSR, and the Association of British studies in post-Soviet Russia (Kapitonova 2011); academician Yu.P. Franzev, who at one time was in charge of the Foreign Ministry's Press Department; and academician L.N. Ivanov, who was an expert of the Ministry of Foreign Trade, as well as an expert of the People's Commissariat for Foreign Affairs on naval issues. Many other well-known scientists and practitioners taught various courses in international relations at MGIMO.

As a result, many graduates of MGIMO became outstanding scientists and diplomats. Consequently, from the batch of first graduates (1948) were there future academicians: G.A. Arbatov, who became director of the Institute of the USA and Canada of the Academy of Sciences of the USSR/Russia; academician V.A. Vinogradov, who headed the Institute of Scientific Information on Social Sciences of the USSR Academy of Sciences/Russia; and academician A.G. Kovalyov, deputy minister of foreign affairs of the USSR (Torkunov 2014).

As for other higher educational institutions of the USSR, a small group of IR specialists was trained at the Institute of International Relations named after T. Shevchenko – Taras Shavchenko National University of Kyev.[47]

In all educational institutions for international relations, there were students from the republics of the Soviet Union, as well as

---

47 Institute of International Relations, Taras Shavchenko University of Kyev: http://www.iir.edu.ua/en/

from socialist countries and from developing countries. Foreign students came to study in the USSR based on intergovernmental agreements. Many of them have become well-known political and diplomatic figures. Among them are the following: Ilham Aliyev — the President of Azerbaijan; Irina Bokova — Director-General of UNESCO; Maros Sefcovic — European Commission Vice President for Energy Union; and Edward Nalbandian — Minister of Foreign Affairs of Armenia.

In other higher educational institutions of the country, including outside Moscow, training was conducted on certain aspects related to international relations. For example, the Oriental faculty of Leningrad State University (currently St. Petersburg State University)[48] as well as the Institute of Asian and African Studies at Lomonosov Moscow State University[49] trained specialists in Asian and African issues. Institutes of foreign languages produced interpreters and teachers of foreign languages. Some historical faculties carried out research and published studies on the history of international relations (e.g., at Irkutsk State University (see, for example, Novikov 1996)). In general, these higher educational institutions and faculties were not focused on teaching and researching international relations as such.

The end of the 1980s became a significant stage in the teaching of international relations in the Soviet Union. Thus, in 1988, for the first time in the USSR, a chair of Political Science was opened at the Philosophical Faculty of Leningrad State University. In 1989, the chair of political science was founded in MGIMO. Then a year later MGIMO opened the first faculty of political science in Russia. International contacts of Russian IR teachers and students began to expand.

---

[48] Oriental faculty at Saint-Petersburg State University: http://www.iir.edu.ua/en/
[49] Institute of Asian and African Studies at Lomonosov Moscow State University: http://www.iaas.msu.ru/

4.2 Teaching International Relations in the Post-Soviet Period

The end of the Cold War and the disintegration of the Soviet Union led to a significant restructuring of the teaching of international relations in Russia. Russia in the late 1980s-early 1990s had experienced the most serious changes in sociopolitical and economic life. Primarily, de-ideologization of education took place, which had a special significance for the sphere of international relations. Marxism-Leninism ceased to be an official theoretical and methodological basis. Many new Western books and articles of different theoretical focus and orientation, previously unknown to the Russian reader, appeared in Russia. All these stimulated interest in the theories of international relations developed in the West, as well as in political science. P.A. Tsygankov made a great contribution to the situation that Russian IR students became acquainted with Western approaches to the theories of international relations. In fact, he was the first to give the description of the main theoretical approaches to the study of international relations in the Russian language. His book *International Relations* (Tsygankov 1996) remains a core textbook in Russia on the theory of international relations. It is included in the curricula of all Russian universities that teach international relations.

The next important moment in the restructuring of education in the field of international relations was that international relations ceased to be only a sphere of diplomatic activity in Russia. The country began to develop international relations in the regions. Businesses, including regional ones, went directly to the international arena, often bypassing the Ministry of Foreign Trade. International tourism began to develop. International nongovernmental organizations and foundations began to operate actively. Chairs and faculties of international relations began to emerge in various Russian cities. From the sphere previously occupied by a relatively narrow group of people in Moscow, the teaching of international relations has spread to various regions of Russia.

One of the first faculties on international relations in new Russia and the first faculty outside of Moscow was the Faculty of International Relations at St. Petersburg State University, established in March 1994.[50] The organizer of the faculty and its first dean was Professor K. K. Khudoley. Two years later—in 1996—the master's program in "European Studies" was opened at the university. Thus, the faculty was one of the first outside Moscow, prior to the Bologna process, which moved to a two-tier system of higher education (Osinskaya 2009).

An important point was that higher education in Russia in the late 1980s and early 1990s experienced problems with insufficient funding; however, these problems were still considered small compared to those in the fields of science. Some of the leading researchers from the institutes of the Academy of Sciences began to teach at universities. This allowed, on the one hand, researchers from academic institutions to maintain an acceptable level financially; on the other hand, the teaching of leading researchers from the Academy of Sciences made it possible to raise the level of teaching in a number of universities. In addition, universities were allowed to receive some of the students on a fee-paying basis. During the Soviet period this was not allowed. This also enabled the universities partially to resolve problems of financing.

In 1992, the Russian Center for Humanitarian Education was established at the institutes of the Russian Academy of Sciences, and two years later, it received the status of a university. Since 2008, the university is known as the State Academic University for Humanities.[51] Academician Alexander O. Chubaryan of the Russian Academy of Sciences played a great role in the organization of this university. The university provided a special emphasis on the training of researchers in the field of humanitarian and social disciplines. The Faculty of World Politics of the State

---

50 Faculty of International Relations at St. Petersburg State University: http://sir.spbu.ru/
51 State Academic University for the Humanities: http://gaugn.ru/en-us/

Academic University for the Humanities, which was established at the Institute of the USA and Canada of the Russian Academy of Sciences, is directly focused on the training of personnel in the field of international relations.

At present, the geography of universities that train cadres for international relations covers the whole country, from Arkhangelsk to Vladivostok. In Moscow, as in St. Petersburg, a number of universities started programs on international relations. There are similar programs in many other Russian cities besides Vladivostok and Arkhangelsk; programs have been implemented in Nizhny Novgorod, Yekaterinburg, Kazan, Krasnoyarsk, Tomsk, Irkutsk, and Krasnodar. Courses on international relations are delivered at some faculties of political science, history, foreign languages, sociology, and others. Rather widespread are summer and winter schools, various seminars for young researchers, graduate students, and teachers of international relations. This work is quite effective and is usually conducted via a framework of various grants.

Since the 1990s, a whole series of educational literature on international relations has been published. Pavel A. Tsygankov, in addition to *International Relations*, published textbooks and readers with the texts of Western scholars (Tsygankov 2002). In a small edition, another reader was published, reflecting the views of American and French researchers (Lebedeva, Tsygankov 2001). In the late 1990s in Irkutsk another textbook on the theory of international relations written by G.N. Novikov was issued (Novikov 1996). Later, other books on the theory of international relations were published (see, for example, Bordachev, Zinovieva, Likhacheva 2015).

Textbooks on conflicts and their settlement (see, for example, Feldman 1998; Lebedeva 1997) the history of international relations (see Protopopov, Kozmenko, Yelmanova 2001) world politics (see Lebedeva 2003), introductions to the IR field (Nikitina), and on other disciplines were also published. Of great importance was the publication of the first Russian textbook on international relations by a team of scholars from MGIMO and other universities, as well as institutes of the Russian Academy of Sciences, edited by A.V.

Torkunov: *Modern International Relations* (Torkunov 1998). Later, the textbook on contemporary international relations, edited by A.V. Torkunov, appeared several times in different versions.

The book *A New Handbook of Political Science* by Robert E. Goodin and Hans-Dieter Klingemann (Goodin, Klingemann 1996) was translated into Russian (*Politicheskaya nauka: novye napravleniya* / Goodin, Klingemann 1999). However, this edition usually is not included in the educational literature when teaching IR students, but was more used by IR researchers, as well as by political scientists. It should be noted that much of the educational literature, especially that released in the late 1990s-early 2000s in Russia, was also scientific literature. The fact is that at that time it was difficult to publish a scientific monograph on international relations in Russia. Grant systems for the publication of academic literature in those days were practically nonexistent, and it was economically unprofitable for publishing houses to publish such work because unlike textbooks, these others were issued in small print runs and did not pay off. But grant support for the publication of textbooks was available. Therefore, educational literature was used by researchers to publish scientific results.

However, later another problem arose with the publication of educational literature on international relations. There was quite a large number of textbooks, which retold two to three other tutorials previously released in Russian. There were even cases where the textbooks contained almost verbatim texts borrowed from textbooks written by another author.

Since the early 1990s, Russia has been differentiating education into area studies, focusing on the study of countries and regions and international relations, with a focus on issues of international relations. Later, the Ministry of Education of the Russian Federation fixed these two approaches in higher education.

The content of education has also changed in post-Soviet time. In Russia, new academic and educational disciplines were formed: world politics, applied international political analysis, and global integrated regional studies (Torkunov 2016). New courses appeared in the programs, including the theory of international relations, analytical methods, tendencies in the development of international processes (in particular, the development of European integration), and theoretical issues of diplomacy (including the theory of negotiations). Active methods of teaching—simulation games, case studies, and so on—began to be used more intensively.

With the accession of Russia to the Bologna process in 2003, Russian higher education switched from a five-year form of study (specialist) to a four-year form (bachelor's degree) plus a two-year form (master's degree) of education. This allowed the Russian education system to be compared with the European one, as well as the possibility of opening a number of joint master's programs in international relations in various universities of the country. In addition, it gave students an opportunity to change the direction of their training. Students who had a bachelor's degree in foreign languages, economics, law, and even natural science and technical specialties began to enter master's programs in international relations.

Russian universities, oriented toward the teaching of international relations, have significantly expanded. In a number of universities, joint master's programs were opened with foreign partners; teachers began to participate much more actively in international conferences and to publish their articles in foreign journals. Two educational institutions—MGIMO and the Faculty of International Relations of St. Petersburg University—became members of the Association of Professional Schools of International Affairs.[52]

The Diplomatic Academy has also changed its focus. Remaining the main center of retraining for the Ministry of Foreign Affairs of Russia (especially for those who received basic bachelor's and master's training not in international relations or area studies), the Diplomatic Academy opened a wide range of all levels of training—bachelor's degrees, master's degrees, and Ph.D. programs.

---

52 Association of Professional Schools of International Affairs: http://www.apsia.org/

Nongovernmental Russian universities and centers also began to provide educational services in the field of international relations. Thus, students in the field of international relations began to be taught at the Moscow Humanitarian University at the Faculty of International Relations and Tourism.[53] First in 1998, the faculty opened the possibility of getting an education in area studies, and in 2004 in international relations.

Other universities and centers also offer different programs. For example, the master's program of a double diploma in the field of nuclear nonproliferation is run by a nongovernmental organization the PIR Center in cooperation with MGIMO, on the Russian side, and the Middlebury Institute for International Studies in Monterey (MIIS, Monterey, California) on the American side.

MGIMO continues to be the leading educational institution in Russia in the field of international relations. In 1994, MGIMO received the status of a university, since it had a large number of programs in various disciplines. This meant expanding the range of specialties for which training was being conducted, as well as an increase in the number of faculties. Accordingly, the areas in which MGIMO graduates began to work has significantly expanded. Along with traditional spheres of employment (the Ministry of Foreign Affairs of Russia, other foreign affairs agencies, and the media), new ones, including private Russian business, foreign companies, and regional structures, became open for graduates.

In 1998 at MGIMO the Faculty of Political Science was established on the basis of the chair of political science of the Faculty of International Relations (FIR). As a result of the foundation of the FIR, international relations are beginning to be taught at two faculties in MGIMO: (1) the Faculty of International Relations and (2) the Faculty of Political Science (later reorganized as the Faculty of Governance and Politics—FGP). The main difference between FIR and FGP was that at the Faculty of International Relations, a significant emphasis was traditionally had on the study of the historical aspects of international relations,

---

[53] Moscow Humanitarian University: http://mosgu.ru/en/

while at the Faculty of Governance and Politics, focus was more on political aspects. At the FGP, much more attention was paid to theoretical aspects, where the chair of Political Theory was established. In addition, the Faculty of Governance and Politics paid special attention to new aspects and problems of contemporary international relations: international activities of non-state actors, role of information technologies in international relations, use of soft power, globalization and integration processes, and so on.

In 1994 MGIMO opened the first joint (and then double) master's degree in international relations in cooperation with the Paris Institute of Political Science (Sci Po). The choice of the two institutions as partners was not accidental: both institutions appeared to prepare graduates for working in the practical sphere of social relations. Also, the two institutions had much in common in terms of teaching (in particular, the use of a multidisciplinary approach—the inclusion in the educational process courses in political science, history, economics, and law). Both institutions were faced with the need to make changes in the process of education in the field of international relations after the end of the Cold War. To run the double degree program, it was necessary not only to create "parallel" French and Russian courses (a kind of "parallel" or "double education"), but also to integrate two national educational programs. This was achieved through the joint development of master's programs and then joint implementation of this program thanks to the efforts of Russian and French teachers (Rousselet, Lebedeva 1997).

While carrying out the changes, MGIMO retained a number of previous traditions. Thus, at MGIMO in the post-Soviet period, academicians and well-known diplomats taught and teach even today. In particular, among them were/are academicians of the Russian Academy of Sciences A.A. Kokoshin, E.M. Primakov, N.P. Laverov, N.A. Simoniya, V.K. Pivovarov, corresponding member of the Russian Academy of Sciences Ivanov, V.I. Salygin, S.A. Afontsev, F.G. Voitolovsky, S.V. Ryazantsev, and others such as Extraordinary and Plenipotentiary Ambassadors V.P. Terekhov,

I.A. Melikhov, A.N. Panov, and P.F. Liadov. The Rector of MGIMO is an academician of the Russian Academy of Sciences, Ambassador Extraordinary and Plenipotentiary, and member of the Board of the Russian Foreign Ministry, Anatoly V. Torkunov.

M. Muller, having spent nine months as a trainee at MGIMO-University, published a book on education at MGIMO. Based on the ideas of poststructuralism he tried to analyze how the University forms great power identities (Muller 2009). Three years later, *Vestnik MGIMO – Universiteta* published a review of this book by P. Demidov. Noting the number of merits of the book (in particular, the use of the included observation method and the interview method), P. Demidov points out that the great power identities of Russian students are due both to Russia's position in the world (permanent member of the UN Security Council) and the future diplomatic activity of many MGIMO students (Demidov 2012).

MGIMO headed the Educational and methodical association (UMO) of higher educational institutions in the areas of training in "International Relations" and "Area Studies", and then the enlarged group - Federal educational and methodical association (FUMO), which includes political science and area studies.[54] UMO and FUMO are public professional associations established under the Ministry of Education and Science of the Russian Federation. The task of UMO, and then of FUMO, is to develop professional requirements for training in the relevant area, particularly in the fields of international relations and area studies. All Russian universities that teach these subjects are required to follow so-called teaching standards, which specify the compulsory set of disciplines that a university must provide. IR students have to study foreign languages (at least two), the history of international relations, world politics, the theory of international relations, and courses in economics and law.

---

54 Federalnoye uchebno-metodicheskoye obyedineniy (FUMO) [Federal educational and methodical association]: http://mgimo.ru/about/structure/ucheb-nauch/fumo/

4.3 Contemporary Issues and Challenges in Teaching International Relations

Significant changes that occurred more than 25 years ago in Russia in the field of teaching international relations, of course, did not solve all problems and did not respond to all existing challenges. Among these unresolved problems and challenges, one can single out those that are common to most states. They also exist in Russia, but, perhaps, with some specificity. The second group of problems and challenges is typical just to Russia.

The first group of problems and challenges include, for example, issues of the commercialization of higher education (see, for example, Stomguest, Monkman 2014). The educational structure in the preparation of training programs increasingly depends on market demand. On the one hand, this makes it possible to generate additional income for both universities and teachers. On the other hand, commercialization limits the ability of applicants to apply. In Russia, education in international relations is very costly. Entrants are attracted by the possibility of mastering at least two foreign languages and the prospect of working in the field of international relations. Despite the fact that educational programs on international relations provide an opportunity to receive education through state financing on a competitive basis, some of the students are paying a fee. This fee, compared to other programs offered by the universities, is usually higher, due to demand for IR education in Russia.

Commercialization of education leads to the fact that the universities and the diplomatic academies in different countries begin to provide educational services that are oriented to the widest possible spectrum: protocol and etiquette, the history of countries and regions, and so on. In Russia, this sphere of educational services is not very well developed.

Another common problem for many countries has been under discussion for several decades. This problem is related to the extent of the combination of academic and practical knowledge for teaching international relations. In Russia, there is a special aspect of this problem. In Moscow's universities, as well as universities in large cities with broad international relations, the problem of practical training is not so critical. However, in smaller Russian cities, issues of internships for students, as well as the involvement of those who worked or work in the field of international relations as a practitioner, are more difficult to solve.

Contemporary international relations have undergone significant changes in the twenty-first century. There are new areas that somehow affect international relations. For example, the development of information technology has sharply intensified international ties; the development of the Bologna process in Europe has led to the expansion of departments of international cooperation between universities. All these facts and events force the educational process to be restructured, including the development and inclusion of courses that were not previously available (e.g. information security and international aspects of the environment).

The problem of creating and developing master's programs with foreign partners (including double diploma programs) is also largely common for different countries, since the phenomenon itself is relatively new, and has become widespread only in the twenty-first century (although such programs were available in the past). The essence of the problem lies in the fact that when creating any joint program, each country, as well as each university, seeks to preserve its requirements and its traditions of higher education. In general, this task is solved if universities themselves choose their partners. Of course, in this case, the general educational principles of various countries have to coincide. A.A. Baykov formulated a number of principles that should be considered when creating IR master's programs in Russia: the opportunity to change specialization in comparison with the bachelor's level (meaning a bachelor's degree can be in any field); training highly professional specialists in all aspects of contemporary international relations; and the possibility of studying rare foreign languages.[55]

In Russia, there is also specificity. First, the Ministry of Education and Science of Russia instructs all universities to follow the accepted standards developed by FUMO. On the one hand, this factor limits flexibility when creating joint-degree programs; on the other hand, it facilitates the creation of programs with other universities in Russia if one university has already run such a program. In other words, the experience of a joint program with one Russian university on international relations can be widely used by other universities (Rousselet, K., Lebedeva 1997).

Second, the transition to a two-level education system — bachelor's and master's degrees (later, Russian universities switched to three-level training, including Ph.D. level) — has become a challenge for Russian universities, as they have not had similar experiences in the past. As a result, they had to build new programs to avoid repetition of topics that were already discussed at the bachelor's level and at the master's level. This task was complicated by master's programs because some students graduated from other universities and studied other programs that were not related to international relations. This problem was solved more or less by implementing self-study courses for students who had no prior education in the field of international relations. Higher education in the Soviet Union did not presuppose self-study courses.

Finally, today IR education in different countries is facing another problem. International contacts are deepening and expanding in the world. As a result, representatives of almost all professions and fields of activity interact with their foreign colleagues in the framework of their professional duties. However, universities do not prepare graduates for work with foreign partners or in an international environment when training doctors, engineers, teachers, or other specialists. Courses on international

---

[55] Baykov, A.A. *Specifika magisterskoy podgotovki po napravleniyu «Mezhdunarodnye otnosheniya»* [The specifics of master's education in international relations]: http://rpp.nashaucheba.ru/docs/index-62808.html

relations, as a rule, are absent in these cases. This is a common problem for many countries. A related question was put by American authors at the conference of the Association of Professional Schools in International Relations (APSIA) (Dibben, Whelan 2005). One of the ways to solve this problem is to provide wide educational services on international relations, including for schoolchildren. For example, in Moscow, the Department of Education encourages such activities by giving grants to universities on a competitive basis for lecturing on international relations to schoolchildren. However, such activity is very limited.

There are also a number of specific challenges for Russian education in the field of international relations. For instance, requirements for writing a Ph.D. dissertation in Russia are different from those in Europe. An analogue of the Ph.D. degree in Russia was and still is an academic, not an educational, degree. This creates difficulties for obtaining a double degree of Ph.D. in Europe and in Russia. As a result, the degree applicant actually has to defend two theses: one in Russia and the other abroad. With the provision of having several universities, the right to award a degree without the approval of VAK, the situation can be resolved.

For Russia, processes related to the internationalization of education also have their specifics. Primarily, the huge Russian territory, its presence in Europe and Asia, raises the question of the need to preserve the integrity of educational space. It is obvious that Russian universities located in the European part are more focused on contacts with European universities, while those that are located in the Asian part are more likely to interact with universities in the Asia-Pacific region. However, the gap of educational space can have consequences in social and economic relations in Russia. At the same time, Russia can become a kind of "bridge" between the European Higher Education Area (EHEA) and the educational spaces of the APR countries, in particular, China, the United States, Japan, and Australia. Such a role of Russia in higher education can have a positive function not only for Russian higher education, but also for the integration of higher education in the world as a whole.

Another problem is that in Russia it is possible to obtain a bachelor's and master's degree in the field of international relations. However, in Russia, the degree of candidate of science (analogue of Ph.D. degree) in international relations is absent. This degree can be obtained either in political sciences or in history. Obviously, this is not a significant problem. Moreover, with the introduction of the third level of higher education, it is largely leveled.

There is a challenge in finding competent teaching staff on international relations in Russia. Many teachers of universities of the older generation who work in the field of international relations actually received an education in history or other disciplines, since in the Soviet period international relations were not taught anywhere except MGIMO. However, this is not a problem in those universities that have many specialists with a basic education in international relations. Moreover, it is rather an advantage for the university because it gives an opportunity to enrich knowledge of close disciplines. In cases where teachers of international relations are from a different background (e.g. history), there is an imminent danger that they could lean more toward teaching history than international relations.

Since Soviet times, in Russia there has been quite a significant distinction between studies which were conducted in the framework of the Russian Academy of Sciences and studies in universities. Studies conducted at the Academy of Sciences usually were more basic scientific research. As in the previous case, it is not a problem for Moscow and other big cities. In big cities, on the one hand, research is actively developing in universities; on the other hand, scholars from the institutes of the Academy of Sciences teach at universities. In smaller cities, the science of international relations has been developing rather poorly, which has had a negative effect on education.

Part 2
The Current State of IR Studies in Russia

Chapter 5
Theoretical Research in the Field of International Relations

5.1 The Place of Theoretical Research in Russian IR Studies

Russian science has always paid great attention to theoretical issues. This is especially clear in the natural sciences and mathematics, where Russian authors proposed many theories. Nevertheless, in the humanitarian sphere also, Russian representatives have contributed significantly: suffice it to mention the names of Mikhail Bakhtin, Vladimir Propp, Yuri Lotman, Lev Vygotskiy, Aleksey Leontiev, Petr Galperin, Aleksander Luria, Dmitry Likhachev, among others. The situation with IR studies is more complicated. Marxism–Leninism, in comparison with other theoretical approaches in international relations, did not make a significant contribution to the development of the theory in this field. This is partly due to a kind of dualism that emerged in the Soviet period, when, on the one hand, it pointed to the existence of national interests of the state — which was a reflection of realism — and, on the other hand, proletarian internationalism was proclaimed.

In contemporary Russia attention to theoretical approaches is an important part of the scientific discourse of Russian IR studies. However, this discourse covers a relatively small circle of Russian scholars.

There are several reasons for interest in theoretical issues in Russia. The absence in the past, not only of research on theoretical problems, but also of acquaintance with foreign studies on the theories of international relations, gave rise to a series of publications on the presentation of the main theoretical directions that were aimed at developing foreign experience. In addition, deep philosophical traditions in Russia became a good basis for the perception of theoretical trends in international relations developed abroad. Finally, a personal factor was important in the development of theoretical research in Russia. A number of Russian authors, including T.A. Alekseeva, D.A. Degterev, V.N. Konyshev, M.M. Lebedeva, A.A. Sergunin, A.P. Tsygankov, P.A. Tsygankov, V.G. Baranovskiy, A.D. Bogaturov, and several others, have been involved in theoretical discussions.

The reason for a small circle of Russian researchers engaged in discussing theoretical issues is also due to Soviet legacy. In the Soviet period, in fact, the only form of presentation of material on international relations was through an essay that did not involve discussion of theoretical problems. For many contemporary Russian authors, this format still remains the only one. However, usually everywhere only a small number of scientists are engaged in actual theoretical research. Most of the research on international relations, both in Russia and in the world, is still represented by applied studies.

Russian theoretical work on international relations can vary. Thus, among the theoretical areas of research of Russian authors A.P. Tsygankov singles out two groups: (1) the universalists and (2) the isolationists. The first group sees the need to integrate Russian IR studies into Western work. The second group considers this integration unacceptable, thereby leading to the elimination of Russian specifics and a Russian theoretical research. These two directions reflect the values of "Westerners" and those who are "soil-bound" (*pochvenniki*) (Tsygankov 2014). A.P. Tsygankov asserts that a Russian theory of international relations cannot be developed, on the one hand, without interacting with global science, and, on the other hand, without reference to analysis of Russian thought.

According to another classification, contemporary theoretical directions in Russia are represented also by two groups. The first group of Russian researchers, the majority, basically follows existing theoretical approaches. On the basis of these approaches, applied research has been developing, which makes this group the largest one. The second group of researchers tries to focus on its own theoretical studies.

5.2 Theoretical Foundations of Russian IR Studies

Russian IR studies are relatively diverse in terms of their theoretical grounds, which is especially noticeable in comparison with the Soviet period. The tendency toward the pluralization of IR studies in the late 1980s and the 1990s, which was mentioned by A.P. Tsygankov and P.A. Tsygankov (Tsygankov, Tsygankov 2005b), continues today. However, the circumstances of 1990 were completely different compared to that of the present.

At the initial stages of the formation of Russian IR studies, its departure from Marxism–Leninism, as well as under the influence of *perestroika* in international relations, the diversity of theoretical approaches in specific IR studies sharply increased. This was unusual for Russia.

Today, a variety of approaches are present in Russian studies of international relations. However, the palette of all theoretical approaches is far from being equally represented. During the period of *perestroika* and the beginning of the 1990s, *liberal* orientations began to be traced in the theory of Russian IR studies. It cannot be said that in those days liberalism was the dominant theoretical trend. But it turned out to be noticeable in the scientific research of international relations in Russia. For example, in 1998, an international conference at Moscow State Institute of International Relations (MGIMO) was dedicated to the 350th anniversary of the Peace of Westphalia. The problematics of the political organization of the contemporary world, which was based on peace treaties of 1648, was largely new for the Russian researchers of international relations. Previously, these issues were considered only from a historical point of view, but not from the point of view of the political organization of the world. Many of the papers presented at the conference focused on a neoliberal approach and were then published in *Kosmopolis. Almanakh*, 1999.

In the late 1990s and early 2000s, articles on globalization (see Kuvaldin 2004; Lebedeva, M.M., Melvil 1999b, Trenin 2001), the democratization of the world (see Kulagin 2000), non-state actors in world politics (see Tsygankov 1995; Lebedeva 2003; Abramova,

Fituni 2015), democratic transit (Melvil 1999; Sergeev 1999), issues on Russian-American relations and security (Kulagin 2001), as well as others were written in the liberal tradition.

Russian liberals drew attention to the transparency of national borders and the interdependence of the world, the activities of non-state actors in the world arena, the role of international institutions in world politics, and so on.

In general, the liberal approach in Russia has been heterogeneous. The work, which was done in the liberal tradition, can be classified according to different parameters. A.P. Tsygankov and P.A. Tsygankov, in particular, single out (1) modernizers who are oriented toward Western values and institutions; (2) institutionalists who support the inclusion of Russia in international institutions; (3) social democrats who are also inclined to support the idea of including Russia in international institutions and to point out the importance of Russian identity (Tsygankov, Tsygankov 2005c).

Liberalism is not homogeneous in other countries also. However, liberalism, which focuses on the perception of the integrity of the world and the interdependence of its parts to a greater extent than other theoretical trends in international relations, is a kind of "cosmopolitanism". Therefore, in part, one can agree with A.P. Tsygankov and P.A. Tsygankov that liberalism, including Russian liberalism, to the greatest extent remains the most dependent theory (Tsygankov, Tsygankov 2007b), but only in the sense that it is less oriented to national specifics. At the same time, since the contemporary world has taken the political organization of the world from the "Western" (Westphalian) model as a basis, it certainly reflects its features. In this sense, it is difficult to talk about any dependence of theoretical approaches, except regarding a "dependence" on reality. By the way, realism, neo-Marxism, and other approaches are also Western ones, and therefore, according to this logic, are "dependent".

During the 25-year-period of history after the dissolution of the USSR and forming Russian IR, the liberal approach in Russia has evolved, becoming less radical on a number of issues. Thus, in the 1990s, ideas of very close rapprochement with European and Euro-Atlantic structures were rather common in Russia, as was partial refusal of sovereignty[56]; currently, there are practically no such views. Now, issues of the relationship between Russia and the West are discussed, but not Russia's inclusion in Western structures.[57] The problems of ecology and climate,[58] security issues (see Zagorskiy 2009), the political organization of the world (Lebedeva 2016a), and other issues are also the focus of discussions within the framework of the liberal approach.

Liberalism did not become a common theoretical approach in Russian IR studies. Currently, liberalism is rather a peripheral theory in Russia, although research continues to be published in the liberal tradition (see, for example, Kuvaldin 2017). Liberalism as a peripheral theory in Russia is caused by a number of reasons. First, this is partly because liberalism had no roots in Soviet traditions of studying international relations. Second, liberalism in the public consciousness (researchers of international relations cannot be isolated from most popular views and trends) was associated in many respects with the 1990s as a period of uncertainty, and then with the withdrawal of Russia as an influential player from the international arena. Third, the general emphasis on the implementation of national interests in the 2000s in Russia gave priority to realism as a theoretical approach. After the 1990s, liberalism rather quickly began to be superseded by other theoretical approaches.

In the early 2000s, *geopolitics* began to be very popular. It should be noted that initially Russian geopolitics in a number of

---

56 See, for example, Rossiya v poiskakh strategicheskoy stabilnosti. «Kruglíy stol» [Russia in search of strategic stability. "Round table"] 14.02.2002. *Fond «Liberalnaya missiya» [Fundation "Liberal mission"]*: http://www.liberal.ru/articles/832

57 See Rossiya v globalnom mire, i kak etot mir vliyaet na Rossiyu. «Kruglíy stol» [Russia in the global world, and how this world affects Russia. "Round table"] 16.05.2013. *Fond «Liberalnaya missiya»* [Fundation "Liberal mission"]: http://www.liberal.ru/articles/6145

58 See Mir na poroge zelenoy revolyutsii. «Kruglyy stol» [The world is on the threshold of a green revolution. "Round table"] 05.04.2016. *Fond Liberalnaya missiya* [Fundation "Liberal mission"]: http://www.liberal.ru/articles/7030

cases had little in common with corresponding theoretical approach in the West. *Geopolitics* and *Introduction to Geopolitics* by K.S. Gadzhiev appeared in the late 1990s and have withstood several publications. Although they contained chapters on the history and the development of geopolitics, they were basically textbooks on international relations that were written in a rather realistic tradition (Gadzhiev 1997, Gadzhiev 2000).

Nevertheless, in the early 2000s in Russia on the shelves of bookstores and in journals, geopolitics took the leading positions. Attention to the geopolitics of Russian authors seems to be primarily due to the term itself, which, apart from its ideological content (which took place in history), involves consideration of geographical factors in international relations. In the Soviet period, geopolitics was under an unofficial ban, because at one time it was officially recognized in fascist Germany. In addition, geopolitics was contrary to the thesis of Marxism-Leninism about the class nature of international relations, which actually minimized the geographical factor. At the end of the twentieth century, lifting the country's restrictions on the introduction and use of various theoretical approaches to international relations has attracted the attention of researchers to different approaches, including geopolitics. But this was not the main factor in the rapid development of geopolitics in Russia. In many respects the geographical position of Russia, namely, the large extent of its territory, its location both in Europe and in Asia, played a major role in the fact that geopolitics proved attractive to Russian authors. In addition, a number of professional groups, in particular the military, saw world politics largely in its geographical dimension. The spectrum of ideas and authors writing within the framework of geopolitics was quite broad: from the rather odious, although often quoted by A. Dugin, to moderate scholars, who, in part, moved away from geopolitics, focusing on the political and economic role of geographical factors (see, for example, Kolosov, Mironenko 2001), as well as ties, including ties in the Eurasian region (see, for example, Tsymburskiy 1999).

The geographical position of Russia made geopolitics attractive, especially for representatives of the Eurasian direction in Russian IR studies. At the same time, as A.P. Tsygankov noted, Russian geopoliticians, despite their negative attitude toward the West, are actively borrowing Western theories (Tsygankov 2014).

In general, geopolitics in Russia, having experienced a certain boom at the end of 1990s to early 2000s largely with a focus on military-strategic aspects, does not represent a holistic trend today. The number of publications on geopolitics has slightly decreased, although they continue to emerge in Russia. However, what is meant by the term "geopolitics" in contemporary Russian studies is very unclear. Some scholars prefer to use the term "political geography", which, by the way, was widely used in the Soviet period and was devoid of ideological content typical of classical geopolitics (see Kolosov 1988).

Since the 2000s, *realism* has become, perhaps, the predominant theoretical approach in Russian IR studies. However, like other approaches in the theories of international relations, it is also diverse and often takes the form that brings it closer to other theories. Within the framework of realism, an absolute majority of studies on the analysis of bilateral relations (see, for example Shakleina 2002, Voskressenski 1999; Voytolovskiy 2016; Luzyanin 2018), international security problems, and Russia-NATO relations (see Shtol 2010), as well as issues of the world order, have been carried out.

Of course, realism in Russia was not formed in the 2000s. As was shown in previous chapters, realism has its roots in the Soviet period, when it was formed as "intuitive realism" in the USSR. In the late 1980s and early 1990s, despite the surge in liberalism, the realist school in Russian IR studies continued to exist and shifted from "intuitive realism" to the forms that exist today. Representatives of realism criticized liberalism, drawing attention to the fact that in Russia "there was a confusion of two close, but, in fact, completely different concepts—the political and value orientations of the Russian Federation and Russian national interest" (Shakleina, Bogaturov 2005: 134-135).

The problem of the world order is one of the central issues in the studies of realists and it is widely discussed in Russian literature. Russian realists see the world order exclusively as a configuration of the leading states of the world. Hence, great attention is paid to the criteria for leadership in the world arena, the policies of leading states, the distribution of zones of influence, and so on (see, for example, Bogaturov, Shakleina 2009; Kortunov 2008; Temnikov 2003).

Since the 1990s, realists have emphasized the untenability of a unipolar system of international relations, and in this connection the idea of the necessity of transition to a multipolar system was formulated. The importance of building a multipolar world was announced by E.M. Primakov (Primakov 2002; Primakov 2009), and it was developed in many publications of Russian politicians and scholars. The requirement of multipolarity sounded quite clearly in studies of Russian authors and politicians. Thus, D. Rogozin wrote: "If the world is preserved as a unipolar one, it will simply be destroyed [...]. Therefore, in the long term, the world can only be multipolar" (Rogozin 2001). It is interesting that the orientation toward the desired future in this case actually brings the realists closer to the liberals, especially those who spoke at the beginning of the twentieth century about the need for disarmament, the creation of international organizations to strengthen peace, and so on.

Such a "blurring" of theoretical approaches between classical schools is quite typical in applied research. For example, in the publications of E.M. Primakov, which are mostly sustained by the realistic tradition, there are also narratives, which are connected with neo-Marxism. Thus, he substantiates multipolarity based on the Marxist thesis of the development of productive forces (Primakov 2009). According to E.M. Primakov, the development of productive forces shaping the world centers in China, India, and Russia. In this respect, multipolarity, according to E.M. Primakov, does not bear in itself the opposition of the centers and does not imply their indispensable confrontation.

It is hardly worth blaming E.M. Primakov for eclecticism. Obviously, reality is always richer than any theoretical constructions, as pointed out by P. Katzenstein and R. Sil (Katzenstein, Sil 2008). For this reason, in analyzing reality, E.M. Primakov resorted to different theoretical directions. A similar statement relates to several other Russian studies of applied character.

In determining Russia's foreign policy course, a discussion within the realistic direction often unfolds as to how geographically the priorities should be set: Should Russia be more focused on the Commonwealth of Independent States (CIS), China, and other countries of the East, or the United States and Western Europe? (see Shakleina, Bogaturov 2005).

Marxism, understood in the broadest sense (including contemporary Marxism-Leninism and neo-Marxism), in Russian political science is more evident when analyzing the internal political situation. However, IR studies also reveal a Marxist orientation. The roots of a Russian Marxist orientation in the study of international relations are partly associated with the Soviet period. Marxism-Leninism is a special direction and is not equal to Marxism. According to A. Kosolapov, Marxism as a method of analysis had little in common with Marxism-Leninism (Kosolapov 2005). For example, E.M. Primakov objected to the thesis of Marxism-Leninism about the inevitability of world revolution and incompatible contradictions between states with different political systems (Primakov 2009).

Thus, in Russian international relations studies, one can trace a certain opposition between Marxism and Marxism-Leninism. However, it does not apply to all Russian studies. Some authors, especially those who strongly criticize *perestroika*, as well as the Russian reforms that followed after 1991, continue to follow many classical principles of Marxism-Leninism. For example, N.S. Leonov proceeds from a belief in the existence of irreconcilable contradictions between socialism and capitalism and the ongoing Cold War of the West against Russia (Leonov 2010). At the same time, A.N. Kosolapov, continuing the Marxist tradition, points out that system analysis and the principles of historicism, taken from Marxism, are important tools for the analysis of contemporary international relations (Kosolapov 2005).

In carrying out applied studies, Marxist orientation is found analyzing a number of issues, including the relationship between the "Global North" and "Global South" (see Borishpolets 2004; Neklessa 2001). In Russia, there are also studies prepared according to a framework of world-system analysis and the theory of dependency. Some authors work in the neo-Marxist tradition in the field of international political economy. These include, for example, A. Neklessa (see Neklessa 2001), who is close in their orientation to the world-system theory of I. Wallerstein. The views of N.A. Simoniya can also be largely attributed to neo-Marxism (see, for example Simoniya 2012). However, in general, neo-Marxist directions in Russia do not constitute the mainstream of IR studies.

Applied research on international relations carried out in postmodernist traditions in Russia are limited. There are a number of interesting publications that to a greater or lesser degree reflect the postmodernist trend (see Sergeev, Akimov, Lukov, Parshin 1990; Ilin 1994). In recent years, constructivism has become popular. However, often the authors largely just point out that they are working in a constructivist direction, but they do not bring something new to it.

5.3 Theoretical Attitudes Toward International Relations in Russia

Ideas about theoretical trends and debates in Russian IR studies are incomplete if the studies of Russian scholars of the "picture of the world" are excluded from it. H. Alker and Th. Biersteker (Alker, Biersteker 1982), among Russian authors—A.P. Tsygankov (Tsygankov 2014)—pointed out the necessity of understanding the "picture of the world" in the study of theoretical views in international relations.

It seems that for Russia the "picture of the world" of scholars involved in the study of international relations is especially important, since it traditionally manifests disputes between Westernizers and Slavophiles, that is, between the Western orientation of Russia, and those who favor the original way of development of Russia. This is well shown in the studies of A.P. Tsygankov (Tsygankov 2007). However, the problem is not confined to the geographical orientation of Russian scholars and their understanding of the current role of a state in the world: whether they are statesmen (focused on a strong state), or not; A.P. Tsygankov has written about this (Tsygankov 2004). "Westerners" adhere mostly to liberal traditions in IR studies, while realists are mainly represented by "statesmen", and Slavophiles are characterized by Eurasian orientation, which reflects the views of both realists and geopoliticians.

At the same time, the "picture of the world" of Russian scholars in the field of international relations is represented by a wider palette of colors than only civilizational ones. This "picture of the world" includes, first of all, ideas about the political organization of the contemporary world. Almost all Russian researchers, regardless of their theoretical orientation or civilizational views, are unanimous in their perception of the political organization of the contemporary world. Russian scholars see states with their sovereignties as the main structural unit of political organization of the world. Hence, great attention in Russian theoretical research is paid to the problem of national sovereignty and its evolution (see, for example, Ilin, Kudryashova 2008; Ilin, I.V. Kudryashova 2011; Kokoshin 2006). In this respect, Russian studies on international relations are a good reflection of the fact that Russia in the classification of states (the Westphalian, the pre-Westphalian, and the post-Westphalian, discussed in Chapter 1) belongs to the category of predominantly Westphalian states.

The issues of the Westphalian system of the world, which were discussed in Russia in the late 1990s and early 2000s, became the periphery of research interest in studies of the second half of the 2010s and represented only a small number of publications (see, for example, Lebedeva 2016a). The study of interstate relations and foreign policies of the leading states determines the main research directions in today's Russia. This situation is largely correlated with the rapid development of realism in Russia. This mainstream entailed the fact that the problem of transforming the political organization of the world led to the search for a new structure of interstate relations after the collapse of the bipolar system. In the 2010s, it became one of the most discussed issues in contemporary Russian international relations. It is noteworthy that not only are realists engaged in the discussion of the structure of interstate relations, but so too are those who positioned themselves, rather, as representatives of the liberal direction at least in some periods (see, for example, Baranovskiy 2012; Baranovskiy 2017a).

When considering the problems of global governance, liberal representatives in Russia often perceive it from the standpoint of strengthening exclusively international institutions (see, for example, Barabanov, Golitsyn, Tereshchenko 2006). At the same time, there are studies that emphasize the need for a system of multilevel global governance, both by representatives of liberalism and constructivism (see, for example, Lebedeva, Kharkevich, Kasatkin 2013) and by those who adhere to a realistic orientation (see, for example, Afontsev 2013) in IR studies. In general, issues of global governance are discussed in Russian theoretical studies on international relations.

The perception of the "picture of the world" is influenced by the education of Russian scholars. It was manifested especially clearly in the 1990s to early 2000s, when Russian IR studies were starting to develop. A.D. Bogaturov has identified two schools in Russian IR studies. The first one is rooted in political sociology and political science (school of world politics), and the second one in history. Representatives of the first school, according to A.D. Bogaturov, were mainly graduates and employees of the philosophical, sociological, and psychological faculties of Moscow State University. Representatives of the second school were scholars, who received an education at MGIMO, as well as at historical faculties of various universities in the country (Bogaturov 2004). Later, as the geography of universities expanded, where international relations were studied and taught, this division into two schools began to be eroded: the initial education ceased to be an important criterion for the watershed.

The school of world politics initiated a discussion in Russian journals on the subject areas of world politics and international relations. If in American and European academic literature there are no clear differences between these disciplines, and both concepts are synonymous, then in Russia it was suggested they be distinguished. There are two directions in the understanding of world politics. The first and the most common direction is the understanding of world politics as a world order or the policy of the leading states of the world. In this sense, it coincides with an understanding of international relations, but focuses on the policies of leading states. The second direction states that world politics is a broader concept that includes the entire complex of political interaction on the world stage (Lebedeva 2003).

Summarizing the discussion on the correlation of the subject areas of world politics and international relations, P.A. Tsygankov gives the following characteristics of an understanding of world politics in Russia. First, world politics emphasizes the existence of the phenomenon of transnationalization. P.A. Tsygankov notes that it is not only the impact of the internal upon the external world but also the reverse process: the penetration of the external to internal relations in states. Second, world politics indicates the activity of non-state actors forming network relationships. Third, the focus of world politics is on different manifestations of interdependence and signs of the formation of a managed global community (Tsygankov 2013).

Another parameter of the "picture of the world" of Russian researchers is determined by whether scholars perceive the world as a whole entity, or primarily as a set of regions (see, for example, Semenenko 2014) that interact with each other and to a large extent compete (see, for example, Gromyko 2015). Now, most IR studies in Russia present the second vision. This is because, first, traditionally, regional studies have a long history in the country, especially the development of oriental studies in Russia, as noted in Chapter 2. Currently in Russia, much attention is paid to China (see, for example, Voskressenski 2004), India (see, for example, Lunev 2003), and other countries of the Asia-Pacific region. Of course, the center of attention of Russian researchers is the United States and Europe, including countries of the former Soviet Union. In recent years, more interest has been shown in Latin American countries, especially in Brazil who is a member of the BRICS countries. As a result of the "Arab Spring", the number of publications in the Middle East and North African countries has sharply increased. To a lesser extent, the focus is on sub-Saharan Africa, with the possible exception of South Africa, which is important for Russia from a strategic point of view, and also from the point of view of its membership in the BRICS group.

Second, in practical terms, the study of countries and regions in Russia is more in demand than general discussion of IR theory, development of international relations, and global issues. Third, in the contemporary world, new associations are being built. One of the initiators or center is Russia, along with the BRICS countries, the Eurasian Economic Union, the SCO, the CSTO, and others. Accordingly, these and other such associations attract the attention of Russian scholars, including of those who deal in a comparative perspective (see Baykov 2012; Nikitina 2011; Afontsev, Lebedeva 2014; Kostyunina 2014). To a large extent, in all these studies, various aspects are examined through the definition of the place and role of Russia.

A special focus of theoretical studies on international relations in Russia is on the search for a Russian theory of international relations. It should be noted that the search for alternatives to Western theories of international relations is conducted in many countries. This applies to theories of international relations (see, for example, Acharya 2011; Behera 2016; Porter 2001; Tsygankov 2014), as well as to some of its parts, especially security issues (see, for example, Khudaikulova 2016). Domination by Western theories in IR studies is difficult to deny. However, the attitude toward this fact is ambiguous. *Non-Western Theories of International Relations* provided a special stimulus for the discussion on the role and possibilities of national schools of international relations (Acharya, Buzan 2010). Russian authors did not stay away from these discussions.

There are two basic approaches to the question of the need for national theories of international relations. Simply put, they can be reduced to the following. The position of the representatives of the first approach is that, unlike natural science, international relations has an ethical and value content. Therefore, non-Western theories have the right to exist; moreover, these theories are obliged to assert and realize non-Western values. This approach has a significant number of supporters in Russia. In particular, P. Tsygankov, A. Tsygankov, A. Voskressenski, and other Russian authors adhere to it (Tsygankov 2013; Tsygankov, Tsygankov 2007b; Voskressenski 2017). Scholars emphasize the inadmissibility of universalization, since each political culture is unique and has its own traditions and customs. According to this point of view, Russian studies in the field of international relations and world politics should depart from Western-centrist theories and begin to develop their own theory. At the same time, a number of scholars point to the need for interaction with representatives of other countries in the study of international relations (see Tsygankov 2014).

The second approach proceeds from the premise that international relations, like any other scientific discipline, do not depend on national characteristics. In this sense, the national theory of international relations can hardly be justified, and Russia is no exception here (Alekseeva 2017; Lebedeva 2017b). The objections of the representatives of the second direction regarding the need for the formation of national schools are reduced to the following points. Today, there is a transformation of the political organization of the world, which is basically Western. This transformation, for the first time in history, encompasses all three levels of political organization of the world: the Westphalian system, the system of interstate relations after the disintegration of the bipolar system, and the political systems of a number of states (Lebedeva 2016a). The crisis of political organization of the world entails a crisis of theory, since theory can either reflect the reality, or act as an impetus for a new political organization of the world. Such a project is out of the question right now. And as a reaction to the crisis of the political organization of the contemporary world (in fact, the Western model of its organization), scholars are attempting to search for theoretical answers outside Western traditions. By the way, researchers who deal with internal political issues also turn to theoretical searches outside the Western world (see Chugrov 2016). This fact also indicates that the crisis covers different levels of political organization of the world, including the domestic one.

In current conditions, embraced by globalization, it is unlikely that the political organization of the world can be built on the basis of this or that national model. Most likely, it will be a synthesis of various national practices; hence, theory will be formed on the basis of the synthesis of various national characteristics (Lebedeva 2017b). In this respect, features of various nations are very important. P.A. Tsygankov, speaking about IR theory, noted that the development of an adequate view of reality involves understanding all of the achievements in the world of political thought with a clear understanding of the need to overcome inherent hitherto hard American- and Eurocentrism, the tendency to exaggerate universality (Tsygankov 2013).

Agreeing with the views of A.P. Tsygankov, it should be added that focus should not only be on political thought but also on the broader scope of scientific achievements. Thus, if we talk about Russian ideas, then as an example, we can mention the research of M.M. Bakhtin, specifically his ideas about dialogue. The concept of "dialogue" is one of the most common concepts in international relations. However, it is often used here to indicate the exchange of information, statements of positions, meetings of representatives, and so on. Such a "dialogue" sometimes does not lead to mutual understanding and sometimes exacerbates conflict. M.M. Bakhtin provides a fundamentally different understanding of the dialogue in his studies. According to him, dialogue is primarily a matter of mutual influence and mutual changes of the participants in communication. M.M. Bakhtin writes about the assertion of someone else's "I" not as an object, but as another subject (Bakhtin

1972). In international relations and world politics, dialogue in its essence must be the opposite of various manipulative technologies. It cannot be one sided, it always has a "two-way traffic". Dialogue requires time and knowledge of one's own, as well as other, culture. And its result is a change in both subjects.

Another example of the possible use of ideas developed in Russian science is connected with psychology. Russian psychologist L.S. Vygotskiy put forward the idea of a "zone of the nearest development" during the development of a child (Vygotskiy 1982). In the context of international relations and world politics, the zone of the nearest development (here it would be more accurate to talk about "the next area of change") can describe how the actions, for example, of a state actor "tighten" the structure and/or direct the activities of other actors in a certain direction. Norms, rules of behavior, the material sphere of the economy, armaments and so on can be seen as structures. The averaged set of changed structures as a result of the activities of various actors forms a "corridor" for new activities. The accumulated changes lead to a breakdown of the old structures and the formation of fundamentally new structures. The very process of influencing structures or other actors can be better or worse realized. For this reason, changes are often perceived as "unexpected" or "sudden" (Lebedeva 2015). The proposed idea of a "zone of proximate changes" is well correlated with what has recently been increasingly asserted in theoretical studies on international relations, especially by constructivists, namely, that actors and factors are not opposing, as previously thought, but complement each other (Tsygankov 2008).

The logical continuation of the approach to the theory of international relations as gathering knowledge and notions, which were accumulated not only by Russian science and culture but also by others, is the direction in the development of the theory of international relations focused on the use of knowledge, including from the natural sciences and mathematics. Thus, in Russian IR studies there is considerable interest in rigorous research methods (see Degterev 2015).

Another direction in this area in Russian international relations is the development of the quantum mind hypothesis by A. Wendt Wendt 2015). In Russia, the ideas of A. Wendt were developed in the studies of T.A. Alekseeva and her colleagues (Alekseeva, T.A., Mineev, A.P., Loshkarev 2016; Alekseeva, T.A., Mineev, A.P., Fenenko, A.V., Loshkarev, I.D., Ananev 2016).

In general, studies related to the development of certain theories and hypotheses that have appeared in the West are quite widespread in Russia. These are issues of the post-bipolar world order (see, for example, Baranovskiy 2012), the comparative study of integration processes (Baykov 2012), theory of democratic peace (Kulagin 2000), and many others.

Ending with a discussion on the theoretical foundations of Russian IR studies, it can be stated that they are developing and for 25 years have come a significant way. Today, it is hardly possible to talk about the long stage of mastering the world's theoretical legacy by Russian researchers or be critical of the lack of theoretical directions being developed in Russia. Moreover, it seems that the theoretical work of Russian authors in the field of international relations can have a good potential for contribution to global science.

Chapter 6
Security Issues in Russian IR Studies

6.1 New Aspects of International Security in Russian IR Studies After the End of the Cold War

Security issues are traditional topics for IR studies in all countries and Russia was not an exception in this respect. Security issues received a lot of attention during the Soviet period, and, in recent years, along with previously discussed security issues related to armaments and disarmaments, as well as conflicts, in Russia as in the whole world, new ones emerged. Primarily, they include terrorism and issues of information security.

At the end of 1980-1990, issues of arms and disarmament in Russia has somewhat gone by the wayside, replaced by the problems of détente, cooperation, integration, and others, although, of course, they never completely disappeared from the Russian scientific agenda. In the 2000s, issues of international security in its classic interstate variant were revived owing to several factors. First, the end of the Cold War and the development of Russia's relations with the West undoubtedly had a significant impact on the assessment of security issues by Russian researchers. In the 1990s, Russian scholars began to discuss widely the opportunities and directions for cooperation with the West in this field. However, the development of the confrontation between Russia and the West in the twenty-first century, the lack of trust between the parties, changed the assessments and tone of Russian security scholars, especially after 2014. In addition, this was facilitated by reaction to the weakening of Russia in the military field in the 1990s, as well as the uncertainty in the configuration of leading states. As a result, according to some Russian scholars, the collapse of the bipolar system did not lead to a safer world (Sergunin 2005b). At the same time, other less common points of view were expressed. Thus, V.M. Kulagin noted that the end of the Cold War did not abolish competition between states, but significantly reduced the degree of confrontation between most of them (Kulagin 2012).

In the 2010s, the Russian academic community began to intensively discuss issues of the role of hard power, the need to ensure national security by armed means, and so on. In 2014, the Russian International Affairs Council (RIAC) and the Moscow State Linguistic University published a handbook on military and IR scholars in Russia, which contained information on Russian experts and organizations involved in the study of military-political aspects, as well as periodical publications in this field (Belozerov, Vladimirov 2014). In the foreword to the handbook, the president of the RIAC, the former minister of foreign affairs of Russia, I.S. Ivanov writes that the force factor again became dominant in international and interstate relations (Ivanov 2014). Understanding of the importance of the power factor in the contemporary world, which is currently quite common in Russia, led to the fact that attention on this issue has intensified in the twenty-first century.

Second, the return of attention of Russian scholars to the problems of security associated with the revolution in military affairs, which looked anew at various types of weapons and disarmament issues in connection with the emergence of precision weapons and a contactless method of its application. According to V.I. Slipchenko, a revolution in military affairs is capable of destroying all existing contractual frameworks in the field of security (Slipchenko 2002).

Third, Russian scholars noted that in the period after the end of the Cold War, opportunities for cooperation at global and regional levels were opened in the world after the end of bipolar confrontation. However, leading states have not broken up arsenals that clearly exceed the level of necessary defense, but they are constantly improving them, including offensive weapons (Kortunov 2010a). In other words, the position of Western countries forced Russia to return to issues of interstate security relations.

All these developments led to new theoretical study of security issues. In Russian IR studies, issues of the correlation of national, international, and global security began to be intensively discussed. Thus, V.M. Kulagin noted that the term "international security" traditionally referred to interstate relations. Therefore, today, when threats arise both externally and internally, as well as being related to non-state actors, it is more accurate to talk about global security. However, the term "international security" is widely used (Kulagin 2006). At the same time, V.M. Kulagin draws attention to the expansion of the subject field of security associated with nonmilitary threats. Starting from the idea of securitization of B. Buzan and O. Waever, he writes about the need to limit the too broad interpretation of the concept of "security" (Kulagin 2007).

In turn, A.G. Arbatov defines international security as the state of international relations ensuring the protection of states, legitimate international organizations, and non-state actors from external and transfrontier threats. A.G. Arbatov emphasizes the need to ensure the sovereignty and territorial integrity of states within the framework of international security (Arbatov 2011).

Russian scholars paid special attention to issues of strategic stability, which in the Soviet period were determined mainly by the relations of the USSR-United States. In the new conditions, when a number of states have nuclear weapons, as A.A. Kokoshin writes, the problem goes beyond bilateral relations, as far as regional conflicts can lead to the use of nuclear weapons (Kokoshin 2009).

The issue of the relationship between regional and global security was discussed in number of articles. Thus, T.B. Yuryeva noted that the problem of determining the region is very ambiguous. For example, European security in its geographical dimension is determined differently by different scholars. But the problem is far more than a simple definition of the region. In the contemporary world, the external borders of the European region are eroding and subregions are emerging, such as the Caucasus, Black Sea-Caspian, and Central Asian. There are a number of other events that go beyond the region. For example, NATO is engaged in supplying security services to Afghanistan, Iraq, and some African countries (Yuryeva 2010). Later, the idea of the continuity of regional and global security can be traced in an article by M.M. Lebedeva and T.V. Yuryeva, in which it is asserted that the worldwide transformation of the late twentieth and early twenty-first centuries led to the fact that the security problem actually goes beyond the region (Lebedeva, Yuryeva 2011).

6.2 Relations Between Russia and NATO, the Issue of Nonproliferation and Arms Control

The special interest of Russian scholars in the field of international security related to interstate relations is focused on a number of issues: first of all, the transformation of NATO, the development of missile defense, the role of the nuclear factor, and control over conventional disarmament.

The structure of European and international security in general, part of which is NATO, has undergone serious changes since the end of the twentieth century. These changes were due to a number of factors, both objective (the disintegration of the bipolar system, the emergence of new challenges and threats, etc.) and subjective in nature (the adoption of a number of strategic and specifically political decisions). Many Russian researchers, analyzing the process of transformation of NATO, noted, above all, the subjective reasons. As V.A. Guseynov writes, having lost its main enemy at the end of the Cold War NATO nevertheless decided to gain a foothold as the prevailing military force on the continent (Guseynov 2001). Enlargement of NATO to the East was perceived very negatively by Russian political leaders and the majority of IR scholars in Russia. S.K. Oznobishchev writes that NATO enlargement was unequivocally perceived in Russia as a violation of previous promises at the highest level (Oznobishchev 2011).

Alexei Arbatov, considering the transformation of NATO after the Cold War, outlined three important parameters: (1) geographic, (2) military and political, (3) operational and technical. In geographical terms, there was the accession to NATO of Eastern European countries, including those formerly part of the USSR (Arbatov 2006). Importantly, according to Russian scholars, there was not only the accession to NATO of new countries, but also the geographical extension of the zones of influence of the Alliance. Thus, Arbatov noted that military actions of NATO became permissible outside the traditional Euro-Atlantic area of responsibility, primarily in the Middle East, the Persian Gulf, and South Asia (Arbatov 2006).

The conceptual framework of its activities developed within NATO also aroused criticism of Russian scholars. Russian researchers perceived the Alliance's new strategic concept, which appeared in 1991, negatively,[59] noting that the strategy was based on a broader understanding of security issues than it had been before (Shtol 2003). The NATO concept of 1999[60] was also critically evaluated. According to V. Shtol, it initially suggested that the main theater of military operations would be in the Balkans (Shtol 2010).

In the late 1990s, Russian scholars were extremely wary of the fact that priority in the peaceful settlement of conflicts within the framework of the UN and OSCE was given to countries belonging to the North Atlantic Alliance (Nikolaev 1998). This meant that international organizations, which included Russia, were excluded from participation in the settlement of conflict relations as leading actors. As for the transformation of the organizational structures of NATO, according to A. Stepanov, this should have ensured the Alliance a leading role in the European security system (Stepanov 2000). In general, according to A.G. Arbatov, NATO moved from a strategy of collective defense of the territory of member countries to active electoral interference outside the zone of its responsibility (Arbatov 2006). As a result, as T.A. Shakleina wrote, the United States and NATO have sought to take on the role of a "global leader" who is responsible for the destinies of the whole world and of nations, based on the right to invade and punish (Shakleina 2013). NATO's intervention in the Yugoslav crisis of 1999, and then in Iraq and Libya, was sharply criticized by Russian experts, as this

---

59 *The Alliance's New Strategic Concept* 1991: http://www.nato.int/cps/en/natohq/official_texts_23847.htm
60 *The Alliance's Strategic Concept* approved by the Heads of State and Government participating in the meeting of the North Atlantic Council in Washington D.C. on 23 and 24 April, 1999: official text. Brussels: NATO Public Diplomacy Division, 1999: http://www.nato.int/cps/ru/natohq/official_texts_27433.htm

was evidence of a violation of international law by the Alliance (see Gus'kova 2013; Ponomareva 2013; Voronin 2012).

Condemnation of NATO's actions is a "red thread" in most Russian IR studies. At the same time, there are studies focused not so much on estimated characteristics of the behavior of NATO, but on an attempt to identify opportunities for European security based on cooperation of Russia with different European structures, including NATO. Thus, T.G. Parkhalina draws attention to the fact that "by 2013 the factor of Russia's non-integration into the Euro-Atlantic system began to play an increasingly serious role" (Parkhalina 2016: 5). This led to dangerous consequences, including one of the most dramatic crises in Europe affecting security — the Ukrainian crisis, "when European institutions were not able to adequately respond to the challenges that emerged, and Russia and the West began to play by the worst rules of bipolar confrontation (and maybe even this was a game without rules)" (Parkhalina 2016, 7). T.G. Parkhalina sees the overcoming of these negative consequences as a departure from the confrontational model of interaction between Russia and the West.

In 2010, O. Antonenko and I. Yurgens proposed a relatively comprehensive program of cooperation between Russia and NATO. They proceeded from the fact that Russia and NATO had much more in common in the contemporary world than security threats. They referred to these commonalities as the strengthening of the development of conflicts, the problem of Afghanistan, the proliferation of weapons of mass destruction and missile technologies, threats that in recent years have come from non-state actors, primarily terrorist organizations, as well as organized criminal groups. O. Antonenko and I. Yurgens noted that despite the fact that the interests and positions of the parties do not always coincide, the benefits from Russia-NATO interaction can be very significant, which they see primarily in overcoming the legacy of the Cold War and building confidence. In this regard, they proposed concrete steps, which were to be implemented in the following four areas:

1. Searching for solutions to arms control, including the treaty on conventional armed forces in Europe (CFE)
2. Achieving agreements between Russia and NATO to reduce armaments on both sides of the border
3. Taking unilateral assurances to resolve concerns on security issues
4. Using public diplomacy to reduce the perception of a mutual threat, improve mutual understanding, and transparency (Antonenko, Jurgens 2010).

After the end of the Cold War, the emphasis related to disarmament and nonproliferation issues were changed. During the Cold War, the main focus for the prevention of nuclear war was on disarmament between the USSR and the United States, and nonproliferation played a subordinate role. In the twenty-first century, these two directions changed places: the main concern for preventing a nuclear catastrophe was the nonproliferation of nuclear and missile technologies (Arbatov 2011).

In the 2010s, the deterioration of Russian-American relations exacerbated disarmament issues, which was reflected in Russian IR studies. Thus, S.M. Rogov noted that after the end of the Cold War, world military spending was declining. At the beginning of the twenty-first century, military expenditures began to increase, primarily due to the growth of the Pentagon budget in the time of George W. Bush. Thirty years ago, American missiles began to be deployed in West Germany with a flying time of 10-12 minutes to Moscow, and from Estonia and Poland the flying time is only 6-7 minutes, which creates for Russia the threat of a "decapitation strike" (Rogov 2015).

START III Treaty was assessed differently by Russian experts. Positive aspects related to overcoming the international legal vacuum, which was formed as a result of the expiry of the START I Treaty, were noted. At the same time, it was critically perceived that this treaty does not provide for any restrictions on US missile defense in Europe (Kortunov 2010b).

The problem of missile defense in general has become one of the most discussed issues by Russian scholars. For analysis of this issue, both Russian and foreign authors were involved (see Arbatov, Dvorkin 2012). In general, the assessments of Russian experts as to how much American missile defense is a threat to Russia differ significantly. Many Russian scholars see US missile defense as a real threat (see, for example, Podberezkin, Parshkova 2014). At the same time, some Russian researchers are not inclined to dramatize this situation (see, for example, Dvorkin 2011).

In the 2000s there were attempts to establish cooperation between Russia and the United States on missile defense, then in 2010 A.G. Arbatov drew attention to the fact that cooperation between Russia and the United States on missile defense is possible only under conditions of allied relations. An attempt to cooperate exclusively on technical aspects, according to A.G. Arbatov, does not lead to success (Arbatov 2016).

The role of the nuclear factor in the contemporary world has become a field of discussion, both in the wider world and in Russia. Questions about the role of nuclear weapons were especially acute in connection with the terrorist acts of 2001. In 2002, the Russian PIR Center published a two-volume issue on nuclear nonproliferation (Orlov 2002), which was then published in several editions. Later, a number of books on nuclear nonproliferation were published (Arbatov, Dvorkin 2005; Arbatov, Dvorkin 2009).

Yu.E. Fedorov wrote that the development of modern technologies, which led to a revolution in military affairs, significantly reduced the importance of nuclear weapons. However, this has not led to the reduction to zero of the role of the nuclear factor because scientific and technical superiority can easily be neutralized by threats to use primitive nuclear or other weapons of mass destruction. The factor of nuclear deterrence remains, as Yu.E. Fedorov wrote, in the sphere of relations of leading powers, but does not work in relations between the countries of the North and extremist groups (Fedorov 2002).

Discussion about the role of nuclear weapons was largely resumed among Russian scholars in connection with articles by George P. Shultz, William J. Perry, Henry A. Kissinger, and Sam Nunn (Shultz, Perry, Kissinger, Nunn 2007). Thus, S.A. Karaganov saw in nuclear weapons, primarily, the factor of deterrence, including the deterrence of conventional arms race. Moreover, according to S.A. Karaganov, changes in the world require an understanding that nuclear powers will continue to increase (Karaganov 2010). In an article published in 2017, S.A. Karaganov continues to develop the idea of nuclear weapons as a deterrent factor (Karaganov 2017). This position was criticized by A.G. Arbatov, who argued that the role of nuclear forces is exaggerated. At one time, A.G. Arbatov wrote that the Soviet Union relied on nuclear weapons as a guarantee of security and prestige, and as a result it disintegrated (Arbatov 2010). This discussion was continued at the Russian International Relations Council (RIAC) portal. It was joined by other Russian scholars. They gave arguments, as well as described the conditions under which the nuclear factor becomes significant, or — on the contrary — useless (Troitskiy 2015a; Troitskiy 2015b; Fenenko 2015).

6.3 Conflicts and Peacemaking

The subjects of conflict research since the end of the Cold War have significantly expanded. If during the Cold War the problematic conflicts in Russia consisted of questions of studying the historical aspects of international conflicts, in the late twentieth and early twenty-first centuries, a considerable number of studies on theoretical issues of conflicts, ethnic conflicts (see, for example, Zvyagelskaya 2008), and others have been done. International conflicts have become the subject of research not only of history (as it was in the time of the Cold War) but also of political science, sociology, and other disciplines.

In fact, all Russian researchers draw attention to the point that contemporary international conflicts have a specificity that significantly distinguishes them from the conflicts of the previous time. First of all, it is noted that an increasing number of conflicts are internal (see, for example, Nikitin 2012; Kulagin 2006). However, they have strong international components, because they

- Analysis of a new geopolitical picture and geopolitical trends of the post-Soviet space
- Consideration of the forms of post-Soviet integration (the CIS, CSTO, SCO, EAEU, etc.) from the point of view of their capacity to prevent and resolve conflicts
- Issues of external intervention of non-regional powers and international organizations in conflicts, including the role of the UN, OSCE, NATO, the EU, and a number of states
- The role and limits of the use of military force in contemporary conflicts
- The problem of the relation between power and law in conflict, legitimacy and the international legal validity of the policies of the countries, including Russia, in the regional conflicts
- Questions of the balance between the sovereignty of states and the need for international intervention
- The consideration of conflicts through the prism of terrorism/counterterrorism
- The study of negotiation and other forms and methods of conflict resolution and conflict management
- The applied analysis of conflicts in a specific country and regional contexts both in the post-Soviet space and far abroad (Nikitin 2016).

Among all areas of conflict studies in Russia named by A.I. Nikitin, perhaps numerous studies are devoted to the analysis of specific regional conflicts, as well as terrorism. Especially many studies are on conflicts in the post-Soviet space (conflicts in Transnistria, in Ossetia and Abkhazia, Nagorno-Karabakh, Central Asia, Ukraine, and others) (see, for example, Kazimirov 2009; Gadzhiev 2003; Pryakhin 2002; Mayerov 2007; Malysheva 1997; Malashenko 2012). Russian scholars also pay attention to those conflicts in which Russia is involved — in particular, to the conflicts in Syria (see, for example, Shepovalenko 2016).

Analyzing Russia's participation in contemporary conflicts, N. Silaev and A. Sushentsov note that in the twenty-first century, the risk of involving Russia in military conflicts of low intensity has increased significantly because of the development of instability along the perimeter of Russian borders, as well as the general unstable situation in the world. As the authors note, Russia is involved in processes within Afghanistan, Syria, and Ukraine. The main danger lies in the risk of the prevalence of ideological priorities over rational calculation and, in the end, the strain on forces of the state (Silaev, Sushentsov 2017).

Obviously, owing to the terrorist threat and instability in the Middle East, Middle Eastern conflicts are becoming one of the central issues in Russian IR studies (see, for example, Naumkin 2011; Naumkin, Zvyagelskaya, Kuznetsov, Soukhov 2016; Bystrov 2011; Doroshenko 2014). Much attention is paid to the history and features of the development of the region. Russian scholars note that nation states began to form in the Middle East rather late, only at the beginning of the twentieth century. Moreover, "the development of the political framework of the nation state has been slow in the region. The Arab public consciousness did not immediately perceive the new political units as states, and for their designation used the term *kurt* that means country, land, region" (Kudryashova 2015: 708). These states were largely formed as authoritarian ones. Their leaders or clans were in power for many years. In the twenty-first century, as a result of mass demonstrations, the statehood of several Middle Eastern countries began to collapse. Vitaly Naumkin and his colleagues emphasize the existence of internal causes that produced these changes. They note that the destruction of the states of the Middle East is primarily connected with internal reasons — political, economic, cultural, and civilizational. At the same time, the authors indicate the presence of certain external factors (Naumkin, Zvyagelskaya, Kuznetsov, Soukhov 2016).

In the context of conflict issues, Russian scholars draw attention to the problems of peacemaking, humanitarian intervention, and conflict resolution procedures. The development of conflicts in the post-Soviet space stimulated research in this area. One of the first studies on peacemaking in Russia after the collapse of the Soviet Union appeared in 1998 (see Nikitin, Khlestov, Fedorov, Demurenko 1998). At the same time, the focus of Russian authors' attention was on UN peacekeeping operations (see Morozov 1999; Nikitin 2009; Zaemskiy 2008). An interesting case study of Russian peacekeeping in conflict settlement in South Ossetia in the early 1990s was presented in the book written by M.V. Mayerov, a Russian diplomat and participant in this peacekeeping process (Mayerov 2007). In recent years, mediation and negotiation methods of conflict resolution, in comparison with peacemaking and humanitarian intervention, have attracted less attention of scholars, although research is also underway in this area in Russia (see, for example, Monoylo 2008; Monoylo 2013; Lebedeva 2016b).

Humanitarian intervention became an important theme in Russian IR studies, first in connection with the operation of the United States in Iraq in 2003, and then especially as a result of NATO operations in Kosovo and Libya, as well as the involvement of the United States in the conflict in Syria. When analyzing humanitarian operations in Russian international relations, much attention is paid to the legal aspects of the problem. All scholars emphasize the need to respect international law, according to which external intervention is possible only in two cases: (1) as a result of a decision of the UN Security Council; and (2) at the invitation of the legally elected leadership of the country. Thus, it is noted that in the late 1990s, in the situation in Kosovo, the UN Security Council adopted three resolutions expressing concern and requiring the Federal Republic of Yugoslavia to withdraw military forces from Kosovo, as well as to ensure international monitoring. In addition, the resolutions condemned the acts of terrorism of the Kosovo Liberation Army. However, there were no direct indications that the situation posed a threat to the world. Nevertheless, the NATO Council decided that in Kosovo there are signs of a humanitarian disaster, and it started an operation that resulted in the destruction of infrastructure, including civilian facilities in Serbia, where civilians were killed (Kulagin 2006). NATO's intervention in Kosovo turned out to be a dangerous precedent and was negatively perceived by Russian scholars (see, for example, Guskova 2013; Ponomareva 2013).

The invasion of the United States and its allies in Iraq in 2003 occurred without a UN Security Council resolution (Kulagin 2006), but those resolutions which were adopted did not imply the independent role of NATO (Nikitin 2012). And in Libya the UN Security Council mandate was exceeded. According to I.N. Kuklina, "The Libyan war was another example of the political and military approaches of the West, and first of all the United States, to solving problems in the era of globalization and deregulation of international relations" (Kuklina 2012: 39). As a result, according to A.V. Fenenko, we can safely say that by the mid-2010s, the great powers have successfully learned how to bypass the UN Charter, which limits their right to conduct wars (Fenenko 2017). At the same time, Russian scholars pay attention to the existing positive experience of interaction between Russia and NATO in the field of peacekeeping (Nikitin 2012).

Issues of conflict, according to some Russian researchers, are closely connected with issues of terrorism. As noted by M.V. Kulagin, "As a rule, in the course of the internal armed conflict, the opposing sides sooner or later start using terrorist methods" (Kulagin 2006: 141).

6.4 Terrorism and the Problems of Countering Terrorism

Since the tragic events of September 11, 2001, the problem of terrorism has become one of the central issues in the research of Russian scholars. In Russia, terrorism is usually seen as a complex political phenomenon. Hence, there is difficulty in defining terrorism. Russian researchers often refer to the history of the development of terrorism (see Kiva, Fedorov 2003), while the appearance of the phenomenon of terrorism is attributed to different epochs, from the ancient world (see Primakov 2002) to a later period. In particular, O.V. Budnitskiy connects the emergence of terrorism with the development of political relations in the nineteenth century (Budnickiy 2010). International terrorism is regarded in most studies as a global threat to humanity (see Kirilenko, Pidzhakov 2008).

Many Russians present a classification of the types of terrorism. Thus, S.S. Veselovskiy cites a variety of existing classifications: on the methods used (physical and psychological terrorism), means for pursuing goals (directed at particular groups or not), and so on (Veselovskiy 2012). V.M. Kulagin identifies local terrorism and transnational (or international) terrorism. Local terrorism is limited in its activities by a certain territory. Examples of local terrorism are the activities of organizations such as the Liberation Tigers of Tamil Eelam operating in the north-east of Sri Lanka and seeking to establish a Tamil state. Other examples of local terrorism are Colombian organizations such as the Revolutionary Armed Forces of Colombia, the National Liberation Army, and the United Self-Defense Forces of Colombia. V.M. Kulagin discusses the emergence of transnational terrorism toward the end of the 1990s, and he names al-Qaeda as an example. Transnational terrorism does not restrict its activities territorially, but it also has a number of special features, including extremist interpretation of Islam, large-scale violence, and globalization of the geography of terrorist acts (Kulagin 2006).

It seems that the differences between local and transnational terrorism are deeper. Transnational terrorist organizations see their task as changing the political system of the world based on Westphalian principles (al-Qaeda and ISIS). In contrast, local terrorism is not only limited by territory but also by its tasks. Local terrorist organizations make up the majority. These are separatist terrorist organizations, organizations fighting for power in the country by terrorist methods. The motives of the local terrorist organizations are not aimed at changing Westphalian principles (Lebedeva 2006).

Therefore, one of the most important features of transnational terrorism, as noted by E.A. Stepanova, is that it eliminates negotiations (Stepanova 2005a). In addition, transnational terrorism increasingly is a business structure as well as an international political and ideological phenomenon (Arbatov, Pikaev, Dvorkin 2006). The largest number of scientific publications in Russia on terrorism, as well as in general in the world, is devoted to the problems of transnational terrorism (Stepanova 2014). This kind of terrorism is also defined in Russia as global terrorism and super-terrorism (Arbatov, Pikaev, Dvorkin 2006). A significant emphasis in its study is placed on the origins and causes of its development.

Different authors distinguish three main reasons for the emergence of transnational terrorism in the contemporary world. The first group of reasons is due to the transformation of the political oarabatrganization of the world and, above all, the erosion of the Westphalian system. This leads to the emergence of alternative projects of political organization in the world, one of which is the formation of a global Caliphate. Its construction is implemented by terrorist methods (Lebedeva 2012). The second group of reasons for the development of transnational terrorism is defined as the result of the emerging world order due to the formation of a new configuration and balance of forces at the global and regional levels, as well as changes in the "center-periphery" relationship. As a result of these processes, competition for participation in the core of the international political system increases and the hierarchy in it becomes more diverse and variable (Baranovskiy 2017b). With this understanding, the main reasons for the development of terrorism lie in the field of independent variables. Within the same group of reasons for the emergence of transnational terrorism, there are studies in which the radicalization of the Arab world is associated with the policy of Western countries (see, for example, Pavlov 2012). This may be the economic interests of the West (primarily oil) or a political game. In other words, the dependent variables come to the fore. V.V. Naumkin also points out the existence of the influence of terrorism and radicalism on the very interstate system of both the region and the world (Naumkin 2011).

Finally, a fairly large group of scholars identifies the internal processes taking place in this region as reasons for the development of cross-border terrorism in the Greater Middle East. Social, political, and economic aspects that contributed to the development of extremism are considered (see, for example, Malashenko 2006; Sapronova 2013; Mirskiy 2015). In this case, both dependent and independent variables are analyzed. A special group of publications are studies on the analysis of ISIS: its history, ideological content, goals, and so on.

A.G. Arbatov, A.A. Pikayev, and V.Z. Dvorkin singled out two criteria for analyzing terrorist threats: (1) the degree of accessibility for terrorists, including the ability to use the threat effectively, and (2) the ability of states to limit or to take control of the consequences in the event of a terrorist attack. Since the degree of damage is inversely proportional to the devastating consequences, the authors build the following scale: at one end of the range is cyberterrorism, which would be increasingly difficult to prevent due to the development of hacking, but the consequences of which are relatively easily eliminated. However, it seems today it is difficult to talk about relatively easy elimination of the consequences of hacker attacks. It is followed by technogenic and radiological terrorism, which is somewhat easier to prevent, but is more difficult to eliminate the consequences of. This is followed by the possible use of chemical and biological weapons by terrorists. Finally, at the opposite end of the scale is terrorism with nuclear weapons (Arbatov, Pikaev, Dvorkin 2006).

Cases of chemical and biological terrorism were witnessed in 1995 (the use of sarin gas in the Tokyo subway) and in 2001 (mailing of envelopes with anthrax). Although the number of victims was not significant in these cases, the possibility of terrorists using weapons of mass destruction (WMD) is of particular concern and continues to be the focus of attention of Russian scholars. The international legal aspects of nuclear terrorism (see, for example, Sinyakina 2012), questions of the possible acquisition of materials, primarily nuclear materials (Arbatov, Pikaev, Dvorkin), the experience of nuclear states in the protection of nuclear facilities (Fenenko 2013), and other issues, are also discussed.

A lot of publications by Russian authors are devoted to the fight against terrorism. These studies cover the following areas of counteraction to terrorism: (1) military counteraction and operations of special services; (2) blocking the economic and financial activities of terrorist organizations, interaction of states and businesses in the fight against terrorism; (3) ideological and psychological resistance to terrorism; and (4) international cooperation in the fight against international terrorism.

It is noteworthy that the understanding of terrorist threats in Russia and in the United States on a number of parameters are rather close, despite the fact that in recent years, Russian-American relations have deteriorated significantly (Stepanova 2017).

At the beginning of the 2000s, some Russian scholars paid attention to the need to involve business in the fight against terrorism (see Safonov 2006; Lebedev 2007). However, later, this theme did not receive proper development in Russian IR studies. At the same time, if we consider the economic sphere of the fight against terrorism, in general, more attention has been paid to these issues in Russian studies (see, for example, Stepanova 2005b; Dobaev, Umarov 2013; Melkumyan 2014). Also, many studies are published on terrorism in various regions of the world (see, for example, Islamic Extremism ... 2015; Belokrenitskiy 2017).

In connection with the danger of Islamic radicalism, as well as the fact that citizens of European countries, including Russia, joined ISIS, and the successful activities of ISIS in the information field, the problem of countering terrorism at the political, ideological, and psychological levels has become very acute. After the terrorist attacks of al-Qaeda, E.M. Primakov wrote that anti-terrorist activities "are ineffective without participation in it, and in the forefront, of Muslim countries and organizations. [...] Moderate Islamic regimes, as well as secular regimes in states with Muslim populations, are not on the same side of the barricade with terrorists" (Primakov 2009: 43). Therefore, a number of Russian researchers note the task of cooperation and building a dialogue with moderate representatives of Islam, with those who see the possibility of the development and evolution of the current political system of the world, and not to replace it with terrorist methods by another system based on the principles of the global caliphate. It is emphasized that understanding of the processes taking place in the Greater Middle East is very important for the realization of this task.

6.5 Studies of Information (Cyber) Security in Russia

The rapid development of information and communication technologies (ICT) and the creation of a global information space have led, on the one hand, to fundamentally changed communications on a global scale, and, on the other hand, to a whole series of challenges and threats in the field of security. In this regard, there has been a clear increase in the information component in the field of research on security issues.

Information security is understood broadly by Russian authors and includes content that is not limited only to its information and technical component, as, for example, it is interpreted in the EU and many states where the concept of cybersecurity is used. The content is understood via political-ideological aspects (manipulation of information, propaganda through global information networks, and information impact) (Zinovieva 2014). Usually, in Russian IR studies, to emphasize a broad interpretation, the term "information security" is used, while for a narrow one, cybersecurity (Krutskikh 2010). At the same time, information security is understood primarily as the security of the state (see, for example, Kucheryaviy 2014).

In addition to terminological differences, the important thing is that to the "triad of threats" to information security (i.e., application of information technologies for 1) military, 2) terrorist, and 3) criminal purposes), formulated in 1999 by the UN General Assembly, in 2013 Russia added a fourth threat of interference in the internal affairs of a sovereign state through ICT, the violation of public stability, the incitement of interethnic hatred.[61] Russia also

---

61 *Osnovy gosudarstvennoy politiki Rossiyskoy Federatsii v oblasti mezhdunarodnoy informacionnoy bezopasnosti na period do 2020 goda* [Fundamentals of the state

initiated the creation of an information security regime and proposed the internationalization of Internet governance, that is, transfer of these functions from the American company ICANN to the International Telecommunication Union.

All these issues specific to the Russian approach to information security, as well as national and international activities of Russia in this, are reflected in the research of Russian scholars (see, for example, Krutskikh 2007; Zinovieva 2014; Zagorskiy, Romashkina 2015; Zagorskiy, Romashkina 2016). At the same time, Russian scholars criticize American approaches to cybersecurity (see, for example, Rogovskiy 2014; Romashkina 2016).

In Russian international studies in the field of information security, a number of trends have emerged. Primarily, scholars analyze the specifics of the new reality associated with information society (see, for example, Inozemtsev 2000a), as well as the impact of ICT on political processes (see Baluev 2006). Thus, P.B. Parshin notes that the problem of the emergence and functioning of the information society began to act as an object of political activity and an important item on the political agenda (Parshin 2009).

Another area of research is the discussion of the technical side of information security, understood as the use of unauthorized access to information (see, for example, Hozikov 2003). At the same time, a special sharpness of the discussion is caused by the fact that the individual received great opportunities to access information that was previously available only to the state (Parshin 2009).

Many publications by Russian scholars are devoted to the analysis of information threats. In particular, they point out that wars have always been waged not only by force of arms but also by means of information impact. However, in the current world, first, the scale of such an impact has sharply increased, and second, its spectrum has expanded. It is noted that in the twenty-first century, the number of attacks happened not only on citizens' computers,

---

policy of the Russian Federation in the field of international information security for the period up to 2020]. Utverzhdena Prezidentom RF 24 iyulya 2013 g. [Approved by the Russian President on July 24, 2013]. No. Pr-1753: http://www.scrf.gov.ru/security/information/document114/

banking structures, and news agencies, but also on state and international organizations, and critical infrastructures, all of which increased significantly (Romashkina 2016). M.M. Kucheryaviy writes that these threats can be quite diverse and aimed primarily against vital values that have a material, spiritual, and geopolitical character (Kucheryaviy 2013). Similar positions were held by E.S. Zinovieva, who wrote that the most important threats to information security were the uses of ICT at the state level in relation to information infrastructures of another state for political and military purposes, via criminal and terrorist activities in cyberspace (Zinovieva 2014). At the same time, it is noted that threats to information security are throwing up real challenges to all of humanity (Kucheryaviy 2014).

N.P. Romashkina identified the following three main types of threats to information security:

> 1. The emergence and rapid spread of meta-technologies (i.e., technologies that create the ability to control a consumer and collect information about him or her from the developer on the basis of various gadgets).
> 2. The digital divide, which implies the emergence of the so-called elite, which has unrestricted access to ICT. This gives it the opportunity to manipulate the opinions of individuals, social groups, and states.
> 3. Computer militarization, information terrorism, and crime, that is, the use of ICT to ensure military–political superiority, power confrontation, and blackmail. As a result, a new direction in the arms race opens up (Romashkina 2016).

A separate line of Russian research in the field of information security is related to terrorism. Russian scholars analyze the characteristics of terrorist propaganda on the Internet. In particular, the high-quality level of the propaganda materials of ISIS; propaganda in several languages (English, Russian, French, Turkish, and others); diversity in the use of channels and formats of advocacy; and attention to video products (Grigoryev, Ignatev, Magerov 2017). Russian scholars pay great attention to the role of social networks in recruiting new supporters of terrorist organizations. Researchers also analyze ways in which recruitment to terrorist organizations takes place through social networks and how terrorists spread destructive ideology (see Zagorskiy,

Romashkina 2016). It has been noted that owing to emerging new challenges, states began to strive to influence the processes of Internet governance (Zinovieva 2014). In particular, a number of states began to close access to certain sites. The problem of the sovereignty of the state in the information space is a topic that is being discussed by Russian scholars. Russian researchers also note the contradiction between sovereignty in its traditional understanding and sovereignty in the information space (Zinovieva 2014).

A fairly large number of studies are devoted to the analysis of information confrontation in the contemporary world, the specifics of information wars, and the functioning of and prospects for the development of information security (Kucheryaviy 2014). In particular, a lot of studies in this area appeared in the 2010s. In connection with information confrontation, Russian researchers pay attention to the phenomenon of the "hybrid war", in which great attention is given to symbols (language, values, identity, etc.) (Tsygankov 2015).

Chapter 7
The Economic Component of Russian IR Studies

7.1 Directions of Russian Studies in the Field of International Political Economy

Marxism, followed by Marxism-Leninism, was largely oriented toward analyzing the economic component of politics. Widely known is the utterance of V. Lenin that "politics is the most concentrated expression of the economy [...] and politics have primacy over the economy" (Lenin 1958-1966: 278). Nevertheless, in Russian IR studies, relatively little attention is paid to issues of international political economy (IPE).

The St. Petersburg researcher S.L. Tkachenko gives an analysis of the formation and development of IPE studies in Russia, from the Soviet time to the present, and notes that Russian IPE studies are developing with a significant delay in relation to American and European IPE (Tkachenko 2015). It should be added that the development rate of this field in Russia is very slow. Moreover, very few scholars in the field of international relations and world politics in Russia are engaged in actual analysis of IPE problems. Rather, it is necessary to talk about the work of economists who begin to work in the field of IPE.

The explanation for this phenomenon may be that the essential aspects of economic processes and their influence on political processes have been little analyzed by Soviet authors with rare exceptions (e.g., the work of E.S. Varga and his colleagues). In the Soviet period, ideological postulates were put forward, at the expense of analysis. In addition, as noted by S.L. Tkachenko, security issues were a priority of the Soviet period in IR studies, and most Russian experts viewed the world's politics primarily as a zero-sum game between "the world of capitalism" and "the world of socialism" (Tkachenko 2015: 110). Therefore, it is not surprising that in Russia a good basis for international political economy research after the collapse of the Soviet Union was absent.

From the 1990s to the 2000s, Russia began active work on entering the world economic system; in particular, on becoming a member of the WTO, as well as joining the regional economic associations and creating them, including the Eurasian Economic Union. These processes were reflected in academic publications of Russian scholars. In particular, there was a wide discussion about the pluses and minuses of Russia's accession to the WTO (see, for example, Primakov 2005).

Russian studies on the problems of international political economy can be divided into two main directions. The first direction of studies is focused on analyzing the opportunities, mechanisms, and prospects for Russia's inclusion in the global economy. In other words, in these studies the emphasis is on Russia. The second direction consists of studies on the problems of political and economic development of the world as such.

The first direction of studies is presented, in particular, by a symbolically entitled article of A.A. Dynkin "Does Russia have a chance in the global economy?" He describes the problems that Russia had faced at the turn of the century: the decline of Russian GDP at the beginning of the 2000s in comparison with 1990, the production structure inherited from Soviet times that was oriented towards industries related to the means of production at the expense of industries that produce consumer goods, as well as low labor productivity, and a number of others. A feature of the development of the Russian economy has also been the growth of the differentiation of the population in terms of income. At the same time, A.A. Dynkin noted the high degree of Russia's involvement in the world economy, indicating that Russia's export quota exceeds 40% of GDP (Dynkin 2002).

A.A. Dynkin singled out two groups of Russian researchers who formulate their views on the inclusion of Russia in the world economy. Representatives of the first group—*dirigisme*—proceed from the need for active state intervention in the management of the economy. They propose to begin to collect export rents from the export sectors of the economy and centralize the redistribution of resources in favor of the manufacturing industry, automotive industry, and other branches of the economy. Assessing this group, S.L. Tkachenko wrote that the views of the *dirigisme*, in particular S. Glazyev, are comparable to the neo-Marxist views of I. Wallerstein. Representatives of this group are critical of closer integration of the Russian economy into the world (Tkachenko 2015).

The second group of Russian authors, according to A.A. Dynkin, is represented by a liberal-institutional school. They are opponents of excessive state intervention in the economy, especially at the regional level. They support the development of institutions in the country and the implementation of reforms, not only in the economy but also on a broader scale, including judicial reform (Dynkin 2002). In the framework of the second direction of Russian research in the field of IPE, more general issues of the development of the world were analyzed, and a comparative analysis of the political and economic development of various states was conducted. In particular, these issues became relevant after the economic crisis of 2008-2009. Thus, M.V. Bratersky formulated the following questions pertaining to international political economy: What is the mechanism of the growth of the world economy instead of credit expansion? What should the financial system be? Whose interests does this financial system serve and how it can be managed? What are the roles of international institutions in the new system? (Braterskiy 2009).

Russian researchers pay much attention to the nature of emerging new political and economic relations of the world. For example, L.M. Grigoryev drew attention to the fact that at the turn of the century, the growth rates of developed, developing, and transitional states became closer and stabilized. According to him, this fact is disturbing, since it means that the gap between these groups of states is not overcome, and these groups will follow divergent roads, gradually moving away from each other (Grigoryev 2002).

In turn, V.L. Inozemtsev believes that the leading place in the economy of the twenty-first century will belong to the postindustrial economic system, concluding that the resources of this system will be information and knowledge. He proposed to define information as public good and knowledge as personalized or customized good, noting that Russian economists often mix these concepts. An analysis of the tendencies of the contemporary world, moving along the path of postindustriality with its information and knowledge, led V.L. Inozemtsev to the following conclusions. First, in postindustrial society, the rate of profit does not have a significant impact on the scale of investment activity. Second, the level of investment activity in its traditional sense does not determine either performance indicators or economic growth in general. Third, economic progress is faster in those countries where economic growth and labor productivity are not absolutized. From this it follows, according to V.L. Inozemtsev, that a self-regulating mechanism is formed in a postindustrial society, main types of consumption are associated with the development of personality (Inozemtsev 2000b).

Later, he did not so clearly refer to the fact that the future will belong to the postindustrial world. He pointed to a number of factors that were not factored into his earlier account when he described the political and economic development of the world. He pointed out that, first, contrary to expectations, the demand for information has not become unlimited. Technology and high-tech products have rapidly become cheaper. Second, the thesis that informatization of the economy will sharply lower the demand for resources and reduce their price was wrong. Third, postindustrial societies, having felt extremely powerful, have focused on the service sector. This sector acquired hypertrophied scales, and its products proved to be highly overrated. As a consequence, V.L. Inozemtsev concluded, trends that emerged in the late 1980s and early 1990s in the economic sphere have not become stable; more precisely, there were countertrends, which in the end turned out to be more significant.

At present, three groups of countries have been formed: postindustrial (the United States and Great Britain), the second group includes countries focused on raw materials (Russia, Saudi

Arabia, Turkmenistan, Venezuela, and others), while the third group is industrial, which includes old industrial countries such as Germany and Japan, and new industrial countries such as South Korea, China, and Brazil. V.L. Inozemtsev believes that the world of the twenty-first century remains the industrial world, athough as a renewed one. In this world, the positions of the United States and Russia, finding themselves in a situation of deindustrialization for various reasons (the United States because it is too "ahead", and Russia as a country that has relied on the export of raw materials), will be the most difficult, because they will have to depend on supply from industrial countries (Inozemtsev 2011).

The study of S.I. Lunev and G.K. Shirokov is also devoted to the differentiation of the regions of the world in the political and economic area. The authors, following largely a neo-Marxist orientation, proceed from the fact that the postindustrial economy based on knowledge is being formed in the global North, which is fundamentally different from what is happening in the global South. Moreover, the gap between these global regions is increasing. Developing countries have relied on the development of industry. Capitalism in these countries increasingly began to take on a national color. At the same time, there is the economic growth of the socialist countries (China, Vietnam, and Cuba). As a result, according to S.I. Lunev and G.K. Shirokov, an integrated capitalist system has not formed. There is redistribution in the world: developed countries are turning from suppliers of finished products into exporters of qualified and capital-intensive services. According to the authors (and in this sense, they largely have solidarity with V.L. Inozemtsev), the emergence of the postindustrial world is possible only if there is an industrial periphery. At the same time, 40–50 countries turn into a "gray zone", for which leaders cannot and/or do not want to be responsible (Lunev, Shirokov 2002).

The regional perspective of IPE is one of the most discussed in Russian IR studies. In part, this seems to be because regional themes in Russia have always taken a leading place in the study of international relations. Specifics of developed and developing countries, and the phenomenon of rapidly developing countries are among the regional plots of IPE. For example, B.V. Martynov analyzes the characteristics of rapidly developing countries. He includes among them the following:

- the presence of an 'imperial' (state) mood of the population, which connects its well-being with the strengthening of the state's influence in the international arena;
- the desire to assume an increasing share of responsibility for international affairs;
- awareness of its 'civilizational mission' in the near geopolitical and geo-economic environment;
- the desire to establish a multipolar world order on the principles of equality, predictability and order; belief in the need of revision of the value framework of human existence, rejection of unlimited consumerism, extreme individualism and moral relativism;
- focus on creating a global culture of ecology, collectivism and spirituality (Martynov 2008).

Emphasis is placed on the rising new economic giants that are beginning to actively influence international political processes. These countries include China, which is now one of the main centers of attention of Russian scholars (see, for example, Mikheev 2005). In addition to China, Russian researchers focus on countries such as India and Brazil. Countries of the "second tier" such as Mexico, Pakistan, Indonesia, and South Africa are also studied (Bobrovnikov, Davydov 2005). V.M. Davydov and A.V. Bobrovnikov conclude that today it is difficult to operate with earlier neo-Marxist concepts such as "center-periphery", "center-semi-periphery-periphery", or first, second, and third worlds. According to the authors, the dynamic aspect, which allows us to identify growing giants, plays great importance in the current world (Davydov, Bobrovnikov 2009).

In recent years, much attention has been paid to the specifics of the development of the BRICS countries, as well as to the

Eurasian Economic Union. It is noted that the understanding of the prospects for BRICS development is closely linked to issues of the transformation of the world system, the contradictory nature of globalization, and assessing the place and role of the nation state in the contemporary world (see, for example, Davydov 2008). Various aspects of BRICS activities are analyzed, namely, the development of the process of internationalization in the currency sphere (see Zharikov 2017), investments of the BRICS's countries (see, for example, Pakhomov 2012), and others. BRICS countries are also being studied, as well as their entering into the global space see, for example, Galishcheva 2017).

The Eurasian Economic Union draws the attention of Russian authors, both from the theoretical point of view (issues of the theory of integration (see, for example, Avdokushin, Tsoy 2016)) and from the applied one (see, for example, Kuznetsov and others 2016).

Theoretical studies in various fields of international political economy are conducted, in particular, by scholars from the Institute of World Economy and International Relations (IMEMO RAS). Thus, the study of S.A. Afontsev is devoted to the problem of the correlation of strategies of interaction. The author asks the question: Is there a shift from noncooperative strategies to cooperative strategies for regulating the world economy? S.A. Afontsev comes to the conclusion that in the current world there is an increase in the comparative weight of cooperative interaction in the economic sphere (Afontsev 2003). S.A. Afontsev has also analyzed economic policies in conditions of globalization (Afontsev 2010), and theoretical issues of global governance in the economy (Afontsev 2001). The studies of A.V. Kuznetsov are devoted to various aspects of integration, including in the post-Soviet space, the activities of transnational corporations, as well as other issues (Kuznetsov 2012; Kuznetsov 2006; Kuznetsov 2008), and research by N.I. Ivanova is on innovative aspects of development (Ivanova 2016; Ivanova, Danilin 2016).

In recent years, new concerns have appeared in Russian studies on international political economy, particularly regarding the influence of rating agencies that have had a significant impact on the development of the global economic crisis of 2008-2009 (see, for example, Tsibulina 2016; Karminskiy, A.M., Trofimova 2011). Issues of international transport corridors are also new for Russian IPE (see, for example, Tsvetkov, Zoidov, Medkov 2012; Babynina 2009; Podberezkina 2015). They acquired a particular importance in connection with projects for the development of transport infrastructure in Eurasia. Russian research in the field of IPE touches on the relationship between business, society, and government in foreign economic activity (see, for example, Zavyalova 2013) as well as issues of sanctions. (Baluev 2014).

Along with the new aspects of IPE for Russia, Russian researchers continue to focus on traditional problems. Among them, one of the most discussed issues is currency relations and their influence on the political development of the world, as well as the institutions regulating these relations (see, for example, Tkachenko 2000; Bardin 2013). In particular, it is noted that "financial development is not isolated from the political processes and motivations of the actors participating in it" (Stolbov 2015: 74). The role of financial issues in the political development of the world has become especially important after the economic crises of 1998 and 2008-2009.

7.2 Economic Crises and Their Impact on World Politics

Economic crises of the late twentieth and early twenty-first centuries forced Russian scholars, as well as researchers from other countries, to turn to an analysis primarily of the world financial system. The surge in the number of such studies falls on 2008-2009, as the period of the most large-scale manifestation of the crisis. A significant number of studies by Russian scholars in connection with the world economic crises were carried out by economists, who pay attention mainly to economic factors. Part of this research is devoted to the impact of the crisis on the economy and politics of Russia. Thus, in 2008, A. Bulatov wrote that the large scale of the economic crisis and the weakness of the Russian economy would lead to the strengthening of the role of the state in the economic life of Russia. At the same time, the author believed that the orientation of state and private Russian companies in the domestic market could become a positive moment (Bulatov 2008). It was noted that the economic crisis exposed the weak points of the Russian economy (see, for example, Melyantsev 2010). Scholars also analyzed the experience of other countries in countering the crisis (see, for example, Timonina, 2010; Karlusov 2010).

Another part of Russian research is aimed at the study of crisis phenomena in the world economy. Therefore, E.S. Khesin saw the reasons for the development of the economic crisis in globalization and in speeding up of innovative development. The logic of his argument is as follows. The pre-crisis rise turned out to be lengthy, intensive, and encompassed all groups of countries. At the same time, the innovation economy has become a strong stimulus for development. Large corporations not only began to move their production to developing countries but also began to transfer their research centers and laboratories there; India and China were the main recipients. Developing countries have become active players in the financial markets. This prompted the development of financial institutions. The other side of these processes was deindustrialization. Globalization was the second factor that influenced the development of the crisis. It is characterized by a sharp internationalization of all segments of the economy, as well as the outstripping development of the international sphere of the economy as a whole in comparison with domestic production. In addition, globalization has stimulated the strengthening of international economic ties. As a result, the crisis that emerged turned out to be global and covered all spheres, in contrast to the financial crisis of 1997-1998 and the information technology crisis in the United States of 2001. The key to understanding the reasons for the financial and subsequent economic crisis was the escape from real assets to financial ones, the introduction of innovations to diversify the latter. Developed countries have become capital importers, and developing countries have become exporters (Khesin 2009).

A number of Russian scholars see the causes of economic crises in the processes of globalization. Thus, O.V. Butorina has compared the crises of the 1930s and 2008-2009 and believes that the causes of both crises are the breaking of market mechanisms. In the first half of the twentieth century, there was the first wave of globalization. In those days, there was a jump in the development of transport and communications; transnational corporations appeared and strengthened. In the twenty-first century, globalization of the economy was completed as a result of the development of information technology and the collapse of the bipolar system. A consequence of this was the spread of capitalism to all regions of the world. The spread of capital and the sharp growth of financial markets have brought the world economy into a new stage. On the one hand, interdependence has sharply increased; on the other hand, the asymmetry of trade and financial flows has become global (Butorina 2009).

According to researchers from the Higher School of Economics (Moscow), L.M. Grigoryev and M.R. Salikhov, financial globalization and the gradual removal of regulatory requirements led to an increase in the concentration of the financial sector at the global level. The authors underline the necessity of changing the criteria for banking activities. They also discuss the role of rating agencies, and informal coordination of political vectors through various international structures (Grigoryev, Salikhov 2009).

Experts in the field of international relations also joined the discussion on these crisis issues. Several important round tables on the issue of global crisis took place in Russia. One of them was organized by the journal *Polis*, and the other one by the journal *Vestnik MGIMO-Universiteta*. In addition, articles were published in leading Russian journals on international relations. Specialists in the field of international relations focused on the political causes, aspects, and consequences of the crisis. The very name of the round table, which was published in the *Vestnik MGIMO-Universiteta*: "Is it economic crisis or world politics crisis?" (Krizis ekonomicheskiy ili ... 2009 [Is it economic crisis or... 2009]) clearly indicates that discussion went beyond economic issues.

The research of specialists in the field of international relations focuses on a number of aspects. In particular, the crisis is viewed as a crisis in the political organization of the world, or the political structure of the world (see, for example, Pantin 2009; Rozov 2009). However, the views of researchers regarding the essence of the transformations are different. A number of researchers demonstrate in varying degrees a neo-Marxist orientation: they see the problem in the development of liberalism and Western models of behavior. Thus, V.I. Pantin saw the essence of the world crisis primarily via the neoliberal model of globalization, which was formed by the end of the twentieth century. Among the most important features of this model he attributed the dominant role of the United States as a world economic, political, and military leader, and complete separation in the economy of the financial sector from the industrial one. The crisis, in the opinion of V.I. Pantin, is a natural phenomenon, conditioned by cycles of development, not only financial or economic but also political (Pantin 2009).

S.A. Makarenko defined the cause of the crisis as the reaction of the West to historical "retreat", which began in the middle of the twentieth century (the collapse of the colonial system, withdrawal from Vietnam, the achievement of Soviet nuclear parity with the United States, etc.). This reaction is expressed in the development of economic liberalism and ensuing financial liberalism. At the same time, the development of democratization has made the world global, narrowing the platform for the development of other types of behavior and interaction (Makarenko 2009).

Another group of Russian researchers after S. Strange, who explained the crisis of the late 1990s as a crisis of the Westphalian system (Srange 1999), views the problem in the contradiction between the interests of nation states and the need for global regulation of the economy. It is noted that the development of globalization in its various hypostases has objectively reduced the significance of territoriality (Kudryashova 2009). At the same time, as M.V. Kharkevich noted, the Westphalian system showed that it is incompatible with the universal interests of systemic regulation.

In the confrontation between the IMF and national states, the victory was of the states (*Krizis ekonomicheskiy ili...* 2009 [Is it economic crisis or... 2009]).

The problem of global political and economic regulation is also noted by other authors. Thus, I.A. Chikharev believed that the crisis was connected with the contradictions of several differently directed political megatrends: integration and manageability on the one hand, and polarization and liberalization on the other. As a result, the contemporary world required the creation of global governance structures, while in practice, different coalitions have been built in analogy with the alliances that started World War I (*Krizis ekonomicheskiy ili...* 2009 [Is it economic crisis or... 2009]).

The erosion of the Westphalian system was manifested not only in the inability to implement the required global regulation of the world economy, but also in the erosion of the traditional functions of various actors. In particular, states begin to act on the international scene like transnational corporations, buying up and selling businesses (Lebedeva 2009). At the same time, non-state actors play an increasingly important role in the globalized but continuing Westphalian world, which contradicts the very structure of the Westphalian system (*Krizis ekonomicheskiy ili...* 2009 [Is it economic crisis or... 2009]; Lebedeva 2009). Along with non-state actors, the number of states and international organizations had significantly increased in the Westphalian system. As a result, according to N.S. Rozov, the global crisis was an unintended systemic consequence of a multitude of national, group, and individual practices and strategies, each of which was completely "rational", yielding considerable income within the existing rules and institutions of economic interaction. In his opinion, it was necessary to realize the necessity of a constant change of institutions and practices of ensuring economic responsibility to the objective requirements of the modern global economy (Rozov 2009).

In any case, the economic crisiws of 2008-2009 set the problem of theoretical understanding of what was happening not only in the economic field but also in the political field. D.M. Feldman noted with regret that none of the theories of international relations could fully explain the origin of the crisis, and could not predict it (Feldman 2009). Agreeing with this statement, D.M. Feldman wrote with regret that it was hardly possible to predict the crisis. Today the political world is undergoing transformation. The choice of the path has not yet been defined, and therefore a theoretical construct is possible only in the form of scenarios.

7.3 Energy Issues in Russian IR Studies

Energy issues occupy a special place in Russian IR studies, largely due to the role of energy in the country's economy. But the reason for the increased attention of Russian authors on the energy sphere is not because this issue is very significant to Russia. Yu.V. Borovskiy noted that if the international community was absorbed by the problem of democratization in the last decade of the twentieth century, then one of the key themes of the twenty-first century is becoming energy (Borovskiy 2008). The problem of energy resources is largely conditioned by the Middle East conflict; it is the responsibility of the Group of Eight (Isakov 2006), and the energy issue was on the agenda of NATO meetings (Borovskiy 2008).

In Russian IR studies, along with consideration of issues of nuclear power, hydropower, and alternative energy sources, the greatest attention is paid to issues of hydrocarbon energy, primarily to oil and gas. Many Russian economists have devoted their work to analysis of energy markets, their dynamics, energy prices, and trade in energy resources, as well as other aspects that somehow address political and economic problems (see, for example, Bushuev, Konoplyanik, Mirkin 2013; Telegina 2012; Makarov, Grigoryev, Mitrov 2015).

Energy security is one of the most discussed areas in Russian IR studies related to problems of world political economics. Thus, the work of V.E. Fortov and his colleagues emphasized that the problem of global energy security has arisen now as an urgent need for reliable provision of the world economy with all kinds of energy without excessive damage to the environment and at prices reflecting basic economic principles. The global nature of threats to energy security and their consequences require concerted international action and the development by the world community of the concept of a sustainable and secure energy future, as well as the implementation of measures to ensure its practical implementation (Fortov, Makarov, Mitrova 2007).

Particular attention in Russian IR studies is paid to Russia's policy in the field of energy security. It is especially noted that Russia has a number of specific features that affect its energy policy. These include the following: (1) Despite the growing domestic demand for energy resources, the country is vitally interested in expanding oil and gas exports; (2) production growth is possible only with the development of new fields in hard-to-reach places of Eastern Siberia, on the shelf of the northern seas, in the Caspian. This will require huge funds to ensure exploration, construction, environmental protection, and road infrastructure; (3) the geographic location of the main fields, from which oil and gas is now extracted in Western Siberia, makes Europe the most profitable export market. The development of fields in Eastern Siberia and the Arctic will allow direct exports to Asia; (4) in the sale of oil and gas, Russia completely transforms to a market economy, refusing to underestimate prices for the CIS countries only because of their entry into the Commonwealth; (5) Russia carries out exploration, production, and transportation of oil and gas with the involvement of foreign participants; and (6) the state has strengthened its participation in the oil and gas sector. In many respects, this is dictated by the need to provide reasonable needs of the domestic market and energy security of Russia (Primakov 2009).

A number of Russian studies focus on regional energy issues (see, for example, Tomberg 2013). Most of the energy Russia supplies is to Europe. Therefore, Russian authors have focused on this region. EU policy and Russia's relations with the EU in the energy field are especially relevant in Russian IR studies (Pashkovskaya 2011). Moreover, the energy component has become one of the main ones in the interaction between Russia and the EU. In 2000, following the results of the EU-Russia Paris summit, the format of the energy dialogue "Russia-EU" was formed. One of the objectives of this format was the development of energy relations between Russia and the EU (Kaveshnikov 2009). The mutual idea of the leaders of Russia and the EU was to single out the energy sphere as one of the priority areas of cooperation. The main issues to be resolved within the framework of this bilateral dialogue lay in the field of energy saving, the formation of production, the construction of transport infrastructure, and control of the relations between supplier companies and consumer countries (Pashkovskaya 2011).

Russian authors also discuss the provisions of the International Energy Charter, signed by Russia in 1994 but not ratified. It is noted that the charter proclaims a number of important principles: encouragement of foreign investments in energy, free trade in energy materials, freedom of transit through pipelines and networks, and reduction of negative environmental impact. But at the same time, it contains provisions that can be interpreted as coming into conflict with the national sovereignty of a country. These provisions were not only confirmed but also strengthened in the Transit Protocol (2003), which was attached to the Energy Charter in 2003 (Primakov 2009).

Criticism by Russian experts was caused by the Third Energy Package of the EU, which was entered into force in 2009 and involved the sale and transfer of gas infrastructure owned by *Gazprom*, with an obligation to grant third-party access to trunk pipelines (see, for example, Gudkov 2010). Russian authors also note that the implementation of certain EU norms of the Third Energy Package on the separation of functions in the most rigid variant may contradict bilateral international agreements of Russia with the EU countries, first of all, pertaining to agreements on investment protection (Salygin, Kaveshnikov 2014).

Despite the fact that gas issues in Russia-EU relations dominate, other aspects of energy cooperation are also being discussed. Thus, as for oil, in early 2010, up to 23% of the import of petroleum products to the European Union came from Russia, and the impact of European sanctions on the oil industry of Russia was significant. Nevertheless, Russian companies were still partly allowed to work with European partners: 1) the obligations under former contracts remain in force in the countries that imposed sanctions; 2) many concepts are interpreted differently, which makes it possible to find opportunities in the imposed restrictions (Mustaparov 2015).

Much attention is paid to the formation and implementation of energy policy and diplomacy. Thus, S. Zhiznin formulates the basic principles of Russia's energy diplomacy. He examines the main methods and means of contemporary energy diplomacy, as well as the specifics of the international activity of leading foreign and Russian companies (Zhiznin 2005). It is noteworthy that the activity of energy companies is included in energy diplomacy, which was relatively new in Russian studies on diplomacy. Although the companies themselves, of course, were previously the object of study, the issues of energy diplomacy were further developed in Russian studies (see, for example, Chernitsyna 2015).

Chapter 8
Development of Social and Humanitarian Issues in Russian IR Studies

8.1 The Growth of Social and Humanitarian Components in World Politics

Social and humanitarian issues in comparison with security issues were at the periphery of the attention of politicians for many decades, and as a consequence also drew the research interest of scholars working in the field of international relations and world politics. All were focused on military-political and partly political-economic issues. A turning point occurred in the late twentieth and early twenty-first centuries. It cannot be said that the problems of security or economic development have attracted the attention of politicians and researchers less and have left the international agenda. It can only be argued that humanitarian aspects began to evoke the increasing interest of both.

The reasons for this orientation lie in the fact that at the beginning of the new century we see an obvious reversal, both in politics and in the scientific sphere, toward human needs. This does not apply only to international relations. For example, it is no coincidence that the Nobel Prize for Economics in 2017 was awarded to Richard H. Thaler for creating such a direction in economic science as a behavioral economy, which is a kind of bridge between economics and psychology.

Social and humanitarian ties, as well as economic ones, create conditions for long-term participant interaction even in situations of deterioration of the overall political climate. For example, even during the Cold War, cultural ties between East and West were maintained.

Contemporary conflicts and wars are accompanied by active actions in the social and humanitarian spheres, hence the emergence of such phenomena as "information wars" and "hybrid wars". The intensification of the activity of economic actors in world politics—TNCs and other business structures—has led to a huge number of human beings involved in the professional international economic sphere. The central figure in this sphere, as well as in the economy as a whole, is a person who goes beyond the national borders of the state. One of the consequences of all these processes can be the fact that in recent years in developed countries more attention is paid to those sectors of the economy that are associated with improving the quality of human life (Ivanova 2016). In addition, the social responsibility of business is increasing. Earlier it was mainly limited to the company or the country of the company's activity; in the twenty-first century it began to acquire a global character. Evidence of this is the UN Global Compact.

As for the social and humanitarian sphere itself, it has been developing rapidly since the end of the twentieth century through the activities of international nongovernmental organizations, international cooperation in the field of education (the Bologna process with its advantages and disadvantages is a good example), social networks, and so on.

It is obvious that the development of ICT has greatly contributed to the involvement of the individual in transnational relations. And if at the end of the twentieth century the transnationalization of states and organizations (primarily business structures and NGOs) became possible, in the twenty-first century the world was faced with the transnationalization of human ties and relations. And the same person is involved in a number of intersecting transnational groups. For example, T. Biersteker notes that in the contemporary world the formation of transnational political networks is taking place, the essence of which is that the subject (in particular, the person) turns out to be included in many networks connected with the study of a particular political phenomenon, the implementation of various proposals, evaluation of political projects, and so on (Biersteker 2014).

Nevertheless, not all people are included in transnational relations. And this generates a new social rift in the world, which is characteristic today of a number of countries. This social rift divides all people into two groups depending on their orientation, either on transnational relations, or — to return to the national state, local connections, and sometimes returns to tribal ties. In the latter case, the archaization of a state often takes place (Lebedeva, Kharkevich, Zinovieva, Koposova 2017). Examples of the archaization of the state, understood as a retreat to a previous stage of development, can be Libya (a return from the national state to tribal relations) and the United Kingdom with Brexit (a return from supranational structures of the European Union to the national state) (Kharkevich, Muzalevskiy, Oskolkov 2018). But, in the case of Libya, the split in society according to this parameter (a person's orientation toward transnational or local relations) is difficult to grasp (rather, there is a split between different tribes and groups), and in the case of Great Britain, it is obvious: large cities, in particular, London, voted to stay in the European Union, that is for greater inclusion in transnational relations, while small settlements saw their future within national borders. The US presidential election of 2016 also demonstrated the split of American society with regard to national or transnational orientation. Here, however, it is necessary to make a reservation connected with the fact that in recent years archaic ties have also sometimes sought to transnationalize. The most vivid examples here are al-Qaeda and ISIS.

However, a clear manifestation of social division in the contemporary world on a significant scale is a relatively new phenomenon which has not yet received an adequate reflection in the scientific literature. It is obvious that it is very significant both in terms of the internal political development of states and on a global scale and needs serious scientific analysis. The same can be said about attempts to transnationalize archaic models of behavior. It seems that this social and humanitarian area will be intensively studied in the near future.

In general, the social and humanitarian sphere can manifest itself in various qualities. This is an area of interaction and cooperation, and a means of development. This is a resource of impact on other countries; it is also an area in which potential for conflict can accumulate.

The attention of researchers on the social and humanitarian aspects of world politics began to increase at the end of the twentieth century. At those times, J. Nye formulated his concept of soft power (Nye 1990), which initially provoked a storm of criticism. The situation began to change in many ways at the beginning of the twenty-first century. The turning point was, to a large extent, the terrorist attacks of September 11, 2001. There was awareness that in countering terrorism one should not confine oneself to military and economic influence alone. A.V. Dolinskiy wrote that the terrorist attacks carried out by out by a small group of people, behind which the great powers did not stand, initiated discussions on how to prevent such tragedies in the future. Quite quickly, the academic community and diplomats-practitioners came to a consensus on the role of communication with foreign societies to prevent the growth of Islamic extremism (Dolinskiy 2011).

8.2 Russian Attention to Social and Humanitarian Issues

Russia, somewhat later, although without such dramatic events as the United States, set itself a similar task: to influence other countries using information and humanitarian resources. The motive in many respects was the political goal of restoring Russia's influence in the world arena. This goal was part of the worldwide trend of the increasing importance of social and humanitarian resources. To restore Russia's influence on the world stage, parity with the United States in the military-political sphere was not sufficient. The Russian economy, although it demonstrated at the beginning of the twenty-first century some improvements, clearly could not claim to ensure Russia's leading position in the world. Under these conditions, humanitarian resources were best suited to achieve this goal. Russia's increasing attention upon the humanitarian aspects of the international arena was reflected in the 2008 *Concept of Russia's Foreign Policy*, which formulated the objectives of achieving an objective perception of Russia in the world, developing its own effective means of informational influence on public opinion abroad, and strengthening the positions of Russian mass media in the global information space.[62] As a result, since the beginning of the twenty-first century, funding for various projects and activities in the social and humanitarian spheres has significantly increased in Russia. There have been several funds established: the "Russian world" Fund of public diplomacy and others, whose task was the maintenance and spread of the Russian language in the world, the development of public diplomacy, and so on. A number of other structures were formed, including in the media. In particular, the television channel *Russia Today* was created. In addition, a number of other practical steps have been taken. As a result, the numbers of Russian studies that discuss humanitarian issues have also increased.

The study of international aspects of social and humanitarian issues in Russia went in three main directions. In the first, attention was paid to issues of soft power, and, in part, public diplomacy, both theoretically and in terms of studying specific examples of use. It is represented by a large number of studies. In addition, the second and third directions are to some extent connected with the first one.

The second direction is also quite extensive in quantitative terms. It is connected with the inclusion of humanitarian and social issues in studies of conflicts and wars. This direction began to develop in Russia a little later than the first one, namely in 2010. Finally, the third direction, which by the number of studies is inferior to the first two, is focused on analysis of human capital. However, it is of particular interest since in a certain respect Russian studies differ in subject matter from Western studies in this field. Thus, Russian scholars in some ways have pioneered the integration of higher education problems as part of international relations and world politics.

---

62 Konceptsiya vneshney politiki Rossiyskoy Federatsii [Foreign policy concept of the Russian Federation]. Utverzhdena Presidentom RF 12.07.2008 [Approved by the Russian President on 12.07.2008]: http://www.kremlin.ru/acts/news/785

8.3 Soft Power and Public Diplomacy in Russian IR Studies

The concept of soft power was not immediately accepted by the scientific community, or by politicians, in Russia. The idea of J. Nye, launched in the early 1990s, was met initially with great skepticism in Russia. Russian scholars did not see any rational element in it. Among many objections put forward to J. Nye by the Russian scholars, perhaps the most frequently used was that this idea did not contain anything new. Arguments were based on the grounds that since the emergence of humankind some groups somehow "softly" influenced others.

Later, after a number of studies in Russia, the situation changed significantly. As a result, the term "soft power" was largely incorporated into the text of the Concept of the Foreign Policy of the Russian Federation, adopted in 2013,[63] and subsequently into the Foreign Policy Concept of 2016,[64] largely due to research findings and practices of its application by other states.

Russian studies on soft power and public diplomacy can be divided into three large groups. The first group is research, in which efforts are being made to theoretically understand these issues. The second group includes many case studies on the use of soft power and public diplomacy by one or another state. Finally, the third group, represented to a large extent by scholars from Yekaterinburg, conducts research on the operationalization of the concept of the effectiveness of the use of soft power.

In theoretical studies, Russian authors are trying to identify the features of soft power, its difference from other means of influence, and so on (see, for example, Zevelev, Troickiy 2006;

---

63 Konceptsiya vneshney politiki Rossiyskoy Federatsii [Foreign policy concept of the Russian Federation]. Utverzhdena Presidentom RF 12 fevralya 2013 [Approved by the Russian President on 12.02.2013]: http://www.mid.ru/foreign_policy/official_documents/-/asset_publisher/CptICkB6BZ29/content/id/122186

64 Konceptsiya vneshney politiki Rossiyskoy Federatsii [Foreign policy concept of the Russian Federation]. Utverzhdena Presidentom RF 30.11.2016]: http://www.mid.ru/foreign_policy/news/-/asset_publisher/cKNonkJE02Bw/content/id/2542248

Pescov, Bobylo 2015; Kazarinova 2011). Today in Russia there are many interpretations of soft power and translations of this term. For example, P.B. Parshin drew attention to two understandings of soft power. According to the first, it is a tool or technology, mainly a communicative one, which involves potentially less damage to the object compared to "hard" tools (technologies). Another understanding of soft power is that it is viewed as the potential impact of some actor, due to its appeal and the desire to have the same values (Parshin 2014).

Nevertheless, the most common understanding of soft power in Russia is any nonmilitary method of influencing the opposite side, that is, rather, what P.B. Parshin called "technological" understandings of soft power. With this approach, economic and political coercion, as well as other types, fall under the definition of soft power. Russian scholars often assume that coercion can be military or economic only. Thus, V.Ya. Wapler, N.E. Gronskaya and their colleagues, citing J. Nye, wrote that soft power is the country's ability to influence others by means other than military and economic coercion (Vapler, Gronskaya, Gusev, Korshunov, Makarychev, Solntsev 2010).

In addition, in Russia (however, not only in Russia) the use of soft power is often identified with propaganda, and in this case, is usually judged negatively. With this understanding, indeed, the differences between soft power, propaganda, nonmilitary and economic means of pressure and so on, disappear. However, in recent years, Russian scientific discourse is increasingly involved in understanding exactly what J. Nye defined as soft power through attractiveness (see, for example, Panova 2010). It was shown that within the framework of the realistic approach, there is an identification of the concepts of "soft power" and "propaganda", whereas in the framework of the neoliberal approach there is a fundamental difference between these concepts. For example, propaganda involves manipulative influence, and soft power excludes it. Propaganda is oriented, as a rule, to short-term goals. With the help of propaganda, you can solve immediate problems, whereas "soft power" provides for a long-term relationship with a partner (Lebedeva 2017c).

Quite a large number of Russian studies are devoted to an analysis of soft power as a foreign policy tool of certain states. In Russian academic literature, the features of Japanese soft power (see Chugrov 2015), that of the United States (see Braterskiy, Skriba 2014), Germany (see Rustamova 2016), the EU (see Baykov 2014), and other actors of world politics, including Russia (see Leonova 2013; Andreev 2016) and the EAEU (see Lebedeva, Kharkevich 2014), are discussed. There are also studies of the different areas which can be used as soft power: education (see Fominykh 2008), media (see Zegonov 2008), cinema (see Teteryuk 2014), sports (see Rusakova 2014), and so on, as well as new areas associated with the negative effects of the application of soft power (see Lebedeva, Rustamova, Sharko 2016), migration (see Kasatkin, Avatkov 2014) and terrorist soft power (see Manoylo 2017).

The third, least numerous groups of studies on soft power is presented by the studies of O.F. Rusakova and her colleagues from Yekaterinburg (Rusakova 2014; Rusakova 2015). For example, according to the authors, Russia ranks 28 among the 40 countries in Soft Power Index Results (2012) (see Rusakova 2014; Rusakova 2015).

Close to the problems of soft power are studies related to the support of compatriots. In Russian academic literature on international relations there have been almost no studies on compatriots. For present-day Russia, emphasis is laid on the importance of a strong diaspora integrated into the society of the country of residence (Chepurin 2009).

Studies on public diplomacy in Russia are fewer in number compared to studies on soft power. Basically, these studies are conducted in Moscow and St. Petersburg and in structure they are similar to the previous group. These are as follows: (1) theoretical understanding of the issues of public diplomacy and (2) the study of specific cases of its use by different states. As in the previous case, interest in public diplomacy in Russia is due, on the one hand, to the involvement of large masses in the world political processes, and, on the other hand, the task of promoting a positive image of Russia abroad. The most common understanding of public diplomacy in the United States, for example, is related to the influence of one state on the society of another state (Snow, Taylor 2009). This cannot be said of the Russian understanding of public diplomacy. In many Russian studies, public diplomacy is identified with the activities of nongovernmental organizations and is synonymous with people's diplomacy (*narodnaya diplomatiya* or *obshchestvennaya diplomatiya*) (see, for example, Mukhametov 2014; Evdokimov 2011). Such identification leads to disregard of the fact that the channels of implementation of public diplomacy can be both state and non-state. In other words, the state can act directly through its official representatives, and indirectly through non-state actors. Moreover, non-state actors do not always act as agents of state policy. As a result, the conceptual apparatus of public diplomacy in Russian-language literature turns out to be extremely unclear. This approach significantly narrows the scope of public diplomacy, as it excludes the official channels for its implementation. A. Dolinskiy draws attention to this aspect. He writes that public diplomacy has a second meaning of the term in Russian — diplomacy at the level of public organizations. This gave rise to a dangerous confusion: even among experts, there is the abiding conviction that public diplomacy is only a dialogue at the level of nongovernmental organizations. Meanwhile, public diplomacy implies a wider range of activities (Dolinskiy).

T. Zonova holds a similar view. She notes that the Russian foreign policy lexicon contains two terms with regard to diplomacy: "public" and "people's". However, the interchangeability of these terms should be treated with extreme caution. The definition of "public" will be translated as a social one, or as civil, and as a people's one. T. Zonova wrote that it is clear that "people's diplomacy" means the diplomacy of nongovernmental organizations (Zonova 2012).

At present, particular attention in Russian studies is drawn to the possibilities of science in the framework of public diplomacy and the search through it for the solution to international problems.

This approach—scientific diplomacy—is relatively new in Russia, although the successful experience of interaction between Soviet and Western scholars to resolve conflicts and prevent a nuclear catastrophe was apparant in the period of the Cold War. V. Panchenko and A. Torkunov note that researchers are not concerned with the need to simplify. Therefore, the interaction of researchers from different countries makes it possible to better understand the problem, and therefore to outline ways to solve it.[65]

A fairly large layer of studies is devoted to public diplomacy of states and intergovernmental organizations. The public diplomacy of the United States (Kubyshkin, A.I., Tsvetkova 2013) as well as Israel, the countries of Central Asia, Iran, the Vatican, the EU, the CIS, NATO, CSTO, and the SCO, as well as historical models of public diplomacy, are studied (Lebedeva 2017d). At the same time, public diplomacy in this context is considered slightly wider than its traditional understanding as the impact of the state on the societies of other countries, because supranational interstate structures appear in the research focus. However, we cannot say that in this respect Russian research is unique. Public diplomacy of intergovernmental structures is studied not only by Russian authors (see, for example, Pagovski 2015).

Among the other states, Russian researchers pay most attention to US public diplomacy as instancing a state that has largely shaped the conceptual framework of public diplomacy and actively uses public diplomacy in practice. It is noted that in recent years, public diplomacy of the United States has undergone significant changes. If at the beginning of the twenty-first century public diplomacy of the United States was focused on a policy of "engagement-involvement" of the foreign target audience in relation to the values and culture of the United States, later there was a sharp change in the conceptual paradigm of public diplomacy of the United States. Instead of a tool of the policy of "engagement-involvement", it has become a strategic

---

65 Panchenko, V., Torkunov, A.V. Ucheniy kak diplomat. *Rossiyskaya gazeta*. 26.06.2017: https://rg.ru/2017/06/26/kak-nauchnoe-sotrudnichestvo-pomog aet-resheniiu-mezhdunarodnyh-problem.html

communication mechanism (Tsvetkova 2015), that is, a purposeful information influence on the external audience with the aim of achieving US goals. In the same context, Russian scholars usually analyze the tools of "color revolutions". In other words, Russian scholars emphasize that if initially public diplomacy was used by the United States within the framework of the neoliberal theoretical paradigm, now it has been used in accordance with a rigid realistic approach.

The understanding of public diplomacy as being close to strategic communication is presented in the study of A.I. Podberezkin and A.V. Zhukov. They note that in the twenty-first century, mass media and the Internet allow us to solve issues that were previously resolved by military, economic, and other means. As a result, public diplomacy has become an integral part of the network-centric hybrid war in which the role of information impacting on the enemy becomes decisive (Podberezkin, Zhukov 2015).

In general, it should be noted that studies of hybrid wars and "color revolutions" are quite trendy in Russia. At the same time, it appears that one should distinguish between public diplomacy and strategic communication, which are two different tools. In conflict situations, hard means of information in order to influence the opposite side are often used. As a result, there are information wars (Manojlo 2016) and hybrid wars (Panarin 2016), which have been widely described, including in Russian academic literature. At the same time, in conflict and crisis, tools of public diplomacy are often used to reduce tensions and reconciliation (Lebedeva 2013). And these are two different instruments. To a certain extent, strategic communication is synonymous with impact, which is called "sharp diplomacy" (Walker, Ludwig 2017), and which actually corresponds to the use of public diplomacy within the framework of a realistic approach, or in the understanding of J. Nye, hard power (Nye 2018).

The development of the Internet and social networks has led to new phenomena in public diplomacy, which include different types of online wars. Thus, E.S. Zinovieva notes that digital diplomacy has helped change diplomacy from a hierarchical type of activity to a network one, involving large numbers of people in solving problems. The use of digital public diplomacy can help reduce tension. However, disabling communication can also be used to reduce tension. Digital public diplomacy is also effective as an instrument for post-conflict settlement (Zinovieva 2017).

8.4 Analysis of Human Capital in Russian IR Studies

Traditionally, economists address issues of human capital. For scholars of international relations and world politics who for a long time focused on problems of high politics, this category usually remained out of sight. At the end of the twentieth century and in the beginning of the twenty-first century, in connection with the increasing role of the social and humanitarian factor in the world, researchers of international relations also turned to its study. However, studies of human capital in international studies turned out to be quite amorphous. Among experts in the field of international relations, A.I. Podberezkin directly wrote on human capital, implying that a wide range of issues related to ideology, values, and socioeconomic relations exist (Podberezkin 2007-2012).

Human rights are among the issues that are related to human capital. The analysis of human rights in Russian foreign policy is devoted, in particular, to the study of S.V. Chugrov. He shows that the discrepancy between Russia and the West in the understanding of fundamental human rights is due to historical developments (Chugrov 2001).

IR scholars, following economists, turn to social and economic problems of human capital. However, such studies are not many. As an example, in his study, V.M. Sergeev showed that the roots of the 2008-2009 crisis were not only in the economic or political developments but also in trust, which was also determined by the social responsibility of members of society (Sergeev 2009). Analysis of migration and demographic processes also belongs to this category of studies. These studies began to be an area of particular interest in recent years, especially due to the migration crisis in Europe (see, for example, Potemkina 2010; Bolshova 2016).

Nevertheless, the greatest number of Russian studies touching upon human capital issues is devoted to aspects of higher education. In many respects, it intersects with issues of soft power, but it is not confined to it, of course.

Higher education issues are the sphere in which Russian IR studies are at the forefront of the world. The main areas of research here are the development of human capital and the strengthening of Russia's role through the development of higher education, its internationalization, and international cooperation. Russian researchers note that in the context of globalization, the functions of education are changed. Along with traditional functions, including those related to the development of human capital, higher education influences the shaping of world politics, acquiring a political function (Lebedeva 2006). Now higher education is characterized by such features as transnationalization, network self-organization, and marketization (Kharkevich 2012).

In connection with the changes that are taking place, university policy is also being transformed. Universities are increasingly involved in internationalization of education, as well as developing training programs for different categories of the population, including for teachers. As a consequence, the role of universities in the development of human capital and in world politics is becoming another area of focus of Russian researchers. The university becomes a kind of discussion platform; it unites the academic community, representatives of state structures and business, and journalists (Lebedeva, Barabanov 2012). It is noted that the university can "combine the strengths of all its units, as well as partners" (Larionova, Suslova: 22). Negative aspects in universities' activities and possible ways to overcome them are also analyzed (Lebedeva 2017a).

Russian scholars write that universities are faced with the need for mass training and retraining of teachers to work with more complex software, similarly to how in the late 1980s the most advanced teachers moved from writing machines to computers and learned the first computer programs (Torkunov 2011).

The educating of specialists in the field of international relations, an area that is particularly important for international relations, is explored in a number of studies by Russian scholars (see, for example, Torkunov 2013; Voevoda 2013). Russian researchers show that training in international relations leads to the development of human capital not only in their own country but also abroad, since specialists in the field of international relations, due to their professional activities, are mostly involved in international processes. Russian scholars also discuss what kind of opportunities open the internationalization of higher education for the implementation of Russia's soft power, both in the short and long terms (see Torkunov 2012b; Lebedeva, Fort 2012). In general, humanitarian issues, which have become some of the most significant in the current world, are now reflected in Russian IR studies. Most of all Russian researchers are attracted to issues of soft power and higher education, as well as analyses of manipulative strategies in the context of hybrid and information wars, "color revolutions". At the same time, it seems that the role that humanitarian issues acquire today in world politics is not fully reflected in Russian international relations studies. Thus, public health, tourism, youth, and professional contacts (including scientific ones) are almost out of focus of research attention. Theoretical studies on the role of the humanitarian component in world politics are also needed, although it should be noted that in other countries these issues are not of much significance and are less intensively studied. Considering the fact that Russia has rich research traditions in the field of culture and psychology, the development of humanitarian issues within the framework of Russian IR studies is important.

Conclusion

It is obviously impossible to present Russian studies in the field of international relations in all their depth in a single book. The task was only to show the process of formation and the main lines of research in the field of international relations in the country. It is possible to agree or not with the formulation of problems by Russian scholars, certain interpretations, and issues that are discussed in the field of international relations and world politics. It is important that they give an idea of how international reality is perceived and understood in Russia. In addition, the history of the development of national schools in the field of international relations, in this case Russia, is certainly a part of the world development of research in the field of international relations and world politics.

Russian IR scholars have come a long way from the first half of the twentieth century to the present day. Political realities have changed and very serious changes have taken place in the field of research and teaching. First of all, it should be noted that research and teaching of international relations in Russia went beyond Moscow; these were developed and are developing in Russian regions. Many new journals and textbooks were invented. The subject of Russian IR studies has also expanded. In this regard, in Russia there have been dramatic shifts in all three layers described by O. Waever: the political layer (factors), institutional layer (factors), and intellectual layer (factors) (Waever 1998). At the same time, the turning point in Russian IR studies is primarily connected with the period of the late 1980s and early 1990s, when, following the political events that developed rapidly, changes began to take place in the latter two layers.

Today in Russian IR studies two trends are clearly discernible. One is aimed toward the integration of Russian IR studies into global science. The second is represented by isolationist aspirations. These two tendencies reflect general political trends both in Russia and in the world. To some extent, they both act all the time, but at one stage or another, one of them dominates.

It can hardly be said that contemporary Russian studies of international relations have become an integral part of global international relations. However, this is not a unique feature of Russia. IR studies to some extent continue to be an "American social science". However, other countries, in particular China, have become more active than Russia in integrating into global science. Nevertheless, Russian researchers began to publish in foreign journals, lecture abroad, and so on. There is also a complementary activity, when foreign researchers are publishing in Russia and lecturing at Russian universities.

The deterioration of relations between Russia and the West in the 2010s undoubtedly had an impact on IR studies. And although there is a certain time lag between political events and scientific and educational activities, academic contacts gradually began to experience a clear atmosphere of "cooling". International studies, being the closest to foreign policy, experienced the deterioration of Russian-American and Russian-European relations to a greater degree than many other disciplines. In Russian IR studies, isolationist aspirations began to intensify. In the mildest form, they are manifested in the attempts by a number of Russian researchers to find their own special path in the study of world politics and international relations. Extremely isolationist views often go beyond academic discussions. Obviously, some isolationism is partly due to language barriers, as well as to the specifics of the construction of research and writing academic articles in Russia. Most Russian scholars publish articles in the form of essays focused on a historical approach. But these factors are not decisive in the formation of isolationism in Russian IR studies.

It is hardly worth feeding illusions that the isolationist tendency will disappear completely anytime soon. However, there is no need for its disappearance. A certain emphasis on the development of national specifics, including in the field of international relations, is certainly necessary. Nevertheless, the break with world science is unacceptable. Moreover, it seems that academic discussion of the most acute problems between Russian researchers and scholars from other countries will make it possible for a better understanding of IR issues and, as a result, improve world politics in the long term. However, for this to happen, constant interaction of scientists with decision-makers is also important.

Bibliography

Acharya, A. (2011). Dialogue and Discovery: In Search of International Relations Theories beyond the West. *Journal of International Studies*. No. 39(3). pp. 619–637.
Acharya, A., B. Buzan, B. (eds.) (2010). *Non-Western International Relations Theory: Perspectives On and Beyond Asia*. NewYork: Routledge.
Afontsev, S.A. (2001). Problema globalnogo upravleniya mirokhozyaystvennoy sistemoy: teoreticheskie aspekty. *Mirovaya ekonomika i mezhdunarodnye otnosheniya*. No. 5. pp. 65–70.
Afontsev, S.A. (2003). Ot borby k rynku: ekonomicheskaya kooperativnost v miropoliticheskom vzaimodeystvii. *Mezhdunarodnye protsessy*. Vol. 11. No. 2. pp. 16–30: http://old.intertrends.ru/two/002.htm
Afontsev, S.A. (2010). *Politicheskie rynki i ekonomicheskaya politika*. Moskva: KomKniga.
Afontsev, S.A. (2013). Budushcheye globalnogo upravleniya. Moskva: *Rossiyskiy sovet po mezhdunarodnym delam (RSMD)*: http://russiancouncil.ru/inner/?id_4=2517#top-content
Afontsev, S.A., Lebedeva, M.M. (red.) (2014). *Rossiya v sovremennykh integratsionnykh protsessakh*. Moskva: MGIMO.
Akhtamzyan, A.A. (2013). Ermolenko, D.V. – perviy prorektor MGIMO iz vypusknikov vuza. *Vestnik MGIMO – Universiteta*. No. 1. pp. 265–267.
Alekseeva, T.A. (2017) «Zapad» i «ne Zapad» v prostranstve teorii mezhdunarodnykh otnosheniy. *Vestnik Rossiyskogo universiteta druzhby narodov. Seriya: Mezhdunarodnye otnosheniya*. Vol. 17. No. 2. pp. 246–256.
Alekseeva, T.A., Mineev, A.P., Fenenko, A.V., Loshkarev, I.D., Ananev, B.I. (2016). Zachem nuzhna «kvantovaya» reforma konstruktivizma v teorii mezhdunarodnykh otnosheniy? *Vestnik MGIMO-Universiteta*. No. 6. pp. 7–13.
Alekseeva, T.A., Mineev, A.P., Loshkarev, I.D. (2016). «Zemlya smyateniya»: kvantovaya teoriya v mezhdunarodnykh otnosheniyakh? *Vestnik MGIMO-Universiteta*. No. 3. pp. 7–16.
Alimov, A.A. (2003). Ekologicheskaya politika i ekologicheskaya diplomatiya. *Vestnik Sankt-Peterburgskogo gosudarstvennogo universiteta*. Series 6. Mezhdunarodnye otnosheniya. Issue 3 (22). pp. 101–109.
Alker, H., Biersteker, Th. (1982). The Dialectics of World Order: Notes for a Future Archeologist of International Savoir Faire. *International Studies Quarterly*. No. 28(2). pp. 121–142.

Allison, G. (1971). *Essence of Decision: Explaining the Cuban Missile Crisis.* Boston: Little & Brown.

Allison, G., Ury, W., Allyn, B. (eds.) (1989). *Windows of Opportunity. From Cold War to Peaceful Competition in U.S.-Soviet Relations.* Cambridge, MA: Cambridge University Press.

Andreev, A.L. (2016). "Myagkaya sila": aranzhirovka smyslov v rossiyskom ispolnenii. *Polis. Politicheskie issledovaniya.* No. 5. pp. 122–133. DOI: https://doi.org/10.17976/jpps/2016.05.10

Antonenko, O., Yurgens, I. (2010). Rossiya i NATO: novaya glava. *Rossiya v globalnoy politike.* 2010. No. 6. pp. 90–99.

Antyukhina-Moskovchenko, V.I., Zlobin, A.A., Khrustalev, M.A. (1980). *Osnovy teorii mezhdunarodnykh otnosheniy.* Uchebnoe posobie. Moskva: MGIMO.

Arbatov, A. (1988). *Lethal Frontiers: A Soviet View of Nuclear Strategy, Weapons, and Negotiations.* New York: Praeger.

Arbatov, A. (1990). *Oboronitelnaya dostatochnost i bezopasnost.* Moskva: Znanie.

Arbatov, A. (2010). Zdraviy smysl i razoruzhenie: o materii i filosofii yadernogo oruzhiya. *Rossiya v globalnoy politike.* No. 4. pp. 178–186.

Arbatov, A., Dvorkin, V. (red.) (2012). *Protivoraketnaya oborona: Protivostoyanie ili sotrudnichestvo?* Moskva: Rossiyskaya politicheskaya entsiklopediya (ROSSPEN): http://carnegieendowment.org/files/pro_book_rus2012.pdf

Arbatov, A.G. (1984). *Voenno-strategicheskiy paritet i politika SShA.* Moskva: Politizdat, 1984.

Arbatov, A.G. (2006). Rasshirenie NATO i natsionalnye interesy Rossii. Doklad na konferentsii ROPC Fonda Rozy Lyuksemburg (Rosa-Luxemburg-Stiftung). *Politiya.* No. 2. pp. 94–103.

Arbatov, A.G. (2011). Mezhdunarodnaya bezopasnost v epokhu peremen i vneshnyaya politika Rossii. *Rossiya v globalnom mire 2000–2011.* Vol. 2. Moskva: Aspekt Press. pp. 12–21.

Arbatov, A.G. (2016). Ne vyshlo i ne viydet? O prichinakh neudachi protivoraketnogo sotrudnichestva Rossii i SShA. *Polis. Politicheskie issledovaniya.* No. 2. pp. 49–61. DOI: 10.17976/jpps/2016.02.05

Arbatov, A.G., Dvorkin, V.Z. (red.) (2005). *Yadernoe sderzhivanie i nerasprostranenie.* Moskva: Moskovskiy tsentr Karnegi.

Arbatov, A.G., Dvorkin, V.Z. (red.) (2009). *Yadernoe rasprostranenie. Novye tekhnologii, vooruzheniya i dogovory.* Moskva: Rossiyskaya politicheskaya entsiklopediya (ROSSPEN).

Arbatov, A.G., Pikaev, A.A., Dvorkin, V.Z. (2006). Yaderniy terrorizm: politicheskie, pravovye, strategicheskie i tekhnicheskie aspekty. *Mirovaya ekonomika i mezhdunarodnye otnosheniya.* No. 11. pp. 3-16.
Avdokushin, E.F., Tsoy, A.V. (2016). EAES v sisteme sovremennykh protsessov mezhdunarodnoy ekonomicheskoy integratsii. *Voprosy novoy ekonomiki.* No. 3(39). pp. 5-12.
Azizian, Rouben, Lukin, Artyom. (eds.) (2012). *From APEC 2011 To APEC 2012: American and Russian Perspectives on Asia-Pacific Security and Cooperation.* Vladivostok: Far Eastern Federal University Press; Honolulu: Asia-Pacific Center for Security Studies: http://ifl.dvfu.ru/images /news/2012_08/03/FEFU-APCSS%20book%20final%201Aug12.pdf
Babynina, L.O. (2009). Transportnye sistemy ES i EvrAzES: perspektivy integratsii. *EvrAzES i integratsionniy opyt ES. Doklady Instituta Evropy.* No. 242 / M.G. Nosov (red.). Moskva: Institut Evropy. pp. 123-144.
Bakhtin, M. (1972). *Problemy poetiki Dostoevskogo.* Moskva: Khudozhestvennaya literatura.
Baluev, D. (2014). Evolyutsiya ekonomicheskikh sanktsiy kak instrumenta vneshney politiki ot Vtoroy mirovoy voyny do sanktsiy protiv Rossii. *Mezhdunarodnye protsessy.* Vol. 12. No. 3(38). pp. 23-33: http://www.intertrends.ru/thirty-eighth/Baluev.pdf
Baluev, D.G. (2006). *Informatsionno-kommunikatsionnye izmereniya politicheskikh protsessov* / O.A. Kolobov (red.). Nizhniy Novgorod: NNGU.
Baluev, D.G., Kaminchenko, D.I. (2012). Politicheskaya rol novykh SMI v liviyskom konflikte. *Vestnik Nizhegorodskogo gosudarstvennogo universiteta im. N.I. Lobachevskogo.* No. 2(1). pp. 307-313: http://cyberleninka. ru/article/n/politicheskaya-rol-novyh-smi-v-liviyskom-konflikte
Barabanov, O.N., Golitsyn, V.A., Tereshchenko, V.V. (2002). *Globalnoe upravlenie.* Moskva: MGIMO-Universitet.
Baranovskiy, V.G. (1983). *Politicheskaya integratsiya v Zapadnoy Evrope: Nekotorye voprosy teorii i praktiki.* Moskva, Nauka.
Baranovskiy, V.G. (2012). Osnovnye parametry sovremennoy sistemy mezhdunarodnykh otnosheniy. *Polis. Politicheskie issledovaniya.* No. 3. pp. 36-44; No. 4. pp. 63-73; No. 5. pp. 148-158.
Baranovskiy, V.G. (2017a). Transformatsiya globalnogo miroporyadka: dinamika sistemnykh izmeneniy. *Polis. Politicheskiye issledovaniya.* No. 3. pp. 71-91.
Baranovskiy, V.G. (2017b). Izmeneniya v globalnom politicheskom landshafte. Puti k miru i bezopasnosti. *Problemy terrorizma, nasilstvennogo ekstremizma i radikalizatsii (rossiyskie i amerikanskie podkhody)* / E.A. Stepanova (red.). Moskva: IMEMO RAN. No. 1(52).

pp. 55-63: http://www.estepanova.net/Addressing_Violent_Extremism.pdf
Bardin, A.L. (2013). Printsipy globalnogo upravleniya na osnove mezhdunarodnykh finansovykh institutov. *Polis. Politicheskie issledovaniya.* No. 4. pp. 168-172.
Barygin, I.N., Lanko, D.A., Fofanova, E.A. (2005). Region kak instrument mira: Analiz Baltiyskogo akademicheskogo diskursa. *Vestnik Sankt-Peterburgskogo gosudarstvennogo universiteta.* Seriya 6. Mezhdunarodnye otnosheniya. No. 2. pp. 100-111.
Batalov, E.Ya. (2005). Antropologiya mezhdunarodnykh otnosheniy. Mezhdunarodnye protsessy. Vol. 3. No. 3(8). pp. 4-16.
Baykov, A.A. (2012). *Sravnitelnaya integratsiya. Praktika i modeli integratsii v zarubezhnoy Evrope i tikhookeanskoy Azii.* Moskva: Aspekt Press.
Baykov, A.A. (2014). «Myagkaya moshch» Evropeyskogo Soyuza v globalnom silovom ravnovesii: evro-rossiyskiy trek. *Vestnik MGIMO-Universiteta.* No. 2(35). pp. 36-46.
Behera, N.G. (2016). Knowledge Production. *International Studies Review.* No. 1. pp. 1-3.
Belokrenitskiy, V.Ya. (2017). Vooruzhenniy ekstremizm v Afganistane, Pakistane i Tsentralnoy Azii: vzglyad iz Rossii. *Puti k miru i bezopasnosti. Problemy terrorizma, nasilstvennogo ekstremizma i radikalizatsii (rossiyskie i amerikanskie podkhody)* / E.A. Stepanova (red.). Moskva: IMEMO RAN. No. 1(52). pp. 205-213.
Belozerov, V.K., Vladimirov, A.I. (sostaviteli) (2014). *Voenno-politicheskie issledovaniya v Rossii.* Moskva: Ves mir: http://russiancouncil.ru/news/spravochnik-voenno-politicheskie-issledovaniya-v-rossii/?sphrase_id=4030570
Bennett, P.R. (1997). *Russian Negotiatiating Strategy: Analytic Case Studies from SALT and START.* New York: Nova Science Publishers.
Berger, Peter, Huntington, Samuel. (eds.) (2002). *Many Globalizations: Cultural Diversity in the Contemporary World.* Oxford, New York: Oxford University Press, 2002.
Biersteker, T.J. (2014). Participating in Transnational Policy Networks: Targeted Sanctions / *Narrowing the Gap: Scholars, Policymakers and International Affairs: Finding Common Cause* // Ed. by M.E. Bertucci, A.F. Lowenthal. Baltimore and London: Johns Hopkins University Press. pp. 137-154.
Bobrovnikov, A.V., Davydov, V.M. (2005). Voskhodyashchie strany-giganty na mirovoy stsene XXI veka. *Latinskaya Amerika.* No. 5. pp. 4-20.

Bogaturov, A. Desyat let paradigmy osvoeniya. *Pro et Contra.* (2000). Zima. Vol. 5. No. 1. pp. 195-198.
Bogaturov, A.D. (2004). Ponyatie mirovoy politiki v teoreticheskom diskurse. *Mezhdunarodnye protsessy.* No. 1. pp. 16-33.
Bogaturov, A.D., Kortunov, A.V. (red.) (1999). *Mezhdunarodnye issledovaniya v Rossii i SNG. Spravochnik.* Sostaviteli: Yu.K. Abramov, V.I. Agayants, A.D. Voskressenski, A.A. Kasyanova and others. Moskva: Moskovskiy rabochiy.
Bogaturov, A.D., Shakleina, T.A. (red.) (2009). *Liderstvo i konkurentsiya v mirovoy sisteme: Rossiya i SShA.* Moskva: Krasand.
Bogdanov, A.A. (1922). *Tektologiya – Vseobshchaya organizatsionnaya nauka.* Berlin, Sankt-Peterburg. V 2-h knigakh. Moskva: Ekonomika.
Bogdanov, A.N. (2012). *Vneshnepoliticheskaya ideologiya SShA i sovremenniy mirovoy poryadok.* Sankt-Peterburg: Izdatelstvo SPbGU.
Bogolyubova, N.M., Nikolaeva, Yu.V. (2013). Mezhdunarodnoe sotrudnichestvo Rossii i Severo-Zapadnogo regiona v oblasti razvitiya ekologicheskogo turizma. *Uchenye zapiski Rossiyskogo gosudarstvennogo gidrometeorologicheskogo universiteta.* No. 27. pp. 165-173.
Bogomolov, O. (1983). Strany SEV i globalnye problemy. *Mezhdunarodnaya zhizn.* No. 4. pp. 22-32.
Bolshova, N.N. (2016). "Pegida" kak primer massovykh protestnykh dvizheniy, voznikshikh v Evrope pod vliyaniem migratsionnogo krizisa. *Polis. Politicheskie issledovaniya.* No. 3. pp. 123-137. DOI: https://doi.org/10.17976/jpps/2016.03.10
Bordachev, T.V., Zinovieva, E.S., Likhacheva, A.B. (2015). *Teoriya mezhdunarodnykh otnosheniy v XXI veke.* Moskva: Mezhdunarodnye otnosheniya.
Borishpolets, K.P. (2004). Razryv mezhdu Yugom i Severom. *Sovremennye mezhdunarodnye otnosheniya i mirovaya politika* / A.V. Torkunov (red.). Moskva: Izdatelstvo «Prosveshchenie», 2004.
Borovskiy, Yu.V. (2008). Politizatsiya mirovoy energetiki. *Mezhdunarodnye protsessy.* Vol. 6. No. 1. pp. 19-28.
Braterskiy, M.V. (2009). Izmeneniya mirovoy sistemy skvoz prizmu politicheskoy ekonomii. *SShA i Kanada: ekonomika, politika, kultura.* No. 11. pp. 3-14.
Braterskiy, M.V., Skriba, A.S. (2014). Kontseptsiya «myagkoy sily» vo vneshnepoliticheskoy strategii SShA. *Vestnik mezhdunarodnykh organizatsiy: obrazovanie, nauka, novaya ekonomika.* Vol. 9. No. 2. pp. 130-144.

Budanova, I.A. (2013). «Aktornost» evroregionov. *Vestnik MGIMO – Universiteta*. No. 3(30). pp. 57–63.
Budnitskiy, O.V. Terrorizm: istoriya i sovremennost (2010) / *Polemika*. No. 10: http://www.ekstremizm.ru/novosti/item/468-terrorizm-istoriya-i-sovremennost
Budyko, M.I. (1977). *Globalnya ekologiya*. Moskva: Mysl.
Bulatov, A. (2008). Shansy i perspektivy finansovogo ozdorovleniya. *Mezhdunarodnye protsessy*. Vol. 6. No. 2 (17). pp. 27–35: http://intertrends.ru/system/Doc/ArticlePdf/604/Bulatov-17.pdf
Burlatskiy, F.M., Galkin, A.A. (1974). *Sotsiologiya. Politika. Mezhdunarodnye otnosheniya*. Moskva: Mezhdunarodnye otnosheniya.
Burnasov, A.S. (2013). Logisticheskie kompanii mira i ikh vliyanie na mirovuyu politiku. *Vestnik MGIMO - Universiteta*. No. 2(29). pp. 52–56.
Bushuev, V.V., Konoplyanik, A.A., Mirkin, Ya.M. (2013). *Tseny na neft: analiz, tendentsii, prognozy*. Moskva: Izdatelskiy dom «Energiya»: http://www.konoplyanik.ru/ru/publications/77m.pdf
Butorina, O.V. (2009). Tantsy s drakonom. *Rossiya v globalnoy politike*. No. 1. pp. 104–116: http://www.globalaffairs.ru/number/n_12449
Bykov, A. (1979). Vliyanie nauchno-tekhnicheskogo progressa na mezhdunarodnye otnosheniya. *Mezhdunarodnaya zhizn*. No. 4. pp. 75–83.
Bystrov, A.A. SShA i Liviya. (2011). Institut Blizhnego Vostoka. *Portal Instituta Blizhnego Vostoka*: http://www.iimes.ru/?p=13031#more-13031
Cambon, Zh. (1946). *Diplomat*. Perevod s angl. Moskva, Leningrad: Gospolitizdat.
Chepurin, A. (2009). «Tri kita» rossiyskoy diasporalnoy politiki. *Rossiya v globalnoy politike*. No. 3. pp. 127–138: http://globalaffairs.ru/number/n_13207
Cherkasov, P.P. (2004). *IMEMO. Portret na fone epokhi*. Moskva: Izdatelstvo «Ves Mir».
Chernitsyna, S.Yu. (2015). *Rol energeticheskoy diplomatii v formirovanii vneshney politiki Rossii*. Moskva: Izdatelskiy Dom «Nauchnoe obozrenie».
Chubaryan, A.O. (1976). *Mirnoe sosushchestvovanie: teoriya i praktika*. Moskva, Politizdat.
Chugrov, S. (2001). K voprosu o pravakh cheloveka v rossiyskoy vneshney politike. *Mirovaya ekonomika i mezhdunarodnye otnosheniya*. No. 6. pp. 3–13.

Chugrov, S.V. (2015). Myagkoe prityazhenie Yaponii. *Polis. Politicheskie issledovaniya.* No. 6. pp. 53-67. DOI: https://doi.org/10.17976/jpps/2015.06.08

Chugrov, S.V. (2016). Sushchestvuet li nezapadnaya politologiya? ("Politicheskaya teoriya" T. Inoguti). *Polis. Politicheskie issledovaniya.* No. 4. pp. 182-191. DOI: https://doi.org/10.17976/jpps/2016.04.14

Davydov, V.M. (2008). Probuzhdayushchiesya giganty BRIK. *Svobodnaya mysl.* No. 5. pp. 131-142.

Davydov, V.M., Bobrovnikov, A.V. (2009). *Rol voskhodyashchikh gigantov v mirovoy ekonomike i politike (shansy Brazilii i Meksiki v globalnom izmerenii).* Moskva: Institut Latinskoy Amerike RAN: http://www.ila ran.ru/pdf/2009/Libros/2009_Davydov_Bobrovnikov.pdf

Degterev, D.A. (2015). Kolichestvennye metody v mezhdunarodnykh issledovaniyakh. *Mezhdunarodnye protsessy.* Vol. 13(2). pp. 35-54. DOI: 10.17994/IT.2015.13.2.41.3

Demidov P.A. (2012) Vzglyad so storony, ili kak MGIMO formiruet velikoderzhavnuyu identichnost Rossii. *Vestnik MGIMO - Universiteta.* No. 3(24). pp. 254-255. http://www.vestnik.mgimo.ru/sites/default/files/pdf/39arecenzii_demidov.pdf

Deriglazova, L.V. (2009). *Asimmetrichnye konflikty: uravnenie so mnogimi neizvestnymi.* Tomsk: Izdatelstvo Tomskogo universiteta.

Dibben, J.E., Whelan, D.J. (2005). U.S. *Undergraduate Genaral Education Curriculum Review.* Paper prepared for APSIA Meeting, December.

Dmitrichev, T.F. (1981). *Mnogostoronnyaya diplomatiya SShA. Teoriya i praktika.* Moskva: Mezhdunarodnye otnosheniya.

Dobaev, I., Umarov, D. (2013). Osobennosti finansirovaniya terroristicheskikh struktur na Severnom Kavkaze. *Mirovaya ekonomika i mezhdunarodnye otnosheniya.* No. 4. pp. 79-86.

Dolinskiy, A. (2012). Chto takoe obshchestvennaya diplomatiya i zachem ona nuzhna Rossii? Moskva: *Rossiyskiy sovet po mezhdunarodnym delam (RSMD).* http://russiancouncil.ru/analytics-and-comments/analytics/chto-takoe-obshchestvennaya-diplomatiya-i-zachem-ona-nuzhna-/

Dolinskiy, A.V. (2011). Evolyutsiya teoreticheskikh osnovaniy publichnoy diplomatii. *Vestnik MGIMO - Universiteta.* No. 2. pp. 275-280.

Doronina, N.I. (1981). *Mezhdunarodniy konflikt.* Moskva: Mezhdunarodnye otnosheniya.

Doroshenko, E.I. (2014). Osobennosti demokratii v nesostoyavshemsya gosudarstve: Liviya. *Rossiya v globalnoy politike.* Vol. 12, No. 3. pp. 177-185.

Dvorkin, V.Z. (2011). Ugrozy net. Otvetnye mery bessmyslenny. *Sayt Moskovskogo tsentra Karnegi*: http://carnegie.ru/publications/?fa=46103

Dynkin, A.A. (2002). Est li u Rossii shans v globalnoy ekonomike? *Pro et Contra*. Vol. 7. No. 2. pp. 42–67.

Dynkin, A.A. (2012). Rossiya v politsentrichnom mire. *Rossiya v globalnom mire* / I.S. Ivanov (red.). Moskva: Aspekt Press. pp. 654–666.

Engels, F. Anti-Dyuring (1955-1974) / Marx K., Engels F. *Sobranie sochineniy*. 2-e izdanie. Vol. 20. Moskva: Izdatelstvo politicheskoy literatury.

Ermolenko, D.V. (1975). *Sotsiologiya i problemy mezhdunarodnykh otnosheniy (nekotorye aspekty i problemy sotsiologicheskikh issledovaniy mezhdunarodnykh otnosheniy)*. Moskva: Mezhdunarodnye otnosheniya.

Evdokimov, E.V. (2011). «Narodnaya diplomatiya». Massovost kak fenomen kitayskoy vneshnepoliticheskoy propagandy. *Vestnik MGIMO – Universiteta*. No. 3. pp. 285–289.

Favre, P. (1996). Politicheskaya nauka vo Frantsii. *Polis. Politicheskie issledovaniya*. No. 6. pp. 109–116.

Fedorov, Yu.E. (2002). Yaderniy faktor v mirovoy politike XXI veka. *Pro et Contra*. Vol. 7. No. 4. pp. 57–71.

Feldman, D.M. (1998). *Politologiya konflikta*. Moskva: Strategiya.

Feldman, D.M. (2009). Kak povliyaet sovremenniy krizis na mezhdunarodnye otnosheniya? Vlast. No. 7. pp. 15–19.

Fenenko, A. (2015). Are Nuclear Weapons Useful? A Response to Mikhail Troitskiy. Moskva: *Rossiyskiy sovet po mezhdunarodnym delam (RSMD)*: http://russiancouncil.ru/en/analytics-and-comments/analytics/po lezno-li-yadernoe-oruzhie-otvet-mikhailu-troitskomu/

Fenenko, A. (2017). Razmyshleniye posle stati I. Timofeeva «Rossiya i mir: povestka na 100 let». Moskva: *Rossiyskiy sovet po mezhdunarodnym delam (RSMD)*: http://russiancouncil.ru/analytics-and-comments/ analytics/za-stoletnim-gorizontom/?sphrase_id=489201

Fenenko, A.V. (2013). *Sovremennaya mezhdunarodnaya bezopasnost. Yaderniy faktor*. Moskva: Aspekt Press.

Fisher, R., Ury W. (1990). *Put k soglasiyu, ili peregovory bez porazheniya*. Perevod s angl. Moskva: Nauka.

Fituni L.L., Abramova I.O. (2015). Negosudarstvennye i kvazigosudarstvennye aktory Bolshogo Blizhnego Vostoka i problema «evrodzhihadizma» / Aziya i Afrika segodnya. No. 11(700). pp. 2–11.

Fominykh, A. (2008). «Myagkaya moshch» obmennyh programm. *Mezhdunarodnye protsessy.* No. 6(16). pp. 76-85: www.intertrends.ru/sixteenth/008.htm

Fortov, V.E., Makarov, A.A., Mitrova, T.A. (2007). Globalnaya energeticheskaya bezopasnost: problemy i puti resheniya. *Vestnik Rossiyskoy akademii nauk.* Vol. 77. No. 2. pp. 99-144.

Frei, Daniel (1984). *Assumptions and Perceptions in Disarmament.* New York: United Nations Publication.

Frolov, I.T. (1980). Filosofiya globalnykh problem. *Voprosy filosofii.* No. 2. pp. 29-44.

Froyanov, I.Ya. (1999). *Pogruzhenie v bezdnu: (Rossiya na iskhode XX veka).* Sankt-Peterburg: Izdatelstvo Sankt-Peterburgskogo universiteta.

Fukuyama, F. (1990). Konets istorii? *Voprosy filosofii.* No. 3. pp. 134-148.

Gadzhiev, K.S. (1997). *Geopolitika.* Moskva: Mezhdunarodnye otnosheniya.

Gadzhiev, K.S. (2000). *Vvedenie v geopolitiku.* Moskva: Logos.

Gadzhiev, K.S. (2003). *Geopolitika Kavkaza.* Moskva: Mezhdunarodnye otnosheniya.

Galishcheva, N.V. (2017). Globalizatsiya indiyskoy ekonomiki: tendentsii i perspektivy. *Vestnik MGIMO – Universiteta.* No. 2. pp. 71-89: http://www.vestnik.mgimo.ru/sites/default/files/pdf/004_gal.pdf

Gantman, V.I. (red.) (1976). *Sovremennye burzhuaznye teorii mezhdunarodnykh otnosheniy: kriticheskiy analiz.* Moskva: Mezhdunarodnye otnosheniya.

Gantman, V.I. (red.) (1983). *Mezhdunarodnye konflikty sovremennosti.* Moskva: Nauka.

Gantman, V.I. (red.) (1984). *Sistema, struktura i protsess razvitiya sovremennykh mezhdunarodnykh otnosheniy.* Moskva: Nauka.

Gauzner, N.D. (1972). Nauchno-tekhnicheskaya revolyutsiya i protivorechiya kapitalizma. *Mirovaya ekonomika i mezhdunarodnye otnosheniya.* No. 10. pp. 14-25.

Golubev, D.S. (2010). Problema ravnoudalennosti tretey storony v etnopoliticheskom konflikte na primere posrednichestva SShA v uregulirovanii arabo-izrailskogo konflikta. *Politicheskaya ekspertiza.* Vol. 6. No. 4. pp. 250-256.

Goodin, R., Klingemann H.-D. (red.). Perevod s angl. (1999). *Politicheskaya nauka: novye napravleniya.* Moskva: Veche.

Goodin, R.E., Klingemann, H.-D. (eds.) (1996). *A New Handbook of Political Science.* Oxford: Oxford University Press.

Gorizontov, B.B. (1982). *Kapitalizm i ekologicheskiy krizis.* Moskva: Politizdat.

Grigoryev, L.M. (2002). XXI vek: raskhodyashchiesya dorogi razvitiya. *Rossiya v globalnoy politike.* No. 1 (noyabr/dekabr): http://global affairs.ru/number/n_17

Grigoryev, L.M. Salikhov, M.R. (2009). Finansovaya arkhitektura: ekstrenniy remont. *Rossiya v globalnoy politike.* No. 4. pp. 8–21: http://globalaffairs.ru/number/n_13628

Grigoryev, M.S., Ignatyev, V.S., Magerov, V.M. (2017). *Protivodeystvie terroristicheskoy propagande.* Moskva: Fond issledovaniya problem demokratii: http://www.oprf.ru/files/1_2017dok/grigoriev_kniga09062017.pdf

Gromyko, A. (2015). Rossiya, SShA, malaya Evropa (ES): konkurentsiya za liderstvo v mire politsentrichnosti. *Sovremennaya Evropa.* No. 4(64). pp. 5–14.

Gromyko, A., M. Hellman, M. and others. (red.) (1988). *Proryv: Stanovlenie novogo myshleniya. Sovetskie i zapadnye uchenye prizyvayut k miru bez voyn.* Moskva: Progress.

Gromyko, A.A., Ponomarev, B.N. (red.) (1981). *Istoriya vneshney politiki SSSR v dvukh tomakh.* Moskva: Nauka.

Gudkov, I.V. (2010). Tretiy energeticheskiy paket Evropeyskogo soyuza. *Neft, gaz i pravo.* No. 3. pp. 58–66: https://mgimo.ru/files2/y11_20 13/243404/10.3.3_gudkov.pdf

Guseynov, V.A. (2001). Rasshirenie NATO: ukreplenie obshcheevropeyskoy bezopasnosti ili ekspansiya bloka? *Vestnik analitiki.* No. 1: http://www.isoa.ru/articles.php?binn_rubrik_pl_art icles=231

Guskova, E. Yu. (2013). *Agressiya NATO 1999 goda protiv Yugoslavii i protsess mirnogo uregulirovaniya.* Moskva: Idrik.

Gvishiani, D.M. (1972). *Organizatsiya i upravlenie.* Moskva: Nauka.

Gvishiani, D.M. (1977). *Metodologicheskie problemy modelirovaniya globalnogo razvitiya.* Preprint No. 1. Moskva: VNIISI.

Gvishiani, D.M. (1979). Pered litsom globalnykh problem. *Mir nauki.* No. 1. pp. 23–27.

Gvishiani, D.M. (1981). Nauka i globalnye problemy sovremennosti. *Voprosy filosofii.* No. 3. pp. 97–108.

Hoffmann, St. (1977). An American Social Science: International Relations. *Daedalus.* No. 106 (3). pp. 41–60.

Huntington, S. (1994). Stolknovenie tsivilizatsiy. Perevod s angl. *Polis. Politicheskie issledovaniya.* No. 1. pp. 33–48.

Huntington, Samuel P. (1991). Democracy's Third Wave. *The Journal of Democracy.* No. 2. pp. 12-34: http://www.ou.edu/uschina/gries/articles/IntPol/Huntington.91.Demo.3rd.pdf

Ilin M.V. (2004). Sluga dvukh gospod. *Polis. Politicheskie issledovaniya.* No. 5. pp. 120-130.

Ilin, M.V. (1994). Politicheskiy diskurs: slova i smysly. *Polis. Politicheskie issledovaniya.* No. 1. pp. 127-140.

Ilin, M.V., Kudryashova, I.V. (red.) (2008). *Suverenitet. Transformatsiya ponyatiy i praktik.* Moskva: MGIMO - Universitet.

Ilin, M.V., Kudryashova, I.V. (red.) (2011). *Asimmetriya mirovoy sistemy suvereniteta. Zony problemnoy gosudarstvennosti.* Moskva: MGIMO.

Inozemtsev, N.N. (red.) (1981). *Globalnye problemy sovremennosti.* Moskva: Mysl.

Inozemtsev, V.L. (2000a). *Sovremennoe postindustrialnoe obshchestvo: priroda, protivorechiya, perspektivy.* Moskva: Logos.

Inozemtsev, V.L. (2000b). Paradoksy postindustrialnoy ekonomiki. *Mirovaya ekonomika i mezhdunarodnye otnosheniya.* No. 3. pp. 3-11.

Inozemtsev, V.L. (2011). Vossozdanie industrialnogo mira: kontury novogo globalnogo ustroystva. *Rossiya v globalnoy politike.* Vol 8. No. 4. pp. 85-98: http://globalaffairs.ru/number/Vossozdanie-industrialnogo-mira-15397

Isakov, Yu.N. (2006). «Vosmerka» i globalnye energeticheskie problemy. Evolyutsiya i perspektivy. *Svobodnaya mysl.* No. 9-10. pp. 25-37.

Isii, K. *Diplomaticheskie kommentarii.* (1942). Perevod s yaponskogo. Moskva: OGIZ, Gospolitizdat.

Islamic Extremism in South-East Asia (2015). *Moskva: Rossiyskiy sovet po mezhdunarodnym delam (RSMD):* http://russiancouncil.ru/en/extremism-asean

Israelyan, V., Lebedeva M. (1991). Peregovory — iskusstvo dlya vsekh. *Mezhdunarodnaya zhizn.* No. 11. pp. 48-55.

Israelyan, V.L. (1988). *Tekhnologiya dvustoronnikh i mnogostoronnikh peregovorov.* Moskva: Diplomaticheskaya Akademiya.

Israelyan, V.L. (1990). *Diplomaty litsom k litsu.* Moskva: Mezhdunarodnye otnosheniya.

Istomin, I., Baykov, A. (2013). Sravnitelnye osobennosti otechestvennykh i zarubezhnykh zhurnalov. *Mezhdunarodnye protsessy.* Vol. 13. No. 2(41). pp. 114-140: http://www.intertrends.ru/forty-fist/Istomin.pdf

Ivanov, I. (2014). Vstupitelnoe slovo. *Voenno-politicheskie issledovaniya v Rossii / V.K. Belozerov, A.I. Vladimirov (sostaviteli).* Moskva: Rossiyskiy sovet po mezhdunarodnym delam (RSMD). p.11.

Ivanov, L.N. (1927). *Mirovaya politika posle Versalya.* Moskva: Moskovskiy rabochiy.
Ivanov, L.N. (1928). *Anglo-frantsuzskoe sopernichestvo 1919 – 1927 gg.* Moskva: Moskovskiy rabochiy.
Ivanov, L.N. (1929). *Liga natsiy.* Moskva: Moskovskiy rabochiy.
Ivanov, Yu.A. *Kongress SShA i vneshnyaya politika. Vozmozhnosti i metody vliyaniya (1970–1980 gg.)* (1982). Moskva: Nauka.
Ivanova, N.I. (2016). Innovatsionnaya politika: teoriya i praktika. *Mirovaya ekonomika i mezhdunarodnye otnosheniya.* Vol. 60. No. 1. pp. 5–16.
Ivanova, N.I. (red.) (2016). *Otraslevye instrumenty innovatsionnoy politiki.* Moskva: Izdatelstvo Instituta mirovoy ekonomiki i mezhdunarodnykh otnosheniy.
Ivanova, N.I., Danilin, I.V. (2016). *Nauka i innovatsii kak faktor mirovogo razvitiya. Politicheskaya nauka pered vyzovami globalnogo i regionalnogo razvitiya.* Moskva: Aspekt Press.
Jorgensen, Knut E., Knudsen, Tonny B. (eds.) (2006). *International Relations in Europe: Traditions, Perspectives and Destinations.* London, New York: Routledge.
Kapitonova, N.K. (2011). Akademik Vladimir Grigoryevich Trukhanovskiy v MGIMO. *Vestnik MGIMO-Universiteta.* pp. 287–294.
Karaganov, S.A. (2010). «Globalniy nol» i zdraviy smysl. *Rossiya v globalnoy politike.* No. 3. pp. 108–118: http://www.globalaffairs.ru/number/Globalnyi-nol-i-zdravyi-sm ysl-14881
Karaganov, S.A. (2017). O novom yadernom mire. *Rossiya v globalnoy politike.* Vol. 15. No. 2. pp. 8–19.
Karlusov, V.V. (2010). Kitay: razvitie vopreki mirovomu krizisu. *Vestnik MGIMO – Universiteta.* No. 4. pp. 191–199.
Karminskiy, A.M., Trofimova, E.A. (2011). Rol reytingov v razvitii biznes-protsessov rossiyskikh bankov. *Vestnik MGIMO-Universiteta.* No. 4. pp. 12–26.
Kasatkin P.I., Avatkov V.A. (2014). The Soft Power of Migration - A Hard Task for European Union. *Defense and Security Analysis.* Vol. 30. No. 4. pp. 311-322.
Katsy, D.V. (2003). Kaliningradskaya problema i interesy Rossii / *Rossiya i Evropeyskiy soyuz v bolshoy Evrope: novye vozmozhnosti i starye baryery.* Sankt-Peterburg: Izdatelstvo SPbGU. pp. 82–93.
Katzenstein, P., Sil, R. (2008). Eclectic Theorizing in the Study and Practice of International Relations. *Oxford Handbook of International Relations.* Oxford: Oxford University Press. pp. 110–130.

Kaveshnikov, N.Yu. (2009). Rol energodialoga Rossiya-ES v obespechenii energeticheskoy bezopasnosti «Bolshoy Evropy». *Vsya Evropa.* No. 5(33). 2009: http://alleuropalux.org/?p=1337
Kazarinova, D. (2011). Fenomen «myagkoy sily». *Svobodnaya mysl.* No. 3(1622). pp. 187-200.
Kazimirov, V.N. (2009). *Mir Karabakhu. Posrednichestvo Rossii v uregulirovanii Nagorno-karabakhskogo konflikta.* Moskva: Mezhdunarodnye otnosheniya.
Keohane, R.O., Nye, J.S. (1971). Transnational Relations and World Politics: An Introduction. *International Organization.* No. 25(3). pp. 329-349.
Kharkevich, M.V. (2010). Gosudarstvo v sovremennoy mirovoy politike. *Vestnik MGIMO - Universiteta.* No. 6. pp. 160-166.
Kharkevich, M.V. (2012). Globalizatsiya i vysshee obrazovanie: vozmozhnosti dlya Rossii. *Vestnik MGIMO – Universiteta.* No. 6. pp. 270-276:
http://vestnik.mgimo.ru/sites/default/files/pdf/harkevich_1.pdf
Kharkevich, M.V., Muzalevskiy, V.A. Oskolkov, P.V. (2018). Arkhaika i praviy povorot v sovremennoy Evrope. *Sovremennaya Evropa.* No. 1. pp. 59-68.
Khesin, E.S. (2009). Anatomiya mirovogo krizisa. *Mezhdunarodnye protsessy.* No. 2. pp. 4-17: http://intertrends.ru/system/Doc/Article Pdf/590/Khesin-20.pdf
Khokhlysheva, O.O. (2000). *Razoruzhenie, bezopasnost, mirotvorchestvo: globalniy masshtab.* Nizhniy Novgorod: Izdatelstvo NNGU.
Khozikov, V.V. (2003). *Informatsionnoe oruzhie.* Sankt-Peterburg: Izdatelskiy dom «Neva».
Khrustalev, M.A. (1987). *Sistemnoe modelirovanie mezhdunarodnykh otnosheniy.* Uchebnoe posobie. Moskva: MGIMO.
Khudaykulova, A.V. (2016). Teorii bezopasnosti tretyego mira. Vestnik Rossiiskogo universiteta druzhby narodov. No. 16(3). pp. 412-423.
Khudoley, K.K. (2000b). Baltic Region: Common Challenges and Similar Response – Russian Point of View / *North-Eastern and South-Eastern dimensions of European security-Regional Cooperation-Similarities and Differences, 10th Partnership for Peace International Research Seminar. NATO Defense College seminar report series* // Dieter Ose, Laure Borgomano-Loup (eds.). No. 13. pp. 105-113.
Khudoley, K.K. (2002a). Rossiya i Evropeyskiy soyuz: nekotorye aspekty otnosheniy / *50-letie Evropeyskogo Soobshchestva i Rossiya: Proshloe, nastoyashchee, budushchee. Materialy mezhdunarodnoy nauchnoy*

konferentsii, 19–20 oktyabrya 2001 g. // V.E. Morozov (red.). Sankt-Pererburg: Izdatelstvo SPbGU. pp. 81–86.

Khudoley, K.K. (2003). Otnosheniya Rossii i Evropeyskogo Soyuza: novye vozmozhnosti, novye problemy / *Rossiya i Evropeyskiy Soyuz: pereosmyslivaya strategiyu vzaimootnosheniy* // A. Moshes (red.). Moskva: Gendalf. pp. 8–30.

Khvostov, V.M. (1940). *Istoriya mezhdunarodnykh otnosheniy i borba za peredel mira (1870 – 1900)*. Moskva: OGIZ.

Kirilenko, V.P., Pidzhakov, A.Yu. (2008). *Sovremenniy terrorizm – globalnaya ugroza chelovechestvu*. Sankt-Peterburg: Izdatelstvo Politekhnicheskogo universiteta.

Kiva, A.V., Fedorov, V.A. (2003). Anatomiya terrorizma. *Obshchestvennye nauki i sovremennost*. No. 1. pp. 130–142.

Knyazhinskaya, L. (1979). Poiski resheniya mirovoy prodovolstvennoy problemy. *Mezhdunarodnaya zhizn*. No. 1. pp. 70–79.

Kokoshin, A.A. (1975). *Prognozirovanie i politika. Metodologiya organizatsii issledovaniya i prognozirovaniya mezhdunarodnykh otnosheniy vo vneshney politike SShA*. Moskva: Mezhdunarodnye otnosheniya.

Kokoshin, A.A. (1984). *SShA v sisteme mezhdunarodnykh otnosheniy 80-kh godov*. Moskva: Mezhdunarodnye otnosheniya.

Kokoshin, A.A. (2006). *Realniy suverenitet*. Moskva: Izdatelstvo «Evropa».

Kokoshin, A.A. (2009). *Obespechenie strategicheskoy stabilnosti v proshlom i nastoyashchem: teoreticheskie i prikladnye voprosy*. Moskva: KRASAND.

Kolobov, O.A. (red.) (2001). *Istoriya mezhdunarodnykh otnosheniy, v 2-kh tomakh*. Nizhniy Novgorod: NNGU.

Kolobov, O.A. (red.) (2005). *NATO i Rossiya v globalnom grazhdanskom obshchestve*. Moskva, Nizhniy Novgorod, Arzamas: AGPI.

Kolobov, O.A., Baluev, D.G. and others. (1997). *Zapad: Novye izmereniya natsionalnoy i mezhdunarodnoy bezopasnosti*. Nizhniy Novgorod: NNGU.

Kolobov, O.A., Kornilov, A.A., Makarychev, A.S., Sergunin, A.A. (1992a). *Protsess prinyatiya vneshnepoliticheskikh resheniy: istoricheskiy opyt SShA, gosudarstva Izrail i stran Zapadnoy Evropy*. Nizhniy Novgorod: NNGU.

Kolobov, O.A., Kornilov, A.A., Makarychev, A.S., Sergunin, A.A. (1992b). *Russia and the Problems of Global Stability*. Nizhniy Novgorod: University of Nizhniy Novgorod Press.

Kolobov, O.A., Kornilov, A.A., Sergunin, A.A. (1991). *Dokumentalnaya istoriya arabo-izrailskogo konflikta*. Nizhniy Novgorod: Izdatelstvo NNGU.

Kolosov, V.A. (1988). *Politicheskaya geografiya: problemy i metody.* Leningrad: Nauka Leningr. Otdelenie.
Kolosov, V.A., Mironenko, N.S. (2001). *Geopolitika i politicheskaya geografiya.* Moskva: Aspekt Press.
Konets istorii ili konets ideologii? Nauchnye diskussii (1990). *SShA i Kanada: ekonomika, politika, ideologiya.* No. 6. pp. 37–47.
Konyshev, V.N., Sergunin, A.A. (2011). Arkticheskoe napravlenie vneshney politiki Rossii. *Obozrevatel-Observer.* No. 3. pp. 13–20.
Konyshev, V.N., Sergunin, A.A. (2013). Teoriya mezhdunarodnykh otnosheniy: Kanun novykh «velikikh debatov»? *— Polis. Politicheskie issledovaniya.* No. 2. pp. 66–78.
Korobkov, A. (2012). Ne nauka, a politicheskaya publitsistika. Moskva: *Rossiyskiy sovet po mezhdunarodnym delam (RSMD):* http://russian council.ru/inner/?id_4=919#top-content
Kortunov, A. (2016). Neizbezhnost strannogo mira. Moskva: *Rossiyskiy sovet po mezhdunarodnym delam (RSMD):* http://russiancouncil.ru/ analytics-and-comments/analytics/neizbezhnost-strannogo-mira/?s phrase_id=68999
Kortunov S.V. (2010b). Dogovor po SNV: Imperativ «zhestkoy sily». *Rossiya v globalnoy politike.* No. 3. pp. 119–132.
Kortunov, S.V. (2008). Rossiya na puti k mirovomu liderstvu / *Bezopasnost Evrazii.* No. 4. pp. 7–35.
Kortunov, S.V. (2010a). Mirovaya voenno-politicheskaya situatsiya. God 2025. *Mezhdunarodnaya zhizn.* No. 3. pp. 93–116.
Kosolapov, N.A. (2005). Rossiya i noviy mirovoy poryadok v otsutstvie levoy alternativy / *Rossiyskaya nauka mezhdunarodnykh otnosheniy: novye napravleniya //* A.P. Tsygankov, P.A. Tsygankov (red.). Moskva: Per Se. 2005. pp. 175–200.
Kosov, Yu. V. (2013). K voprosu stanovleniya evraziyskoy integratsii: politiko-ekonomicheskiy aspect. *Upravlencheskoe konsultirovanie.* No. 2. pp. 62–67.
Kosov, Yu.V. (2008). Rossiya i transgranichnye svyazi na Baltike. *Kosmopolis.* No. 2. pp. 130–133.
Kostyunina, G.M. (2014). *Integratsionnye protsessy v Zapadnom polusharii.* Moskva: MGIMO.
Kovalev, A.G. (1988). *Azbuka diplomatii.* 5-e izd., dopoln. Moskva: Mezhdunarodnye otnosheniya.
Kovaleva, O.M., Lebedeva, M.M. (1981). Metodika otsenki pozitsiy uchastnikov mezhdunarodnykh peregovorov na osnove analiza vystupleniy (na primere vystupleniy predstaviteley Frantsii na I i III

etapakh Soveshchaniya po bezopasnosti i sotrudnichestvu v Evrope) / *Voprosy modelirovaniya mnogostoronnikh diplomaticheskikh peregovorov* // I.G. Tyulin, M.A. Khrustalev (red.). Moskva: MGIMO. pp. 113-129.

Kremenyuk, V.A. (1977). *Politika SShA v razvivayushchikhsya stranakh. Problemy konfliktnykh situatsiy 1945-1976*. Moskva: Mezhdunarodnye otnosheniya.

Kremenyuk, V.A. (1979). *SShA i konflikty v stranakh Azii*. Moskva: Nauka.

Kremenyuk, V.A. (1982). Sovetsko-amerikanskie otnosheniya i nekotorye problemy osvobodivshikhsya gosudarstv. *SShA i Kanada: ekonomika, politika, ideologiya*. 1982. No. 6. pp. 7-18.

Kremenyuk, V.A. (1990). Na puti uregulirovaniya konfliktov. *SShA i Kanada: ekonomika, politika, ideologiya*. No. 12. pp. 47-52.

Kremenyuk, V.A. (1991). Problemy peregovorov v otnosheniyakh dvukh derzhav. *SShA i Kanada: ekonomika, politika, ideologiya*. No. 3. pp. 43-51.

Kremenyuk, V.A. (ed.) (1991). *International Negotiation: Analysis, Approaches, Issues*. San Francisco, Oxford: Jossey-Bass.

Krizis ekonomicheskiy ili krizis miropoliticheskiy? («krugliy stol»). (2009). *Vestnik MGIMO – Universiteta*. No. 5(8). pp. 157-177: http://www.vestnik.mgimo.ru/sites/default/files/vestnik/2009-5.pdf

Krutskikh, A.V. (2007). K politiko-pravovym osnovam globalnoy informatsionnoy bezopasnosti. *Mezhdunarodnye protsessy*. Vol. 5. No. 1. pp. 28-37.

Krutskikh, A.V. (red.) (2010). *Innovatsionnye napravleniya sovremennykh mezhdunarodnykh otnosheniy*. Moskva: Aspekt Press.

Kubyshkin, A.I., Tsvetkova, N.A. (2013). *Publichnaya diplomatiya SShA*. Moskva: Aspekt-Press.

Kucheryaviy, M.M. (2013). Problemy mezhdunarodnoy bezopasnosti v kontekste sovremennoy politicheskoy nauki. *Upravlencheskoe konsultirovanie*. No. 11. pp. 23-32: https://cyberleninka.ru/article/v/problemy-mezhdunarodnoy-bezopasnosti-v-kontekste-sovremenno y-politicheskoy-nauki

Kucheryaviy, M.M. (2014). *Informatsionnoe izmerenie politiki natsionalnoy bezopasnosti v usloviyakh sovremennogo globalnogo mira*. Dissertatsiya na soiskanie stepeni doktora politicheskikh nauk. Sankt-Peterburg: https://disser.spbu.ru/disser2/disser/Kucheryavy.pdf

Kudryashova, I.V. (2009). Krizis i gosudarstvo. *Polis. Politicheskie issledovaniya*. No. 3. pp. 17-20.

Kudryashova, I.V. (2015). Formirovanie i razvitie politicheskikh sistem stran arabskogo Vostoka. *Sravnitelnaya politologiya* / O.V. Gaman-Golutvina (red). Moskva: Aspekt Press. pp. 701-724.

Kuklina, I.N. (2012). Operatsiya NATO v Livii. *Sever-Yug-Rossiya. 2011. Ezhegodnik* / V.G. Khoros, D.B. Malysheva (red). Moskva: IMEMO RAN. pp. 34-39.
Kukulka, Yu. (1980). *Problemy teorii mezhdunarodnykh otnosheniy*. Perevod s polskogo. Moskva: Progress.
Kulagin, V.M. (2000). Mir v XXI v.: mnogopolyusniy balans sil ili globalniy Pax Democratica (Gipoteza demokraticheskogo mira v kontekste alternativ mirovogo razvitiya). *Polis. Politicheskie issledovaniya.* No. 1. pp. 23-37.
Kulagin, V.M. (2001). Rossiya—SShA. Koe-chto nachinaet poluchatsya. *Mezhdunarodnaya zhizn.* No. 12. pp. 10-18.
Kulagin, V.M. (2006). *Mezhdunarodnaya bezopasnost.* Moskva: Aspekt Press.
Kulagin, V.M. (2007). Globalnaya ili mirovaya bezopasnost. *Mezhdunarodnye protsessy.* Vol. 5. No. 2. pp. 38-51.
Kulagin, V.M. (2012). Mezhdunarodnaya bezopasnost. *Sovremennye mezhdunarodnye otnosheniya* / A.V. Torkunov, A.V. Malgin (red.). Moskva: Aspekt Press. pp. 415-439.
Kurilla, I.I. (red.) (2007). *Mezhdunarodnaya integratsiya rossiyskikh regionov.* Moskva: Logos.
Kurilla, Ivan, Zhuravleva, Victoria I. (eds.) (2016). *Russian / Soviet Studies in the United States: Mutual Representations in Academic Projects.* Lanham, Maryland: Lexington Books.
Kuvaldin, V. (2017). *Globalniy mir. Politika. Ekonomika. Sotsialnye otnosheniya.* Moskva: Ves mir.
Kuvaldin, V.B. (2001). Globalizatsiya: rozhdenie megaobshchestva / *Postindustrialniy mir i Rossiya* // V.G. Khoros, V.A. Krasilshchikov (red.). Moskva: Editorial URSS. pp. 105-116.
Kuznetsov, A.V. (2006). Dva vektora ekspansii rossiyskikh TNK— Evrosoyuz i SNG. *Mirovaya ekonomika i mezhdunarodnye otnosheniya.* No. 2. pp. 95-102.
Kuznetsov, A.V. (2008). Evroregiony: polveka «maloy» integratsii. *Sovremennaya Evropa.* No. 2 (34). pp. 48-59.
Kuznetsov, A.V. (2012). Transnatsionalnye korporatsii stran BRIKS. *Mirovaya ekonomika i mezhdunarodnye otnosheniya.* No. 3. pp. 3-11.
Kuznetsov, A.V. and others (red.) (2016). *EAES i strany Evraziyskogo kontinenta: monitoring i analiz pryamykh investitsiy. Doklad.* Vol. No. 41. Sankt-Peterburg: Evraziyskiy bank razvitiya.
Ladyzhenskiy, A.M., Blishchenko, I.P. (1963). *Mirnye sredstva razresheniya sporov mezhdu gosudarstvami.* Moskva: Gosyurizdat.

Larionova, M., Suslova, D. (2012). Mezhdunarodnoe sotrudnichestvo kak resurs razvitiya vuza. *Rektor vuza*. No. 7. pp. 22–27: http://intpr.ntf.ru/DswMedia/nfpk+07-2.pdf

Lebedev, M.V. Mezhdunarodnoe sotrudnichestvo v borbe s terrorizmom: rol biznesa. (2007). *Mirovaya ekonomika i mezhdunarodnye otnosheniya*. No. 3. pp. 47–54.

Lebedeva, M. (2006). The Terrorist Threat to the World Political System. *Connections*. Winter. No. 1. pp. 115–124.

Lebedeva, M.M. (1997). *Politicheskoe uregulirovanie konfliktov: Podkhody, resheniya, tekhnologii*. Moskva: Aspekt-Press.

Lebedeva, M.M. (2003). *Mirovaya politika*. Moskva: Aspekt Press.

Lebedeva, M.M. (2004a). International Relations Studies in the USSR/Russia: Is there a Russian National School of IR Studies. *Global Society*. July. No. 18(3). pp. 263–278.

Lebedeva, M.M. (2004b). Problemy razvitiya mirovoy politiki. *Polis. Politicheskie issledovaniya*. No. 5. pp. 106–113.

Lebedeva, M.M. (2006). Politikoobrazuyushchaya funktsiya vysshego obrazovaniya v sovremennom mire. *Mirovaya ekonomika i mezhdunarodnye otnosheniy a*. No. 10. pp. 69–75.

Lebedeva, M.M. (2008). Politicheskaya sistema mira: proyavleniya «vnesistemnosti», ili novye aktory—starye pravila / *"Privatizatsiya" mirovoy politiki: lokalnye deystviya - globalnye rezultaty* // M.M. Lebedeva (red.). Moskva: Golden-Bi. pp. 53–66.

Lebedeva, M.M. (2009). Politicheskaya osnova sovremennogo mirovogo krizisa. *Politiya*. No. 3. pp. 51–57.

Lebedeva, M.M. (2012). Sovremennye trendy mirovogo razvitiya: novoe kachestvo mira / *Metamorfozy mirovoy politiki*. Moskva: MGIMO. pp. 9–32.

Lebedeva, M.M. (2013). *Rossiyskiye issledovaniya i obrazovaniye v oblasti mezhdunarodnykh otnosheniy: 20 let spustya*. Moskva: Rossiyskiy sovet po mezhdunarodnym delam (RSMD). Izdatelstvo «Spetskniga».

Lebedeva, M.M. (2014). Resursy vliyaniya v mirovoy politike. *Polis. Politicheskie issledovaniya*. No. 1. pp. 99–108.

Lebedeva, M.M. (2015). Publichnaya diplomatiya v uregulirovanii konfliktov. *Mezhdunarodnye protsessy*. Vol. 13. No. 4(43). pp. 45–56: http://www.intertrends.ru/forty-third/Lebedeva.pdf DOI: 10.17994/IT.2015.13.4.43.3

Lebedeva, M.M. (2016a). Sistema politicheskoy organizatsii mira: «idealniy shtorm. *Vestnik MGIMO – Universiteta*. No. 2. pp. 125–133:

http://www.vestnik.mgimo.ru/sites/default/files/pdf/015_lebede vamm.pdf

Lebedeva, M.M. (2016b). *Tekhnologiya vedeniya mezhdunarodnykh peregovorov*. Moskva: Aspekt Press.

Lebedeva, M.M. (2017a). Mezhdunarodno-politicheskie protsessy integratsii obrazovaniya. *Integratsiya obrazovaniya*. Vol. 21. No. 3. pp. 385–394: http://edumag.mrsu.ru/content/pdf/17-3/03.pdf DOI: 10.15507/1991-9468.088.021.201703.385-394

Lebedeva, M.M. (2017b). Nezapadnye teorii mezhdunarodnykh otnosheniy: mif ili realnost? *Vestnik Rossiyskogo universiteta druzhby narodov. Seriya 6: Mezhdunarodnye otnosheniya*. Vol. 17. No. 2. pp. 246–256.

Lebedeva, M.M. (2017c). «Myagkaya sila»: ponyatie i podkhody. *Vestnik MGIMO - Universiteta*. 3(54). pp. 212–223. DOI: 10.24833/2071-8160-2017-3-54-212-223: http://www.vestnik.mgimo.ru/razdely/issledovatelskie-stati/mya gkaya-sila-ponyatie-i-podhody

Lebedeva, M.M. (red.) (2017d). *Publichnaya diplomatiya: Teoriya i praktika*. Moskva: Aspekt Press.

Lebedeva, M.M., Barabanov, O.N. (2012). Globalnye tendentsii razvitiya universitetov i transformatsiya rossiyskoy obrazovatelnoy politiki. *Vestnik MGIMO – Universiteta*. No. 6. pp. 265–279: http://www.mg imo.ru/publications/?id=1003587

Lebedeva, M.M., Fort, J. (2009). Vysshee obrazovanie kak potentsial «myagkoy sily» Rossii. *Vestnik MGIMO – Universiteta*. No. 4. pp. 200–205.

Lebedeva, M.M., Kharkevich, M.V. (2014). «Myagkaya sila» Rossii v razvitii integratsionnykh protsessov na Evraziyskom prostranstve. *Vestnik MGIMO – Universiteta*. No. 2(35). pp. 10–13: http://www.vestnik.mgimo.ru/sites/default/files/pdf/lebedeva_h arkevich.pdf

Lebedeva, M.M., Kharkevich, M.V., Kasatkin, P.I. (2013). *Globalnoe upravlenie*. Moskva: MGIMO.

Lebedeva, M.M., Melvil, A.Yu. (1999a). Sravnitelnaya politologiya, mirovaya politika, mezhdunarodnye otnosheniya: razvitie predmetnykh oblastey. *Polis. Politicheskie issledovaniya*. No. 4. pp. 130–140.

Lebedeva, M.M., Melvil, A.Yu. (1999b). «Perekhodniy vozrast» sovremennogo mira. *Mezhdunarodnaya zhizn*. No. 10. pp. 76–84.

Lebedeva, M.M., Rustamova, L.R., Sharko, M.V. (2016). «Myagkaya sila»: tyemnaya storona (na primere Germanii). *Vestnik MGIMO-Universiteta*. No. 3. pp. 144-153: http://www.vestnik.mgimo.ru/sites/default/files/pdf/013_lebedevamm_rustamovalr_sharkomv.pdf

Lebedeva, M.M., Tsygankov, P.A. (red.) (2001). *Mirovaya politika i mezhdunarodnye otnosheniya v 1990-e gody: Vzglyady amerikanskikh i frantsuzskikh issledovateley*. Moskva: MONF.

Lebedeva, M.M., Yuryeva, T.V. (2011). Arhitektura evropeyskoy bezopasnosti: globalniy i regionalniy aspekty. *Vestnik MGIMO - Universiteta*. No. 5. pp. 122-131.

Lebedeva, M., Kharkevich, M., Zinovieva, E., Koposova, E. (2017). The impact of information technologies on development of archaic state structures. *Storia constituzionale*. No. 3. pp. 195-205.

Lenin, V.I. (1958—1966). *Polnoe sobranie soch*. 5-e izdanie. Vol. 42. Moskva: Politizlat.

Leonov, N.S. (2010). *Kholodnaya voyna protiv Rossii*. Moskva: Izdatelstvo Eksmo Algoritm.

Leonova, O.G. (2013). Myagkaya sila—resurs vneshney politiki gosudarstva. *Obozrevatel*. No. 4. pp. 27-40.

Light, M. (1988). *Marxism and Soviet International Relations*. London: Wheatsheaf Books.

Lukov, V.B. (1988). Sovremennye diplomaticheskie peregovory: problemy razvitiya /*Diplomaticheskiy vestnik. God 1987* // O.G. Peresypkin (red.). Moskva: Mezhdunarodnye otnosheniya. pp. 117-127.

Lukov, V.B., Sergeev, V.M. (1981). Metodologicheskie i metodicheskie osnovy informatsionno-logicheskoy sistemy "SBSE" / *Voprosy modelirovaniya mnogostoronnikh diplomaticheskikh peregovorov* // I.G. Tyulin, M.A. Khrustalev (red.). Moskva: MGIMO. pp. 48-70.

Lukov, V.B., Sergeev, V.M. (1982). Opyt postroeniya indikatorov konflikta i sotrudnichestva v mezhdunarodnykh otnosheniyakh / *Analiticheskie metody v issledovanii mezhdunarodnykh otnosheniy* // I.G. Tyulin, M.A. Khrustalev (red.). Moskva: MGIMO. pp. 74-84.

Lunev, S.I. (2003). Indiyskaya tsivilizatsiya v globaliziruyushchemsya mire. *Mirovaya ekonomika i mezhdunarodnye otnosheniya*. 2003. No. 3. pp. 74-83.

Lunev, S.I. Shirokov, G.K. (2002). Skladyvanie novoy mirovoy sistemy i Rossiya. *Pro et Contra*. Vol. 7. No. 4. pp. 26-46.

Luzyanin S.G. (2018). *Rossiya - Kitay: formirovanie obnovlennogo mira*. Moskva: Institut Dalnego Vostoka Rossiyskoy akademii nauk.

Makarenko, S.A. (2009). O gnoseologii krizisa. *Polis. Politicheskie issledovaniya*. No. 3. pp. 13-15.

Makarov, A.A., Grigoryev, L.M., Mitrov, T.A. (red.) (2015). *Evolyutsiya mirovykh energeticheskikh rynkov i eye posledstviya dlya Rossii*. Moskva INEI RAN, AC pri Pravitelstve RF: https://www.eriras.ru/files/evolyutsiya-mirovyh-energeticheskikh-rynkov-i-ee-posledstviya-dlya-rossii.pdf

Makarychev, A., Morozov, V. (2013). Is "Non-Western Theory" Possible? The Idea of Multipolarity and the Trap of Epistemological Relativism in Russian IR. *International Studies Review*. No. 15(3). pp. 328-350.

Maklyarskiy, B.M. (1980). *Ekologicheskiy bumerang: klassovye aspekty problemy okhrany okruzhayushchey sredy*. Moskva: Mezhdunarodnye otnosheniya.

Maksimova, M.M. (1982). *Globalnye problemy i mir mezhdu narodami*. Moskva: Nauka.

Malashenko, A. (2012). *Tsentralnaya Aziya: na chto rasshchityvaet Rossiya?* Moskva: ROSSPEN.

Malashenko, A.V. (2006). *Islamskaya alternativa i islamistskiy proekt*. Moskva: Ves mir: http://carnegieendowment.org/files/11352_islam_project_malash.pdf.

Malysheva, D.B. (1997). *Konflikty v razvivayushchemsya mire, Rossii i Sodruzhestve Nezavisimykh Gosudarstv: religiozniy i etnicheskiy aspekty*. Moskva: IMEMO RAN.

Manoylo, A. (2017). «Myagkaya sila» terroristov. Rossiya i musulmanskiy mir. No. 3 (297). pp. 137-149.

Manoylo, A.V. (2013). Uregulirovanie i razreshenie mezhdunarodnykh konfliktov. *Mir i politika*. No. 10. pp. 130-140.

Manoylo, A.V. (2008). Mirnoe razreshenie konfliktov: natsionalnye kontseptsii, modeli, tekhnologii. *Vlast*. No. 8. pp. 79-84.

Manoylo, A.V. (2015). Tsvetnye revolyutsii v kontekste gibridnykh voyn. *Pravo i politika*. No. 10. pp. 1400-1405.

Manoylo, A.V. (2016). Informatsionnaya voyna kak ugroza rossiyskoy natsii. *Vestnik rossiyskoy natsii*. No. 6. pp. 174-184.

Martynov, B.F. (2008). «Gruppovoy portret» stran bystrogo razvitiya. *Mezhdunarodnye protsessy*. Vol. 6. No. 1. pp. 41-51: http://www.intertrends.ru/sixteenth/004.htm

Marx, K., Engels, F. (1955-1974). Manifest kommunisticheskoy partii / Marx K., Engels F. *Sobranie sochineniy*. 2-e izdanie. Vol. 7. Moskva: Izdatelstvo politicheskoy literatury.

Mayerov, M.V. (2007). *Mirotvortsy. Iz opyta rossiyskoy diplomatii v posrednichestve.* Moskva: Mezhdunarodnye otnosheniya.
Melikhov, S.V. (1979). *Kolichestvennye metody v amerikanskoy politologii.* Moskva: Nauka.
Melkumyan, K.S. (2014). FATF v protivodeystvii finansirovaniyu terrorizma (spetsifika podkhoda). *Vestnik MGIMO-Universiteta.* No. 1. pp. 88–96.
Melvil, A. Yu. (2004). Eshche raz o sravnitelnoy politologii i mirovoy politike. *Polis. Politicheskie issledovaniya.* No. 5. pp. 114–119.
Melvil, A.Yu. (1999). *Vneshnie i vnutrennie faktory demokraticheskikh tranzitov.* Moskva: MGIMO.
Melyantsev, V.A. (2010). Perspektivy mirovoy ekonomiki: menyayushchayasya rol osnovnykh uchastnikov. *Vestnik MGIMO – Universiteta.* No. 4. pp. 163–173: http://www.vestnik.mgimo.ru/sites/default/files/vestnik/2010-13-4.pdf
Mesto i rol SSSR v mirovom tsivilizacionnom protsesse. Materialy nauchnoy diskussii. Nauchnye diskussii. (1991). *Vestnik Akademii nauk SSSR.* No. 3. pp. 3–17.
Mezhdunarodnye otnosheniya v XXI veke. Regionalnoe v globalnom, globalnoe v regionalnom. (2000). Nizhniy Novgorod: NGLU.
Mezhdunarodnye otnosheniya, politika, lichnost. (1976). Moskva: Nauka.
Mikhaylenko, V.I. (1998). *Evolyutsiya politicheskikh institutov sovremennoy Italii. Metodologicheskiy aspekt.* Yekaterinburg: Bank kulturnoy informatsii.
Mikheev, V.V. (red.) (2005). *Kitay: ugrozy, riski, vyzovy razvitiyu.* Moskva: Moskovskiy Tsentr Karnegi.
Milner, H.V. (1998). Rationalizing Politics: The Emerging Synthesis of International, American, and Comparative Politics. *International Organization.* No. 52(4). pp. 759–786.
Mirskiy, G.I. (2015). Radikalniy islamizm: ideyno-politicheskaya motivatsiya i vliyanie na mirovoe musulmanskoe soobshchestvo. Doklad Mezhdunarodnogo diskussionnogo kluba «Valday». Moskva: *Rossiyskiy sovet po mezhdunarodnym delam (RSMD):* https://www.sli deshare.net/RussianCouncil/ss-50399197
Morozov, G.I. (1999). OON na rubezhe XXI veka (krizis mirotvorchestva OON). *Doklad Instituta Evropy.* No. 55. Moskva: Institut Evropy RAN.
Mukhametov, R.S. (2014). Specifika obshchestvennoy diplomatii kak instrumenta vneshney politiki gosudarstva. *Izvestiya Uralskogo federalnogo universiteta. Seriya 3. Obshchestvennye nauki.* No. 2(128).

pp. 84-90: http://elar.urfu.ru/bitstream/10995/25264/1/iuro-2014-128-10.pdf
Muller, Martin (2009). *Making Great Power Identities in Russia: An Ethnographic Discourse Analysis of Education at a Russian Elite University*. Zürich: LIT Verlag.
Muradyan, A.A. (1990). *Samaya blagorodnaya nauka. Ob osnovnykh ponyatiyakh mezhdunarodno-politicheskoy teorii*. Moskva: Mezhdunarodnye otnosheniya.
Mustaparov, R.M. (2015). Sotrudnichestvo Rossii i ES v obespechenii neftyu v usloviyakh sanktsiy. *Gorizonty ekonomiki*. No. 4(23). pp. 131-135.
Naumkin, V., Zvyagelskaya, I., Kuznetsov, V., Soukhov, N. (2016). The Middle East: From Conflicts to Stability. *Valdai Discussion Club*: http://valdaiclub.com/files/10099/
Naumkin, V.V. (2011). Vliyanie «arabskoy vesny» 2011 g. na globalnuyu mezhdunarodnuyu sistemu. *Blizhniy Vostok v mirovoy politike i kulture* / V.V. Naumkin (red.). Moskva: Institut vostokovedeniya RAN. pp. 288-307.
Neklessa, A. (2001). Konets epokhi Bolshogo Moderna. *Postindustrialniy mir i Rossiya* / V.G. Khoros, V.A. Krasilshchikov (red.). Moskva: Editorial URSS. pp. 37-63.
Nicolson, H. (1941). *Diplomatiya*. Perevod s angl. Moskva: OGIZ — gosudarstvennoe izdatelstvo politicheskoy literatury.
Nicolson, H. (1945). *Kak delalsya mir v 1919 g*. Perevod s angl. Moskva: Gospolitizdat.
Nicolson, H. (1965). *Diplomaticheskoe iskusstvo ("Evolyutsiya diplomaticheskogo metoda")*. Perevod s angl. Moskva: Institut mezhdunarodnykh otnosheniy.
Nikitin, A.I. (2009). *Konflikty, terrorizm, mirotvorchestvo*. Moskva: Aspekt Press.
Nikitin, A.I. (2012). Vooruzhennye konflikty i mirotvorchestvo. *Sovremennye mezhdunarodnye otnosheniya* / A.V. Torkunov, A.V. Malgin (red.). Moskva: Aspekt Press. pp. 480-496.
Nikitin, A.I. (2016). Evolyutsiya problematiki konfliktov v kontekste mezhdunarodnoy bezopasnosti v postsovetskoy Rossii. *Vestnik MGIMO - Universiteta*. No. 5(50). pp. 48-62: http://www.vestnik.mgimo.ru/sites/default/files/pdf/04_nikitinai.pdf
Nikitin, A.I., Khlestov, O.N., Fedorov, Yu.E., Demurenko, A.V. (1998). *Mirotvorcheskie operatsii v SNG. Mezhdunarodno-pravovye, politicheskie, organizacionnye aspekty*. Moskva, MONF.

Nikitina, Yu.A. (2009). *Mezhdunarodnye otnosheniya i mirovaya politika. Vvedenie v spetsialnost.* Moskva: Aspekt Press.

Nikitina, Yu.A. (2011). ODKB i ShOS kak modeli vzaimodeystviya v sfere regionalnoy bezopasnosti. *Indeks bezopasnosti.* Vol. 17. No. 2(97). pp. 45-53.

Nikolaev, A. (1998). Voennaya doktrina NATO na sovremennom etape. *Zarubezhnoe voennoe obozrenie.* No. 3. pp. 2-5.

Novikov, G.N. (1996). *Teorii mezhdunarodnykh otnosheniy.* Irkutsk: Izdatelstvo IGU.

Nye, J. (1990). *Bound to Lead: The Changing Nature of American Power.* New York: Basic Books.

Nye, J. (2002). *The Paradox of American Power: Why the World's Only Superpower Can't Go It Alone.* New York: Oxford University Press.

Nye, J. (2018). How Sharp Power Threatens Soft Power. *Foreign Affairs.* January / February. #1: https://www.foreignaffairs.com/articles/china/2018-01-24/how-sharp-power-threatens-soft-power

Orlov, V.A. (red.) (2002). *Yadernoe nerasprostranenie. V dvukh tomakh.* Moskva: Pir-tsentr.

Osinskaya, D. (2009). Pyatnadtsat let rosta i uspekha. *Sankt-Peterburgskiy gosudarstvenniy universitet.* No. 6(3728): http://www.spbumag.nw.ru/2009/06/2.shtml

Oznobishchev, S.K. (2011). Noviy mir i otnosheniya Rossii – NATO. *Polis. Politicheskie issledovaniya.* No. 3. pp. 50-57.

Pagovski, Z.Z. (2015). *Public Diplomacy of Multilateral Organizations: The Cases of NATO, EU, and ASEAN.* Los Angeles: Figueroa Press: http://uscpublicdiplomacy.org/sites/uscpublicdiplomacy.org/files/useruploads/u25044/Public%20Diplomacy%20of%20Multilateral%20-%20Full%20June%202015.pdf

Pakhomov, A.A. (2012). BRIKS nabiraet ves. Strany BRIKS v mirovom «klube investorov». *Aziya i Afrika segodnya.* No. 4. pp. 16-23.

Panarin, I.N. (2016). Gladiatory gibridnoy voyny. *Ekonomicheskie strategii.* Vol. 18. No. 2. pp. 60-65: http://www.inesnet.ru/wp-content/mag_archive/2016_02/ES2016-02-060-65_Igor_Panarin.pdf

Panova, E.P. (2010). Sila privlekatelnosti: ispolzovanie «myagkoy sily» v mirovoy politike. *Vestnik MGIMO – Universiteta.* No. 4. pp. 91-97.

Pantin V.I. (2009). Krizis kak rubezh mirovogo razvitiya. *Polis. Politicheskie issledovaniya.* No. 3. pp. 9-11.

Parkhalina, T.G. (2016). Vvedenie. *Problemy evropeyskoy bezopasnosti.* Sbornik nauchnykh trudov. Vypusk 1. Moskva: Institut nauchnoy informatsii RAN. pp. 5-17.

Parshin, P.A. (2009). Globalnoe informatsionnoe obshchestvo i mirovaya politika. *Analiticheskie doklady MGIMO.* Moskva: MGIMO - Universitet MID Rossii. No. 2(23): http://imi-mgimo.ru/images/pdf/analiticheskie_doklady/ad-23.pdf

Parshin, P.B. (2014). Dva ponimaniya «myagkoy sily»: Predposylki, korrelyaty i sledstviya. *Vestnik MGIMO-Universiteta.* No. 2(35). pp. 14-21: http://vestnik.mgimo.ru/sites/default/files/pdf/parshin.pdf

Pashkovskaya, I.G. (2011). *Energeticheskaya politika Evropeyskogo soyuza v otnoshenii Rossii. Analiticheskie doklady MGIMO-Universiteta.* Issue 5(29). Moskva: MGIMO-Universitet. 2011: http://www.mgimo.ru/files2/y09_2011/211115/pashkovskaya.pdf

Pavlov, O.V. (2012). Prichiny alyansa Zapada i radikalnogo islama. *Blizhniy Vostok, Arabskoe probuzhdenie i Rossiya: chto dalshe?* / V.V. Naumkin and others (red.). Moskva: MGU, Institut Vostokovedenya RAN. pp. 131-137: http://test.ivran.alpite.ru/attachments/585_middleast-russia2012.pdf

Pestsov, S.K., Bobylo, A.M. (2015) «Myagkaya sila» v mirovoy politike: problema operatsionalizatsii teoreticheskogo kontsepta. *Vestnik Tomskogo gosudarstvennogo universiteta. Istoriya.* No. 2(34). pp. 108-114.

Petrovskiy, V.F. (1976). *Amerikanskaya vneshnepoliticheskaya mysl. Kriticheskiy obzor organizatsii, metodov i soderzhaniya burzhuaznykh issledovaniy v SShA po voprosam mezhdunarodnykh otnosheniy i vneshney politiki.* Moskva: Mezhdunarodnye otnosheniya.

Petrovskiy, V.F. (1982). *Razoruzhenie: konceptsii, problemy, mekhanizm.* Moskva: Politizdat.

Podberezkin, A.I. (2007-2012). *Natsionalniy chelovecheskiy kapital.* V 5-ti tomakh. Moskva: MGIMO-Universitet.

Podberezkin, A.I., Parshkova, Yu.Yu. (2014). Ugroza EvroPro natsionalnoy bezopasnosti Rossii. *Vestnik MGIMO -Universiteta.* No. 1. pp. 54-63: http://vestnik.mgimo.ru/sites/default/files/pdf/podberezkin_parshkova.pdf

Podberezkin, A.I., Zhukov, A.V. (2015). Publichnaya diplomatiya v silovom protivostoyanii tsivilizatsiy. *Vestnik MGIMO-Universiteta.* No. 6(45). pp. 106-116.

Podberezkina, O.A. (2015). Transportnye koridory v rossiyskikh integratsionnykh proektakh na primere EAES. *Vestnik MGIMO-Universiteta.* No. 1(40). pp. 55-75: http://www.vestnik.mgimo.ru/sites/default/files/pdf/018_politologiya_podberezkinaoa.pdf

Poggi, G. (2007). States and State Systems: Democratic, Westphalian or Both? *Review of International Studies*. No. 33. pp. 577-595.

Pokhlebkin, V.V. (1992). *Vneshnyaya politika Rusi, Rossii i SSSR za 1000 let v imenakh, datakh i faktakh" (Spravochnik)*. Vypusk I: Vedomstva vneshney politiki i ikh rukovoditeli. Moskva: Mezhdunarodnye otnosheniya.

Polyvyanniy, D.I. (2015). «Balkanizatsiya i «evropeizatsiya» na yugo-vostoke Evropy. *Sovremennaya Evropa*. No. 5(65). pp. 36-47.

Ponomareva, E.G. (2013). «Proekt Kosovo»: Mafiya, NATO i bolshaya politika. *De Conspiratione* / Fursov A. (sostavitel). Moskva: KMK. pp. 101-145.

Porter, T. (2001). Can There Still Be National Perspectives on International Relations? / *International Relations – Still an American Social Science: Towards Diversity in International Thought* // Ed. by Robert M.A. Crawford, Daril S.L. Jarvis. Albany, New York: State University of New York Press. pp. 131-147.

Potemkin, V.P. (red.) (1941-1955). *Istoriya diplomatii v 3-kh tomakh*. Moskva: OGIZ.

Potemkina, O.Yu. (2010). *Immigratsionnaya politika Evropeyskogo soyuza*. Moskva: Russkiy suvenir.

Pozdnyakov, E.A. (1976). *Sistemniy podkhod i mezhdunarodnye otnosheniya*. Moskva: Nauka.

Primakov, E.M. (1978). *Anatomiya blizhnevostochnogo konflikta*. Moskva: Mysl.

Primakov, E.M. (2002). *Mir posle 11 sentyabrya*. Moskva: Mysl.

Primakov, E.M. (2005). Alternativy vstupleniya Rossii v VTO net. *Mezhdunarodnaya zhizn*. No. 7/8. pp. 79-81.

Primakov, E.M. (2006). Situatsionniy analiz kak analiticheskiy zhanr. *Situatsionnye analizy. Metodika provedeniya*. Moskva: Nauchno-obrazovatelniy forum po mezhdunarodnym otnosheniyam: http://www.obraforum.ru/pdf/broshura1.pdf

Primakov, E.M. (2009). *Mir bez Rossii? K chemu vedet politicheskaya blizorukost*. Moskva: Rossiyskaya gazeta.

Primakov, E.M. (red.) (1983). *Problemy razoruzheniya i razvivayushchiesya strany*. Moskva: Nauka.

Problemy okruzhayushchey sredy, energii i prirodnykh resursov. Mezhdunarodniy aspect. (1974). Moskva: Progress.

Problemy teorii mezhdunarodnykh otnosheniy. (1969). *Mirovaya ekonomika i mezhdunarodnye otnosheniya*. No. 9. pp. 88-106; *Mirovaya ekonomika i mezhdunarodnye otnosheniya*. No. 10. pp. 78-99.

Protopopov, A.S., Kozmenko, V.M., Yelmanova, N.S. (2001). *Istoriya mezhdunarodnykh otnosheniy i vneshney politiki Rossii (1648–2000)*. Moskva: Aspekt Press.

Pryakhin, V.F. (2002). *Regionalnye konflikty na postsovetskom prostranstve: (Abhaziya, Yuzhnaya Osetiya, Nagorniy Karabakh, Pridnestrove, Tadzhikistan)*. Moskva: GNOM i D.

Pushmin, Ye.A. (1970). *Posrednichestvo v mezhdunarodnom prave*. Moskva: Mezhdunarodnye otnosheniya.

Pushmin, Ye.A. (1974). *Mirnoe razreshenie mezhdunarodnykh sporov (mezhdunarodno-pravovye voprosy)*. Moskva: Mezhdunarodnye otnosheniya.

Putnam, R. (1988). *Diplomacy and Domestic Policy: The Logic of Two-Level Games*. International Organization. Summer. No. 42(3). pp. 427–460.

Rogov S.M. (2015). Reinkarnatsiya kholodnoy voyny. Moskva: *Rossiyskiy sovet po mezhdunarodnym delam (RSMD)*: http://russiancouncil.ru/analytics-and-comments/comments/reinkarnatsiya-kholodnoy-voyny/

Rogov, S.M. (1989). *Sovetskiy Soyuz i SShA: poisk balansa interesov*. Moskva: Mezhdunarodnye otnosheniya.

Rogovskiy, E.A. (2014). *Kiber-Vashington: globalizatsiya ambitsiy*. Moskva: Mezhdunarodnye otnosheniya.

Rogozin, D.O. (2001). Novye izmereniya mezhdunarodnoy bezopasnosti i problemy uregulirovaniya v Afganistane. *Posle 11 sentyabrya (sbornik statey i dokumentov)*. Moskva: Sovet po vneshney politike. Komitet Gosudarstvennoy Dumy po vneshney politike: http://velikoross.org/wp-content/uploads/2014/05/mir-posle-11-sentyabrya-2001.pdf

Romanova, T.A. (2002). Inostrannye investitsii v stanovlenii ES kak aktora na mirovoy arene. *Vestnik Sankt-Peterburgskogo gosudarstvennogo universiteta*. Seriya 6. Mezhdunarodnye otnosheniya. No. 2. pp. 142–149.

Romanova, T.A. (2013). Energeticheskoe sotrudnichestvo Rossii i Evrosoyuza: Osnovnye napravleniya evolyutsii i sovremennoe sostoyanie. *Baltiyskiy region*. No. 3 (17). pp. 7–19.

Romashkina N.P. (2016). Sovremennye ugrozy natsionalnoy bezopasnosti: ot praktiki k teorii. *Problemy informatsionnoy bezopasnosti v mezhdunarodnykh voenno-politicheskikh otnosheniyakh* / A.V. Zagorskiy, N.P. Romashkina. Moskva: IMEMO RAN: http://www.imemo.ru/files/File/ru/publ/2016/2016_037.pdf

Rossiya pered globalnymi vyzovami. (2002). Nizhniy Novgorod: NGLU, 2002.

Rossiyskie regiony kak mezhdunarodnye aktory. (2000). Nizhniy Novgorod: NGLU.
Rousselet, K., Lebedeva, M.M. (1997). Une experience internationale d'enseignement des relations internationales: le dialogue des traditions. *Kosmopolis. Almanakh.* Issue 1. pp. 29–31.
Rozov, N.S. (2009). Krizis kak globalnyy imperativ obnovleniya strukturnoy otvetstvennosti v epokhu rastsveta natsionalnogo i gruppovogo egoizma. *Polis. Politicheskie issledovaniya.* No. 3. pp. 15–17.
Rusakova, O.F. (2015). Diskurs soft power v gumanitarnoy diplomatii: instrumentalno-izmeritelniy analiz. *Gumanitarnye nauki.* No. 2(30). pp. 91–97.
Rusakova, O.F. (red.) (2014). *Soft power: teoriya, resursy, diskurs.* Yekaterinburg: Izdatelskiy dom «Diskurs-Pi»: http://polit.ispn.urfu.ru/fileadmin/user_upload/site_15780/uploads/Doc/SoftPower.pdf
Rustamova, L.R. (2016). Osobennosti «myagkoy sily» vo vneshney politike FRG. *Vestnik MGIMO – Universiteta.* No. 1. pp. 118–128: https://mgimo.ru/upload/iblock/614/011_mirovaya_politika_rustamovalr.pdf
Rykhtik, M.I. (2012). Natsionalnaya innovatsionnaya sistema SShA: istoriya formirovaniya, politicheskaya praktika, strategii razvitiya. *Vestnik Nizhegorodskogo gosudarstvennogo universiteta im. N.I. Lobachevskogo.* No. 6(1). pp. 263–268: http://www.unn.ru/pages/issues/vestnik/99999999_West_2012_6(1)/42.pdf
Rykhtik, M.I. Kvashnin, D.A. (2009). Sovremennaya biopolitika i voprosy upravleniya novymi riskami (postanovka problemy). *Vlast.* No. 8. pp. 28–31.
Safonov, A.E. (2006). Terrorizm apokalipsisa. *Mezhdunarodnaya zhizn.* No. 5. pp. 12–17.
Safronova, O.V. (2001). *Teoriya mezhdunarodnykh otnosheniy.* Nizhniy Novgorod: NNGU.
Salygin V.I., Kaveshnikov, N.Yu. (2014). «Gazprom» na rynke Evrosoyuza: neobkhodim balans printsipov konkurentsii i energeticheskoy bezopasnosti. *Vestnik MGIMO-Universiteta.* No. 4. pp. 45–53.
Sapronova, M.A. (2013). *Arabo-musulmanskiy mir: istoriya, geografiya, obshchestvo.* Kazan: Kazanskiy universitet.
Satou, E. (1961). *Rukovodstvo po diplomaticheskoy praktike.* Perevod s angl. Moskva: Izdatelstvo Instituta mezhdunarodnykh otnosheniy.

Semenenko, I.S. (red.) (2014). *Globalnyy mir: k novym modelyam natsionalnogo i regionalnogo razvitiya.* V dvukh tomakh. Moskva: IMEMO RAN.
Sergeev, V.M. (1999). *Demokratiya kak peregovorniy protsess.* Moskva: MONF.
Sergeev, V.M. (2009). O glubinnykh kornyakh sovremennogo finansovogo krizisa. *Polis. Politicheskie issledovaniya.* No. 3. pp. 47-53.
Sergeev, V.M., Akimov, V.P., Lukov, V.B., Parshin, P.B. (1990). Interdependence in a Crisis Situation. A Cognitive Approach to Modelling the Caribbean Crisis. *Journal of Conflict Resolution.* No. 34(2). pp. 179-207.
Sergeev, V.S. (1938). *Ocherki istorii Drevnego Rima.* Moskva: Sotsekgiz.
Sergunin, A. (2000). Russian Post-Communist Foreign Policy Thinking at the Cross-Roads. *Journal of International Relations and Development.* No. 3. pp. 23-50.
Sergunin, A.A. (2005b). Mezhdunarodnaya bezopasnost: novye podkhody i kontsepty. *Polis. Politicheskie issledovaniya.* No. 6. 126-138.
Sergunin, A.A., Makarychev, A.S. (1999). *Sovremennaya politicheskaya mysl Zapada: «postpozitivistskaya revolyutsiya».* Nizhniy Novgorod: NGLU.
Sergunin, Alexander A. (2005a). Discussions of International Relations in Post-Communist Russia / *New Directions in Russian International Studies //* Ed. by Andrei P. Tsygankov, Pavel A. Tsygankov. Stuttgart: Ibidem Verlag. pp. 37-59.
Sevastyanov, S. (2005). The Russian Far East's Security Perspective: Interplay of Internal and External Challenges and Opportunities / *Siberia and the Russian Far East in the 21st Century: Partners in the Community of Asia //* Ed. by A. Iwashita. Sapporo: Slavic Research Center. pp. 21-38.
Shagalov, V.A., Grishin, Y.Y., Akhmetova, A.R. (2015). Regional Conflicts in Africa and Evolution of Conceptual Bases of Peace-Keeping of P.R. China. *Social Sciences.* No. 10 (2). pp. 114-116.
Shakh, G. (Shakhnazarov, G.). (1981). *Gryadushchiy miroporyadok. O tendentsiyakh i perspektivakh mezhdunarodnykh otnosheniy.* Moskva: Politizdat.
Shakleina, T.A. (2002). *Rossiya i SShA v novom mirovom poryadke. Diskussii v politiko-akademicheskikh soobshchestvakh Rossii i SShA (1991-2002).* Moskva: Institut SShA i Kanady RAN.
Shakleina, T.A. (2013). Obshchnost i razlichiya v strategiyakh Rossii i SShA. *Mezhdunarodnye protsessy.* Vol. 11. No. 2(33). pp. 6-19.
Shakleina, T.A., Bogaturov, A.D. (2005). Mesto realizma v rossiyskikh issledovaniyakh mezhdunarodnykh otnosheniy / *Rossiyskaya nauka*

mezhdunarodnykh otnosheniy: novye napravleniya / A.P. Tsygankov, P.A. Tsygankov (red.). Moskva: Per Se. pp. 123–146.

Shamakhov, V.A. (red.) (2003). *Vneshnie svyazi Severo-Zapada Rossiyskoy Federatsii*. Sankt-Peterburg: Izdatelstvo SZAGS.

Shepovalenko, M.Yu. (red.) (2016). *Siriyskiy rubezh*. S predisloviem S.K. Shoygu i poslesloviem S.V. Lavrova. Moskva: Tsentr analiza strategiy i tekhnologiy.

Shevardnadze, E.A. (1990). Priglashenie k sotrudnichestvu. *Vestnik Rossiyskoy Akademii Nauk*. No. 3. pp. 3–7: http://www.ras.ru/publishing/rasherald/rasherald_articleinfo.aspx?articleid=d03db83 5-0917-4f5b-a881-8ddbee75a476

Shirin, S.S. (2007). Problema postroeniya edinogo informatsionnogo prostranstva Rossii i Evropeyskogo Soyuza / *Otnosheniya Rossii i ES v poiskakh optimalnoy modeli sblizheniya*. Sankt-Peterburg: Izdatelstvo SPbGU. pp. 72–78.

Shiryaev, B. A. (2011). Interesy SShA na Tikhom okeane (proshloe i nastoyashchee). *Nauchnye trudy Severo-Zapadnogo instituta upravleniya*. Vol. 2. No. 2(3). pp. 137-146.

Shishkov, Yu.V., Mirovitskaya, N.S. (1983). *Mezhdunarodnye aspekty prodovolstvennoy problemy*. Moskva: Mezhdunarodnye otnosheniya.

Shmelev, N.P. (1983). Globalnye problemy i razvivayushchiysya mir. *Kommunist*. No. 14. pp. 83–94.

Shtol, V.V. (2003). *Novaya strategiya NATO v epokhu globalizatsii*. Moskva: Nauchnaya kniga.

Shtol, V.V. (2010). *Armiya «novogo mirovogo poryadka»*. Moskva: OGI.

Shtol, V.V. (2010). O novoy strategicheskoy konceptsii NATO. *Obozrevatel*. No. 8. pp. 47–56.

Shultz, George P., Perry, William J., Kissinger, Henry A., Nunn, Sam. (2007). A World Free of Nuclear Weapons. *The Wall Street Journal*. January 4.

Silaev, N., Sushentsov, A. (2017). Soyuzniki Rossii i geopoliticheskiy frontir v Evrazii. *Diskussionniy klub «Volday»*. *Analiticheskie zapiski* No. 66: http://valdaiclub.com/files/14720/

Simoniya, N.A. (2012). Politicheskaya ekonomiya mezhdunarodnykh otnosheniy / *Sovremennye mezhdunarodnye otnosheniya* // A.V. Torkunov, A.V. Malgin (red.). Moskva: Aspekt Press. pp. 73–89.

Sinyakina, I.I. (2012). *Terrorizm s ispolzovaniem oruzhiya massovogo unichtozheniya: mezhdunarodno-pravovye voprosy protivodeystviya*. Moskva. Norma.

Sitnikov, B.P. (1979). Mineralnye resursy: gosudarstvennoe regulirovanie. *SShA i Kanada: ekonomika, politika, ideologiya.* No. 7. pp. 44-55.
Slipchenko, V.I. (2002). *Voyny shestogo pokoleniya.* Moskva: Veche.
Snow, N., Taylor, Ph. M. (eds.) (2009). *Routledge Handbook of Public Diplomacy* (2009). New York: Routletge.
Sogrin, V.V. (1992). M. Gorbachev. (1992). Lichnost i istoriya. *Obshchestvennye nauki i sovremennost.* 1992. No. 3. pp. 136-146.
Stepanov, A. (2000). Novaya struktura organov upravleniya OVS NATO. *Zarubezhnoe voennoe obozrenie.* No. 3. pp. 2-7.
Stepanova, E.A. (2005a). *Rol narkobiznesa v politekonomii konfliktov i terrorizma.* Moskva: IMEMO RAN.
Stepanova, E.A. (2005b). Protivodeystvie finansirovaniyu terrorizma. *Mezhdunarodnye protsessy.* Vol. 3. No. 2. pp. 66-73.
Stepanova, E.A. (2014). IGIL i transnatsionalniy islamistskiy terrorizm. *Puti k miru i bezopasnosti.* No. 2(47). dekabr. pp. 13-27.
Stepanova, E.A. (2017). Rossiya i SShA v borbe s terrorizmom (sravnitelnye ugrozy i podkhody, Siriya, Afganistan, protivodeystvie nasilstvennomu ekstremizmu). *Puti k miru i bezopasnosti. Problemy terrorizma, nasilstvennogo ekstremizma i radikalizatsii (rossiyskie i amerikanskie podkhody)* / E.A. Stepanova (red.). Moskva: IMEMO RAN, 2017. No. 1(52). pp. 13-54: http://www.estepanova.net/Addressing_Violent_Extremism.pdf
Stetsko, E.V. (2015). Amerikanskie nepravitelstvennye organizatsii: ikh vidy, rol i otsenka vliyaniya na formirovanie grazhdanskogo obshchestva. *Obshshestvo. Sreda. Razvitie.* No. 1. pp. 49-54.
Stolbov, M. (2015). Politicheskaya ekonomiya finansovogo razvitiya. *Mezhdunarodnye protsessy.* Vol. 13. No. 3. pp. 68-77: http://intertrends.ru/system/Doc/ArticlePdf/521/Stolbov-42.pdf
Stomguest, Nelly P., Monkman, Karen. (eds.) (2014). *Globalization and Education: Integration and Contestation Across Cultures.* 2nd edn. Anham, Boulder a.o.: Rowman & Littlefield.
Strange, S. (1999). The Westfailure System. *Review of International Studies.* No. 25(3). pp. 345-354.
Studenetskiy, S.A., Parin, N.V. (red.) (1980). *Ispolzovanie biologicheskikh resursov mirovogo okeana.* Moskva: Nauka.
Tarle, E. (1936). *Napoleon.* Moskva: Zhurnalno-gazetnoe obyedinenie.
Tarle, E.V. (1941-1944). *Krymskaya voyna. V dvukh tomakh.* Moskva-Leningrad: Izdatelstvo Akademii nauk SSSR.
Telegina, E.A. (2012). *Uglevodorodnaya ekonomika.* Moskva: Rossiyskiy gosudarstvennyy universitet im. I.M. Gubkina.

Temnikov, D.M. (2003). Ponyatie mirovogo liderstva v sovremennom politicheskom diskurse. *Mezhdunarodnye protsess.* No. 2. pp. 80-90.

Teteryuk, A.S. (2014). «Myagkaya sila»: faktor kinematografa. *Aktualnye problemy sovremennoy mirovoy politiki. Ezhegodnik IMI.* Moskva: MGIMO. No. 2(8). pp. 170-177: http://imi-mgimo.ru/images/pdf/Ezegodnik_IMI/ez_28_2014.pdf

Timofeev, I. (2017). Rossiya i mir: povestka na 100 let». Moskva: *Rossiyskiy sovet po mezhdunarodnym delam (RSMD)*: http://russiancouncil.ru/analytics-and-comments/analytics/rossiya-i-mir-povestka-na-100-let/

Timofeev, T.T. (red.) (1989). *Perestroyka i sovremenniy mir.* Moskva: Mezhdunarodnye otnosheniya.

Timonina, I.L. (2010). Zhizn posle krizisa: napravleniya transformatsii ekonomicheskoy modeli Yaponii. *Vestnik MGIMO – Universiteta.* No. 4. pp. 183-190.

Tkachenko, S.L. (2000). *Valyutnoe regulirovanie pri perekhode ot zolotogo standarta k plavayushchemu kursu natsionalnoy valyuty.* Sankt-Peterburg: Izdatelstvo Sankt-Peterburgskogo universiteta.

Tkachenko, S.L. (2015). Mezhdunarodnaya politekonomiya – rossiyskaya shkola. *Vestnik Sankt-Peterburgskogo universiteta.* Series 6. No. 4. pp. 106-118: http://vestnik.spbu.ru/html15/s06/s06v4/10.pdf

Tomashevskiy, D.G. (1972). *Politika, otvechayushchaya interesam narodov. O mirnom sosushchestvovanii gosudarstv dvukh sistem.* Moskva: Politizdat.

Tomberg, I.R. (2013). Energetika KNR v mirokhozyaystvennom kontekste. Moskva: Institut Vostokovedeniya RAN: http://book.ivran.ru/f/tombergverstkafinal2.pdf

Torkunov, A.V. (2011). Zadachi i vyzovy universitetskoy politiki. *Mezhdunarodnye protsessy.* Vol. 9. No. 1(25). pp. 50-57: http://www.intertrends.ru/twenty-fifth/006.htm

Torkunov, A.V. (2012a). Sovremennaya istoriya Rossii v mezhdunarodnom kontekste. *Vestnik MGIMO - Universiteta.* No. 5. pp. 45-48.

Torkunov, A.V. (2012b). Obrazovanie kak instrument «myagkoy sily» vo vneshney politike Rossii. *Vestnik MGIMO – Universiteta.* No. 4. pp. 85-93.

Torkunov, A.V. (2013). Pedagogika i podgotovka spetsialistov-mezhdunarodnikov. Vestnik MGIMO – Universiteta. No. 1. pp. 7-8.

Torkunov, A.V. (2016). Proshloe i budushchee mezhdunarodno-politicheskikh issledovaniy. *Mezhdunarodnye protsessy.* Vol. 14. No. 1(44). pp. 77-85.

Torkunov, A.V. (red.) (1998). *Sovremennye mezhdunarodnye otnosheniya.* Moskva: MGIMO, 1998.

Torkunov, A.V. (red.) (2014). *MGIMO-Universitet: Traditsii i sovremennost. 1944-2014.* Moskva: Izdatelstvo «Aspekt Press».
Trenin, D. (2001). *The End of Eurasia.* Washington, D.C.: Carnegie Moscow Center: http://jozefdarski.pl/uploads/zalacznik/7134/dmitritreni n-theendofeurasiarussiaontheborderbetweengeopoliticsandglobaliza tion2002.pdf
Troitskiy, M. (2015a). The Nuclear Factor in Global Politics: Myths and Reality. Moskva: *Rossiyskiy sovet po mezhdunarodnym delam (RSMD)*: http://russiancouncil.ru/en/analytics-and-comments/analytics/ya dernyy-faktor-v-mirovoy-politike-mify-i-realnost/
Troitskiy, M. (2015b). Why Nuclear weapons are strategically useless? Response to Alexei Fenenko. Moskva: *Rossiyskiy sovet po mezhdunarodnym delam (RSMD)*: http://russiancouncil.ru/en/analyt ics-and-comments/analytics/strategicheskaya-bespoleznost-yadern ogo-oruzhiya-otvet-aleks/
Trotsky, L. (2005). *Permanentnaya revolyutsiya. Sbornik.* Moskva: Izdatelstvo AST.
Tsibulina, A. (2016). Reytingovye agentstva v globalnom upravlenii. *Mezhdunarodnye protsessy.* Vol. 14. No. 3(46). pp. 143-150: http://intertrends.ru/system/Doc/ArticlePdf/1655/6cl57veGMh.pdf
Tsvetkov, V.A., Zoidov, K.Kh., Medkov, A.A. (2012). *Problemy integratsii i innovatsionnogo razvitiya transportnykh sistem Rossii i stran Vostochnoy Azii.* Moskva: TsEMI RAN.
Tsvetkova, N.A. (2015). Publichnaya diplomatiya SShA. *Mezhdunarodnye protsessy.* Vol. 13. No. 3. pp. 121-133. DOI: 10.17994/IT.2015.13.2.42.8
Tsygankov, A.P. (2007). Funding a Civilizational Idea: "West," "Eurasia," and "Euro-East" in Russia's Foreign Policy. *Geopolitics.* Vol. 12. No. 3. pp. 375-399.
Tsygankov, A.P. (2014). Rossiyskaya teoriya mezhdunarodnykh otnosheniy: kakoy ey byt? *Sravnitelnaya politika.* No. 2. pp. 65-83.
Tsygankov, A.P., Tsygankov, P.A. (2005b). New Directions in Russian International Studies: Pluralization, Westernization, and Isolationism / *New Directions in Russian International Studies* // Ed. by Andrei P. Tsygankov, Pavel A. Tsygankov. Stuttgart: Ibidem Verlag. pp. 13-35.
Tsygankov, A.P., Tsygankov, P.A. (2005c). Dilemmas and Promises of Russian Liberalism / *New Directions in Russian International Studies* // Ed. by A.P. Tsygankov, P.A. Tsygankov. Stuttgart: Ibidem Verlag. pp. 83-106.
Tsygankov, A.P., Tsygankov, P.A. (2007a). *A Sociology of Russian Liberal IR.* Paper prepared for presentation at an annual meeting of International

Studies Association, San Diego, February 28: http://polit.msu.ru/pub/unn_mpmo/library/A%20Sociology%20of%20Russian%20Liberal%20IR.pdf

Tsygankov, A.P., Tsygankov, P.A. (2007b). A Sociology of Dependence in International Relations Theory: A Case of Russian Liberal IR. International Political Sociology. Volume 1, Issue 4. pp. 307-324.

Tsygankov, A.P., Tsygankov, P.A. (2014). Rossiyskiye mezhdunarodniki-teoretiki: opyt avtoporteta. *Mirovaya ekonomika i mezhdunarodnye otnosheniya*. No. 9. pp. 92-102.

Tsygankov, A.P., Tsygankov, P.A. Predislovie (2005a) / *Rossiyskaya nauka mezhdunarodnykh otnosheniy: novye napravleniya* // A.P. Tsygankov, P.A. Tsygankov (red.). Moskva: Per Se. pp. 9-16.

Tsygankov, Andrei P. (2004). *Whose World Order? Russia's Perception of American Ideas after the Cold War*. Notre Dame, IN: University of Notre Dame.

Tsygankov, Andrei P., Tsygankov, Pavel A. (eds.) (2005d). *New Directions in Russian International Studies*. Stuttgart: ibidem-Verlag.

Tsygankov, P. (2013). Mezhdunarodnye otnosheniya i mirovaya politika: konsolidatsiya uchebno-nauchnoy discipliny? *Mezhdunarodnye protsessy*. No. 3-4(34-35). pp. 7-20: http://www.intertrends.ru/anniversary%20issue/Tsygankov.pdf

Tsygankov, P.A. (1995). Mirovaya politika: soderzhanie, dinamika, osnovnye tendentsii. *Obshchestvennye nauki i sovremennost*. No. 5. pp. 131-141.

Tsygankov, P.A. (1996). *Mezhdunarodnye otnosheniya*. Moskva: «Novaya shkola».

Tsygankov, P.A. (2003). *Teoriya mezhdunarodnykh otnosheniy*. Moskva: Gardariki.

Tsygankov, P.A. (2008). Aktory i faktory v mezhdunarodnykh otnosheniyakh i mirovoy politike. *«Privatizatsiya» mirovoy politiki* / M.M. Lebedeva (red.). Moskva: Golden Bi.

Tsygankov, P.A. (2015). «Gibridnye voyny»: ponyatie, interpretatsii i realnost. *Gibridnye voyny v haotiziruyushchemsya mire XXI veka* / A.P. Tsygankov (red.). Moskva: Izdatelstvo Moskovskogo universiteta.

Tsygankov, P.A. (red.) (2002). *Teoriya mezhdunarodnykh otnosheniy. Khrestomatiya*. Moscow: Gardariki.

Tsymburskiy, V.L. (1999). Geopolitika dlya evraziyskoy Atlantidy. *Pro et Contra*. No. 4. pp. 141-175.

Tyulin, I.G. (1988). *Vneshnepoliticheskaya mysl sovremennoy Frantsii*. Moskva: Mezhunarodnye otnosheniya.

Tyulin, I.G. (1997). Issledovaniye mezhdunarodnykh otnosheniy v Rossii: vchera, segodnya, zavtra. *Kosmopolis. Almanakh.* Issue 1. pp. 18-28.

Tyulin, I.G. (2005). Institutsionalnoe izmerenie rossiyskoy nauki mezhdunarodnykh otnosheniy / *Rossiyskaya nauka mezhdunarodnykh otnosheniy: novye napravleniya //* A.P. Tsygankov, P.A. Tsygankov (red.). Moskva: Per Se. pp. 49-67.

Tyulin, I.G., Khrustalev, M.A. (red.) (1981). *Voprosy modelirovaniya mnogostoronnikh diplomaticheskikh peregovorov.* Moskva: MGIMO.

Udalov, V. (1990). Balans sil i balans interesov. *Mezhdunarodnaya zhizn.* No. 5. pp. 16-25.

Usachev, I.G. (1974). *SShA: militarizm i razoruzhenie. Ot konfrontatsii k peregovoram.* Moskva: Mezhdunarodnye otnosheniya.

Vapler, V.Ya., Gronskaya, N.Ye., Gusev, A.S., Korshunov, D.S., Makarychev, A.S., Solntsev, A.V. (2010). Ideya imperii i «myagkaya sila»: mirovoy opyt i rossiyskie perspektivy. *Voprosy upravleniya.* No. 1(10). pp. 22-27: http://vestnik.uapa.ru/ru/issue/2010/01/02/

Varga, E.S. (1991a). Vskryt cherez 25 let. *Polis. Politicheskie issledovaniya.* No. 2. pp. 175-184.

Varga, E.S. (1991b). Vskryt cherez 25 let.*Polis. Politicheskiye issledovaniya* No. 3. pp. 148-164.

Vasilev, Yu.S., Lebedeva, M.M. (1988). Konflikt i politiko-psikhologicheskie osobennosti lidera (na osnove analiza ofitsialnykh rechey liderov Pakistana / *Regionalnye i lokalnye konflikty: genezis, uregulirovanie, prognozirovanie //* A.V. Torkunov (red.). Moskva: MGIMO. pp. 59-70.

Veselovskiy, S.S. (2012). Fenomen mezhdunarodnogo terrorizma. *Sovremennye mezhdunarodnye otnosheniya /* A.V. Torkunov, A.V. Malgin (red.). Moskva: Aspekt Press. pp. 497-518.

Vneshnepoliticheskie konflikty i mezhdunarodnye krizisy (1979). Moskva: INION AN SSSR.

Voevoda, E.V. (2013). Professionalnaya yazykovaya podgotovka studentov-mezhdunarodnikov: voprosy didaktiki. *Vestnik MGIMO – Universiteta.* No. 1. pp. 9-12.

Voprosy teorii i praktiki diplomaticheskikh peregovorov (1981). (referativniy sbornik). Moskva: INION AN SSSR.

Voronin, E. (2012). *Liviyskaya operatciya NATO: strategiya, «tverdaya» i «myagkaya» sila, itogi.* Moskva: MGIMO.

Voskressenskiy, A.D. (1999). *Rossiya i Kitay: teoriya i istoriya mezhgosudarstvennykh otnosheniya.* Moskva: Moskovskiy obshchestvenniy nauchniy fond.

Voskressenski, A.D. (2004). *Kitay i Rossiya v Evrazii: istoricheskaya dinamika politicheskikh vzaimovliyaniy.* Moskva: Muravey.

Voskressenski, A.D. (2017). *Non-Western Theories of International Relations: Conceptualizing World Regional Studies.* Springer Global (Europe-America): Palgrave Macmillan.

Voytolovskiy F.G. (2016). Predely i perspektivy normalizatsii povestki rossiysko-amerikanskikh otnosheniy. *Puti k miru i bezopasnosti.* No. 2(51). pp. 7-14.

Vygotskiy, L.S. *Myshlenie i rech.* (1982). Sobr. soch. T. 2. Moskva: Pedagogika.

Vzaimosvyaz i vzaimovliyanie vnutrenney i vneshney politiki. (1982). Moskva: Nauka.

Waever, O. (1998). The Sociology of a Not So International Discipline: American and European Developments in International Relations. *International Organization.* No. 52(4). pp. 687-727.

Walker, Ch. Ludwig, J. (2017). The Meaning of Sharp Power. *Foreign Affairs.* November / December. No. 6: https://www.foreign affairs.com/articles/china/2017-11-16/meaning-sharp-power

Wendt, A.E. (2015). *Quantum Mind and Social Science. Unifying Physical and Social Ontology.* Cambridge: Cambridge University Press.

Werner, S., de Mosquita, B. (2003). Desolving Boundaries: Introduction. *International Studies Review.* No. 5(4). pp. 1-8.

Wiatr, Jerzi J. (1979). *Sotsiologiya politicheskikh otnosheniy.* Perevod s polskogo. Moskva: Progress.

Yagya, V.S. (red.) (2011). *Aktualnye problemy mirovoy politiki v XXI veke.* Sankt-Peterburg: Izdatelstvo Sankt-Peterburgskogo gosudarstvennogo universiteta.

Yegorova, E.V. (1988). *SShA v mezhdunarodnykh krizisakh (politiko-psikhologicheskie aspekty).* Moskva: Nauka.

Yuryeva, T.V. (2010). Problemy regionalnoy bezopasnosti: sovremenniy opyt Evropy. *Vestnik MGIMO – Universiteta.* No. 6. pp. 126-133.

Zaemskiy, V.F. (2008). *Teoriya i praktika mirotvorcheskoy deyatelnosti OON.* Moskva: MGIMO – Universitet.

Zagladin, V.V., Frolov, I.T. (1976). Globalnye problemy sovremennosti. Socialno-politicheskie i ideyno-teoreticheskie aspekty. *Kommunist.* No. 16. pp. 93-104.

Zagorskiy, A.V. (2009). Razgovory ob ugroze so storony NATO ne imeyut pod soboy realnoy voennoy osnovy / *Rossiya i Zapad: Vneshnyaya politika Kremlya glazami liberalov* // I.M. Klyamkin (red.). Moskva: Fond «Liberalynaya missiya». pp. 10-18.

Zagorskiy, A.V., Romashkina, N.P. (red.) (2015). *Ugrozy informatsionnoy bezopasnosti v krizisakh i konfliktakh XXI veka*. Moskva: IMEMO RAN: http://picxxx.info/pml.php?action=GETCONTENT&md5=d5efe38f df59802d7b13bf4ed18e3875

Zagorskiy, A.V., Romashkina, N.P. (red.) (2016). *Problemy informatsionnoy bezopasnosti v mezhdunarodnykh voenno-politicheskikh otnosheniyakh*. Moskva: IMEMO RAN: http://www.imemo.ru/files/File/ru/publ/2016/2016_037.pdf

Zagorskiy, An.V., Lebedeva, M.M. (1989). *Teoriya i metodologiya analiza mezhdunarodnykh peregovorov*. Moskva: MGIMO.

Zalett, R. (1956). *Diplomaticheskaya sluzhba: eye istoriya i organizatsiya vo Frantsii, Velikobritanii i Soedinennykh Shtatakh*. Perevod s nemetskogo. Moskva: Izdatelstvo inostrannoy literatury.

Zamoshkin, Yu.A. (1966). *Krizis burzhuaznogo individualizma i lichnost: sotsiologicheskiy analiz nekotorykh tendentsiy v obshchestvennoy psikhologii SShA*. Moskva: Znanie.

Zavyalova, E.B. (2013). Gosudarstvenno-chastnoe partnyorstvo vo vneshneekonomicheskoy deyatelnosti. *Rossiyskiy vneshneekonomicheskiy vestnik*. No. 2. pp. 52–61.

Zegonov, O.V. (2008). Rol SMI kak setevogo aktora v miropoliticheskikh protsessakh. *«Privatizatsiya» mirovoy politiki: lokalnye deystviya – globalnye rezultaty*. Moskva. Golden-Bi. pp. 140–178.

Zevelev, I.A., Troitskiy, M.A. (2006). Sila i vliyanie v amerikano-rossiyskikh otnosheniyakh: semioticheskiy analiz. *Ocherki tekushchey politiki*. Issue 2. Moskva: Nauchno-obrazovatelnyy forum po mezhdunarodnym otnosheniyam: http://www.obraforum.ru/pdf/Semiotics-US-Russian-relations-WP2.pdf

Zharikov, M.V. (2017). Finansoviy minilateralizm kak instrument antikriznoy politiki stran BRIKS. *Obshchestvo: yekonomika, politika, pravo*. No. 6. pp. 60–62: http://dom-hors.ru/rus/files/arhiv_zhurnala/pep/2017/6/economics/zharikov.pdf

Zhiritskiy, A.K. (1979). *Plata za bezotvetstvennost. Ekologicheskiy krizis v sovremennom burzhuaznom obshchestve i ideyno-politicheskaya borba*. Moskva: Politizdat.

Zhiznin, S. (2005). *Energeticheskaya diplomatiya Rossii: ekonomika, politika, praktika*. Moskva: Ist Bruk.

Zhurkin, P.V. Primakov, E.M. (red.) (1972). *Mezhdunarodnye konflikty*. Moskva: Mezhdunarodnye otnosheniya.

Zhurkin, V., Karaganov, S., Kortunov, A. (1989). *Razumnaya dostatochnost i novoe politicheskoe myshlenie*. Moskva: Nauka.

Zhurkin, V.V. (1975). *SShA i mezhdunarodno-politicheskie krizisy*. Moskva: Nauka.

Zinovieva, E.S. (2014). *Mezhdunarodnaya informatsionnaya bezopasnost*. Moskva: MGIMO.

Zinovieva, E.S. (2017). Tsifrovaya publichnaya diplomatiya kak instrument uregulirovaniya konfliktov. *Publichnaya diplomatiya: Teoriya i praktika*. Moskva: Aspekt Press.

Zobnin, A.V. (2015). Konsultatsii G. Kissindzhera i A. Dobrynina po voprosu razrabotki Helsinskogo akta. *Vestnik Ivanovskogo gosudarstvennogo universiteta. Seriya: Gumanitarnye nauki*. No. 4(15). pp. 11–20.

Zonova, T.V. (2012). Publichnaya diplomatiya i eye aktory. NPO— instrument doveriya ili agent vliyaniya? Moskva: *Rossiyskiy sovet po mezhdunarodnym delam (RSMD)*: http://russiancouncil.ru/inner/?id_4=681

Zorin, V.A. (1977). *Osnovy diplomaticheskoy sluzhby*. 2-e izd., ispr. i dopoln. Moskva: Mezhdunarodnye otnosheniya.

Zvyagelskaya, I.D. (2008). *Spetsifika etnopoliticheskikh konfliktov i podkhodov k ikh uregulirovaniyu*. Moskva: Navona.

Annex

Main abbreviations

CFDP (Engl.) / SVOP (Russ.)
    Council for Foreign and Defense Policy / Sovet po vneshney i oboronnoy politike

DA
    Diplomatic Academy / Diplomaticheskaya Akademiya

EAEU (Eng.) / EAES (Russ.)
    The Eurasian Economic Union / Evraziyskiy ekonomicheskiy souz

FEFU (Engl.) / DVFU (Russ.)
    The Far Eastern Federal University / Dalnevostochniy federalniy universitet

FUMO (Russian abbreviation is used)
    The Federal Educational and Methodical Association / Federalnoye uchebno-metodicheskoe obyedinenie

IMEMO (Engl./ Russ.)
    Primakov National Research Institute of World Economy and International Relations Russian Academy of Sciences / Natsionalniy issledovatelskiy Institut mirovoy ekonomiki i mezhdunarodnykh otnosheniy Rossiyskoy Akademii Nauk

INION (Russian abbreviation is used)
    The Institute of Scientific Information on Social Sciences Russian Academy of Sciences / Institut nauchnoy informatsii po obshchestvennym naukam Rossiyskoy Akademii Nauk

IR (Engl.) / MO (Russ.)
    International Relations / mezhdunarodnye otnosheniya

MGIMO or MGIMO-University (Russian abbreviation is used) - Moscow State Institute of International Relations / Moskovskiy institut mezhdunarodnikh otnosheniy (Universitet)

MPSF (Engl.) / MONF (Russ.)
    Moscow Public Science Foundation / Moskovskiy obshchestvenniy nauchniy fond

MSU (Engl.) / MGU (Russ.)
Lomonosov Moscow State University / Moskovskiy gosudarstvenniy universitet im. M.V. Lomonosova

RANEPA (Eng.) / RANKhiGS (Russ.)
The Russian Presidential Academy of National Economy and Public Administration / Rossiyskaya akademiya narodnogo khozyaystva i gosudarstvennoy sluzhby

RAS (Engl.) / RAN (Russ.)
Russian Academy of Sciences / Rossiyskaya Akademiya Nauk

RFBR (Eng.) / RFFI (Russ.)
Russian Foundation for Basic Research / Rossiyskiy fond fundamentalnykh issledovaniy

RHF (Eng.) / RGNF (Russ.)
Russian Humanitarian Science Foundation or Russian Foundation for Humanities and social sciences / Rossiyskiy gumanitarniy nauchniy fond

RIAC (Eng.) / RSMD (Russ.)
Russian International Affairs Council / Rossiyskiy sovet po mezhdunarodnym delam

RISA (Engl.) / RAMI (Russ.)
Russian International Studies Association / Rossiyskaya assotsiatsiya mezdunorodnykh issledovaniy

RPSA (Engl.) / RAPN (Russ.)
Russian Political Science Association / Rossiyskaya assotsiatsiya politicheskikh nauk

RSF (Eng.) / RNF (Russ.)
Russian Science Foundation / Rossiyskiy nauchniy fond

RUDN or RUDN University (Russian abbreviation is used)
The Peoples' Friendship Universityof Russia named after Patrice Lumumba / Universitet druzhby narodov im. Patrisa Lumumby

SPbGU (Russian abbreviation is used)
St. Petersburg University or St. Petersburg State University / Sanktpereburgskiy gosudarstvenniy universitet

UMO (Russian abbreviation is used)
Educational and Methodical Association / Uchebno-metodicheskoe obyedineniye

UNN (Eng.)/NNGU (Russ.)
Lobachevski University / Nizhegorodskiy Gosudarsnvenniy Universitet im. N.I. Lobachevskogo

UrFU
Ural Federal University/ Uralskiy Federalniy Universitet named after the first President of Russia B.N. Yeltsin

VAK (Russian abbreviation is used)
Higher Attestation Commission under the Ministry of Higher Education and Science / vysshaya attestatsionnaya komissiya

Titles of Russian journals

Azya i Afrika segodnya [Asia and Africa Today]

Bezopasnost Evrazii [Eurasian Security]

Kosmopolis [Cosmopolis]

Kosmopolis. Almanakh [Cosmopolis. Almanac]

Mezdunarodnye protsessy [International Trends]

Mezhdunarodnaya zhizn [International Affairs]

Mirovaya ekonomika i mezhdunarodnye otnosheniya [World Economy and International Relations]

Obozrevatel-Observer [Observer]

Obshchestvennye nauki i sovremennost [Social Sciences and Modernity]

Politicheskaya ekspertiza [Political expertise]

Polis. Politicheskie issledovaniya [Polis. Political Studies]

Politiya [Politia]

Pro et Contra [Pro et Contra]

Problemy Dalnego Vostoka [The Far East Issues]

Puti k miru i bezopasnosti [Pathways to Peace and Security]

Rossiya v globalnoy politike [Russia in Global Politics]

Rossiyskiy vneshneekonomicheskiy vestnik [Russian Foreign Economic Journal]

Sovremennaya Evropa [Contemporary Europe]

Sravnitelnaya politika [Comparative Politics]

SShA i Kanada: ekonomika, politika, kultura [USA and Canada: Economy, Policy, Culture] Former: *SShA i Kanada: ekonomika, politika, ideologiya* [USA and Canada: Economy, Policy, Ideology]

Svobodnaya mysl [Free Thought]

Upravlencheskoe konsultirovanie [Administrative Consulting]

Uralskoe vostokovedenie: Mezhdunarodniy almanakh [Ural Oriental Studies. International Almanac].

Vestnik Ivanovskogo gosudarstvennogo universiteta. Seriya: Gumanitarnye nauki [Ivanovo State University Bulletin]

Vestnik MGIMO – Universiteta [MGIMO Review of International Relations]

Vestnik Nizhegorodskogo gosudarstvennogo universiteta im. N.I. Lobachevskogo [Vestnik of Lobachevsky State University of Nizhni Novgorod]

Vestnik Rossiyskogo universiteta druzhby narodov. Seriya: Mezhdunarodnye otnosheniya [Vestnik RUDN. Serie. International Relations]

Vestnik Rossiyskoy akademii nauk [Herald of the Russian Academy of Sciences]

Vestnik Sankt-Peterburgskogo gosudarstvennogo universiteta. Seriya 6. Mezhdunarodnye otnosheniya [Vestnik of Saint Petersburg University. Seria 6. Political Science. International Relations]

Voprosy filosofii [Russian Studies in Philosophy]

Vostok. Afro-Aziatskiye obshchestva; istoriya i sovremennost [East. Afro-Asian societies: history and modernity. Shortened name is "Oriens"].

Vsya Evropa [All Europe]

SOVIET AND POST-SOVIET POLITICS AND SOCIETY

Edited by Dr. Andreas Umland

ISSN 1614-3515

1   Андреас Умланд (ред.)
    Воплощение Европейской
    конвенции по правам человека в
    России
    Философские, юридические и
    эмпирические исследования
    ISBN 3-89821-387-0

2   Christian Wipperfürth
    Russland – ein vertrauenswürdiger
    Partner?
    Grundlagen, Hintergründe und Praxis
    gegenwärtiger russischer Außenpolitik
    Mit einem Vorwort von Heinz Timmermann
    ISBN 3-89821-401-X

3   Manja Hussner
    Die Übernahme internationalen Rechts
    in die russische und deutsche
    Rechtsordnung
    Eine vergleichende Analyse zur
    Völkerrechtsfreundlichkeit der Verfassungen
    der Russländischen Föderation und der
    Bundesrepublik Deutschland
    Mit einem Vorwort von Rainer Arnold
    ISBN 3-89821-438-9

4   Matthew Tejada
    Bulgaria's Democratic Consolidation
    and the Kozloduy Nuclear Power Plant
    (KNPP)
    The Unattainability of Closure
    With a foreword by Richard J. Crampton
    ISBN 3-89821-439-7

5   Марк Григорьевич Меерович
    Квадратные метры, определяющие
    сознание
    Государственная жилищная политика в
    СССР. 1921 – 1941 гг
    ISBN 3-89821-474-5

6   Andrei P. Tsygankov, Pavel
    A. Tsygankov (Eds.)
    New Directions in Russian
    International Studies
    ISBN 3-89821-422-2

7   Марк Григорьевич Меерович
    Как власть народ к труду приучала
    Жилище в СССР – средство управления
    людьми. 1917 – 1941 гг.
    С предисловием Елены Осокиной
    ISBN 3-89821-495-8

8   David J. Galbreath
    Nation-Building and Minority Politics
    in Post-Socialist States
    Interests, Influence and Identities in Estonia
    and Latvia
    With a foreword by David J. Smith
    ISBN 3-89821-467-2

9   Алексей Юрьевич Безугольный
    Народы Кавказа в Вооруженных
    силах СССР в годы Великой
    Отечественной войны 1941-1945 гг.
    С предисловием Николая Бугая
    ISBN 3-89821-475-3

10 Вячеслав Лихачев и Владимир
    Прибыловский (ред.)
    Русское Национальное Единство,
    1990-2000. В 2-х томах
    ISBN 3-89821-523-7

11 Николай Бугай (ред.)
    Народы стран Балтии в условиях
    сталинизма (1940-е – 1950-е годы)
    Документированная история
    ISBN 3-89821-525-3

12 Ingmar Bredies (Hrsg.)
    Zur Anatomie der Orange Revolution
    in der Ukraine
    Wechsel des Elitenregimes oder Triumph des
    Parlamentarismus?
    ISBN 3-89821-524-5

13 Anastasia V. Mitrofanova
    The Politicization of Russian
    Orthodoxy
    Actors and Ideas
    With a foreword by William C. Gay
    ISBN 3-89821-481-8

14 *Nathan D. Larson*
Alexander Solzhenitsyn and the
Russo-Jewish Question
ISBN 3-89821-483-4

15 *Guido Houben*
Kulturpolitik und Ethnizität
Staatliche Kunstförderung im Russland der neunziger Jahre
Mit einem Vorwort von Gert Weisskirchen
ISBN 3-89821-542-3

16 *Leonid Luks*
Der russische „Sonderweg"?
Aufsätze zur neuesten Geschichte Russlands im europäischen Kontext
ISBN 3-89821-496-6

17 Евгений Мороз
История «Мёртвой воды» – от страшной сказки к большой политике
Политическое неоязычество в постсоветской России
ISBN 3-89821-551-2

18 Александр Верховский и Галина Кожевникова (ред.)
Этническая и религиозная интолерантность в российских СМИ
Результаты мониторинга 2001-2004 гг.
ISBN 3-89821-569-5

19 *Christian Ganzer*
Sowjetisches Erbe und ukrainische Nation
Das Museum der Geschichte des Zaporoger Kosakentums auf der Insel Chortycja
Mit einem Vorwort von Frank Golczewski
ISBN 3-89821-504-0

20 Эльза-Баир Гучинова
Помнить нельзя забыть
Антропология депортационной травмы калмыков
С предисловием Кэролайн Хамфри
ISBN 3-89821-506-7

21 Юлия Лидерман
Мотивы «проверки» и «испытания» в постсоветской культуре
Советское прошлое в российском кинематографе 1990-х годов
С предисловием Евгения Марголита
ISBN 3-89821-511-3

22 *Tanya Lokshina, Ray Thomas, Mary Mayer (Eds.)*
The Imposition of a Fake Political Settlement in the Northern Caucasus
The 2003 Chechen Presidential Election
ISBN 3-89821-436-2

23 *Timothy McCajor Hall, Rosie Read (Eds.)*
Changes in the Heart of Europe
Recent Ethnographies of Czechs, Slovaks, Roma, and Sorbs
With an afterword by Zdeněk Salzmann
ISBN 3-89821-606-3

24 *Christian Autengruber*
Die politischen Parteien in Bulgarien und Rumänien
Eine vergleichende Analyse seit Beginn der 90er Jahre
Mit einem Vorwort von Dorothée de Nève
ISBN 3-89821-476-1

25 *Annette Freyberg-Inan with Radu Cristescu*
The Ghosts in Our Classrooms, or: John Dewey Meets Ceauşescu
The Promise and the Failures of Civic Education in Romania
ISBN 3-89821-416-8

26 *John B. Dunlop*
The 2002 Dubrovka and 2004 Beslan Hostage Crises
A Critique of Russian Counter-Terrorism
With a foreword by Donald N. Jensen
ISBN 3-89821-608-X

27 *Peter Koller*
Das touristische Potenzial von Kam''janec'–Podil's'kyj
Eine fremdenverkehrsgeographische Untersuchung der Zukunftsperspektiven und Maßnahmenplanung zur Destinationsentwicklung des „ukrainischen Rothenburg"
Mit einem Vorwort von Kristiane Klemm
ISBN 3-89821-640-3

28 *Françoise Daucé, Elisabeth Sieca-Kozlowski (Eds.)*
Dedovshchina in the Post-Soviet Military
Hazing of Russian Army Conscripts in a Comparative Perspective
With a foreword by Dale Herspring
ISBN 3-89821-616-0

29 Florian Strasser
    Zivilgesellschaftliche Einflüsse auf die
    Orange Revolution
    Die gewaltlose Massenbewegung und die
    ukrainische Wahlkrise 2004
    Mit einem Vorwort von Egbert Jahn
    ISBN 3-89821-648-9

30 Rebecca S. Katz
    The Georgian Regime Crisis of 2003-
    2004
    A Case Study in Post-Soviet Media
    Representation of Politics, Crime and
    Corruption
    ISBN 3-89821-413-3

31 Vladimir Kantor
    Willkür oder Freiheit
    Beiträge zur russischen Geschichtsphilosophie
    Ediert von Dagmar Herrmann sowie mit
    einem Vorwort versehen von Leonid Luks
    ISBN 3-89821-589-X

32 Laura A. Victoir
    The Russian Land Estate Today
    A Case Study of Cultural Politics in Post-
    Soviet Russia
    With a foreword by Priscilla Roosevelt
    ISBN 3-89821-426-5

33 Ivan Katchanovski
    Cleft Countries
    Regional Political Divisions and Cultures in
    Post-Soviet Ukraine and Moldova
    With a foreword by Francis Fukuyama
    ISBN 3-89821-558-X

34 Florian Mühlfried
    Postsowjetische Feiern
    Das Georgische Bankett im Wandel
    Mit einem Vorwort von Kevin Tuite
    ISBN 3-89821-601-2

35 Roger Griffin, Werner Loh, Andreas
    Umland (Eds.)
    Fascism Past and Present, West and
    East
    An International Debate on Concepts and
    Cases in the Comparative Study of the
    Extreme Right
    With an afterword by Walter Laqueur
    ISBN 3-89821-674-8

36 Sebastian Schlegel
    Der „Weiße Archipel"
    Sowjetische Atomstädte 1945-1991
    Mit einem Geleitwort von Thomas Bohn
    ISBN 3-89821-679-9

37 Vyacheslav Likhachev
    Political Anti-Semitism in Post-Soviet
    Russia
    Actors and Ideas in 1991-2003
    Edited and translated from Russian by Eugene
    Veklerov
    ISBN 3-89821-529-6

38 Josette Baer (Ed.)
    Preparing Liberty in Central Europe
    Political Texts from the Spring of Nations
    1848 to the Spring of Prague 1968
    With a foreword by Zdeněk V. David
    ISBN 3-89821-546-6

39 Михаил Лукьянов
    Российский консерватизм и
    реформа, 1907-1914
    С предисловием Марка Д. Стейнберга
    ISBN 3-89821-503-2

40 Nicola Melloni
    Market Without Economy
    The 1998 Russian Financial Crisis
    With a foreword by Eiji Furukawa
    ISBN 3-89821-407-9

41 Dmitrij Chmelnizki
    Die Architektur Stalins
    Bd. 1: Studien zu Ideologie und Stil
    Bd. 2: Bilddokumentation
    Mit einem Vorwort von Bruno Flierl
    ISBN 3-89821-515-6

42 Katja Yafimava
    Post-Soviet Russian-Belarussian
    Relationships
    The Role of Gas Transit Pipelines
    With a foreword by Jonathan P. Stern
    ISBN 3-89821-655-1

43 Boris Chavkin
    Verflechtungen der deutschen und
    russischen Zeitgeschichte
    Aufsätze und Archivfunde zu den
    Beziehungen Deutschlands und der
    Sowjetunion von 1917 bis 1991
    Ediert von Markus Edlinger sowie mit einem
    Vorwort versehen von Leonid Luks
    ISBN 3-89821-756-5

44 *Anastasija Grynenko in Zusammenarbeit mit Claudia Dathe*
Die Terminologie des Gerichtswesens der Ukraine und Deutschlands im Vergleich
Eine übersetzungswissenschaftliche Analyse juristischer Fachbegriffe im Deutschen, Ukrainischen und Russischen
Mit einem Vorwort von Ulrich Hartmann
ISBN 3-89821-691-8

45 *Anton Burkov*
The Impact of the European Convention on Human Rights on Russian Law
Legislation and Application in 1996-2006
With a foreword by Françoise Hampson
ISBN 978-3-89821-639-5

46 *Stina Torjesen, Indra Overland (Eds.)*
International Election Observers in Post-Soviet Azerbaijan
Geopolitical Pawns or Agents of Change?
ISBN 978-3-89821-743-9

47 *Taras Kuzio*
Ukraine – Crimea – Russia
Triangle of Conflict
ISBN 978-3-89821-761-3

48 *Claudia Šabić*
"Ich erinnere mich nicht, aber L'viv!"
Zur Funktion kultureller Faktoren für die Institutionalisierung und Entwicklung einer ukrainischen Region
Mit einem Vorwort von Melanie Tatur
ISBN 978-3-89821-752-1

49 *Marlies Bilz*
Tatarstan in der Transformation
Nationaler Diskurs und Politische Praxis 1988-1994
Mit einem Vorwort von Frank Golczewski
ISBN 978-3-89821-722-4

50 *Марлен Ларюэль (ред.)*
Современные интерпретации русского национализма
ISBN 978-3-89821-795-8

51 *Sonja Schüler*
Die ethnische Dimension der Armut
Roma im postsozialistischen Rumänien
Mit einem Vorwort von Anton Sterbling
ISBN 978-3-89821-776-7

52 *Галина Кожевникова*
Радикальный национализм в России и противодействие ему
Сборник докладов Центра «Сова» за 2004-2007 гг.
С предисловием Александра Верховского
ISBN 978-3-89821-721-7

53 *Галина Кожевникова и Владимир Прибыловский*
Российская власть в биографиях I
Высшие должностные лица РФ в 2004 г.
ISBN 978-3-89821-796-5

54 *Галина Кожевникова и Владимир Прибыловский*
Российская власть в биографиях II
Члены Правительства РФ в 2004 г.
ISBN 978-3-89821-797-2

55 *Галина Кожевникова и Владимир Прибыловский*
Российская власть в биографиях III
Руководители федеральных служб и агентств РФ в 2004 г.
ISBN 978-3-89821-798-9

56 *Ileana Petroniu*
Privatisierung in Transformationsökonomien
Determinanten der Restrukturierungs-Bereitschaft am Beispiel Polens, Rumäniens und der Ukraine
Mit einem Vorwort von Rainer W. Schäfer
ISBN 978-3-89821-790-3

57 *Christian Wipperfürth*
Russland und seine GUS-Nachbarn
Hintergründe, aktuelle Entwicklungen und Konflikte in einer ressourcenreichen Region
ISBN 978-3-89821-801-6

58 *Togzhan Kassenova*
From Antagonism to Partnership
The Uneasy Path of the U.S.-Russian Cooperative Threat Reduction
With a foreword by Christoph Bluth
ISBN 978-3-89821-707-1

59 *Alexander Höllwerth*
Das sakrale eurasische Imperium des Aleksandr Dugin
Eine Diskursanalyse zum postsowjetischen russischen Rechtsextremismus
Mit einem Vorwort von Dirk Uffelmann
ISBN 978-3-89821-813-9

60   *Олег Рябов*
     «Россия-Матушка»
     Национализм, гендер и война в России XX века
     С предисловием Елены Гощило
     ISBN 978-3-89821-487-2

61   *Ivan Maistrenko*
     Borot'bism
     A Chapter in the History of the Ukrainian Revolution
     With a new introduction by Chris Ford
     Translated by George S. N. Luckyj with the assistance of Ivan L. Rudnytsky
     ISBN 978-3-89821-697-5

62   *Maryna Romanets*
     Anamorphosic Texts and Reconfigured Visions
     Improvised Traditions in Contemporary Ukrainian and Irish Literature
     ISBN 978-3-89821-576-3

63   *Paul D'Anieri and Taras Kuzio (Eds.)*
     Aspects of the Orange Revolution I
     Democratization and Elections in Post-Communist Ukraine
     ISBN 978-3-89821-698-2

64   *Bohdan Harasymiw in collaboration with Oleh S. Ilnytzkyj (Eds.)*
     Aspects of the Orange Revolution II
     Information and Manipulation Strategies in the 2004 Ukrainian Presidential Elections
     ISBN 978-3-89821-699-9

65   *Ingmar Bredies, Andreas Umland and Valentin Yakushik (Eds.)*
     Aspects of the Orange Revolution III
     The Context and Dynamics of the 2004 Ukrainian Presidential Elections
     ISBN 978-3-89821-803-0

66   *Ingmar Bredies, Andreas Umland and Valentin Yakushik (Eds.)*
     Aspects of the Orange Revolution IV
     Foreign Assistance and Civic Action in the 2004 Ukrainian Presidential Elections
     ISBN 978-3-89821-808-5

67   *Ingmar Bredies, Andreas Umland and Valentin Yakushik (Eds.)*
     Aspects of the Orange Revolution V
     Institutional Observation Reports on the 2004 Ukrainian Presidential Elections
     ISBN 978-3-89821-809-2

68   *Taras Kuzio (Ed.)*
     Aspects of the Orange Revolution VI
     Post-Communist Democratic Revolutions in Comparative Perspective
     ISBN 978-3-89821-820-7

69   *Tim Bohse*
     Autoritarismus statt Selbstverwaltung
     Die Transformation der kommunalen Politik in der Stadt Kaliningrad 1990-2005
     Mit einem Geleitwort von Stefan Troebst
     ISBN 978-3-89821-782-8

70   *David Rupp*
     Die Rußländische Föderation und die russischsprachige Minderheit in Lettland
     Eine Fallstudie zur Anwaltspolitik Moskaus gegenüber den russophonen Minderheiten im „Nahen Ausland" von 1991 bis 2002
     Mit einem Vorwort von Helmut Wagner
     ISBN 978-3-89821-778-1

71   *Taras Kuzio*
     Theoretical and Comparative Perspectives on Nationalism
     New Directions in Cross-Cultural and Post-Communist Studies
     With a foreword by Paul Robert Magocsi
     ISBN 978-3-89821-815-3

72   *Christine Teichmann*
     Die Hochschultransformation im heutigen Osteuropa
     Kontinuität und Wandel bei der Entwicklung des postkommunistischen Universitätswesens
     Mit einem Vorwort von Oskar Anweiler
     ISBN 978-3-89821-842-9

73   *Julia Kusznir*
     Der politische Einfluss von Wirtschaftseliten in russischen Regionen
     Eine Analyse am Beispiel der Erdöl- und Erdgasindustrie, 1992-2005
     Mit einem Vorwort von Wolfgang Eichwede
     ISBN 978-3-89821-821-4

74   *Alena Vysotskaya*
     Russland, Belarus und die EU-Osterweiterung
     Zur Minderheitenfrage und zum Problem der Freizügigkeit des Personenverkehrs
     Mit einem Vorwort von Katlijn Malfliet
     ISBN 978-3-89821-822-1

75 Heiko Pleines (Hrsg.)
    Corporate Governance in post-
    sozialistischen Volkswirtschaften
    ISBN 978-3-89821-766-8

76 Stefan Ihrig
    Wer sind die Moldawier?
    Rumänismus versus Moldowanismus in
    Historiographie und Schulbüchern der
    Republik Moldova, 1991-2006
    Mit einem Vorwort von Holm Sundhaussen
    ISBN 978-3-89821-466-7

77 Galina Kozhevnikova in collaboration
    with Alexander Verkhovsky and
    Eugene Veklerov
    Ultra-Nationalism and Hate Crimes in
    Contemporary Russia
    The 2004-2006 Annual Reports of Moscow's
    SOVA Center
    With a foreword by Stephen D. Shenfield
    ISBN 978-3-89821-868-9

78 Florian Küchler
    The Role of the European Union in
    Moldova's Transnistria Conflict
    With a foreword by Christopher Hill
    ISBN 978-3-89821-850-4

79 Bernd Rechel
    The Long Way Back to Europe
    Minority Protection in Bulgaria
    With a foreword by Richard Crampton
    ISBN 978-3-89821-863-4

80 Peter W. Rodgers
    Nation, Region and History in Post-
    Communist Transitions
    Identity Politics in Ukraine, 1991-2006
    With a foreword by Vera Tolz
    ISBN 978-3-89821-903-7

81 Stephanie Solywoda
    The Life and Work of
    Semen L. Frank
    A Study of Russian Religious Philosophy
    With a foreword by Philip Walters
    ISBN 978-3-89821-457-5

82 Vera Sokolova
    Cultural Politics of Ethnicity
    Discourses on Roma in Communist
    Czechoslovakia
    ISBN 978-3-89821-864-1

83 Natalya Shevchik Ketenci
    Kazakhstani Enterprises in Transition
    The Role of Historical Regional Development
    in Kazakhstan's Post-Soviet Economic
    Transformation
    ISBN 978-3-89821-831-3

84 Martin Malek, Anna Schor-
    Tschudnowskaja (Hrsg.)
    Europa im Tschetschenienkrieg
    Zwischen politischer Ohnmacht und
    Gleichgültigkeit
    Mit einem Vorwort von Lipchan Basajewa
    ISBN 978-3-89821-676-0

85 Stefan Meister
    Das postsowjetische Universitätswesen
    zwischen nationalem und
    internationalem Wandel
    Die Entwicklung der regionalen Hochschule
    in Russland als Gradmesser der
    Systemtransformation
    Mit einem Vorwort von Joan DeBardeleben
    ISBN 978-3-89821-891-7

86 Konstantin Sheiko in collaboration
    with Stephen Brown
    Nationalist Imaginings of the
    Russian Past
    Anatolii Fomenko and the Rise of Alternative
    History in Post-Communist Russia
    With a foreword by Donald Ostrowski
    ISBN 978-3-89821-915-0

87 Sabine Jenni
    Wie stark ist das „Einige Russland"?
    Zur Parteibindung der Eliten und zum
    Wahlerfolg der Machtpartei
    im Dezember 2007
    Mit einem Vorwort von Klaus Armingeon
    ISBN 978-3-89821-961-7

88 Thomas Borén
    Meeting-Places of Transformation
    Urban Identity, Spatial Representations and
    Local Politics in Post-Soviet St Petersburg
    ISBN 978-3-89821-739-2

89 Aygul Ashirova
    Stalinismus und Stalin-Kult in
    Zentralasien
    Turkmenistan 1924-1953
    Mit einem Vorwort von Leonid Luks
    ISBN 978-3-89821-987-7

90 *Leonid Luks*
Freiheit oder imperiale Größe?
Essays zu einem russischen Dilemma
ISBN 978-3-8382-0011-8

91 *Christopher Gilley*
The 'Change of Signposts' in the Ukrainian Emigration
A Contribution to the History of Sovietophilism in the 1920s
With a foreword by Frank Golczewski
ISBN 978-3-89821-965-5

92 *Philipp Casula, Jeronim Perovic (Eds.)*
Identities and Politics During the Putin Presidency
The Discursive Foundations of Russia's Stability
With a foreword by Heiko Haumann
ISBN 978-3-8382-0015-6

93 *Marcel Viëtor*
Europa und die Frage nach seinen Grenzen im Osten
Zur Konstruktion ‚europäischer Identität' in Geschichte und Gegenwart
Mit einem Vorwort von Albrecht Lehmann
ISBN 978-3-8382-0045-3

94 *Ben Hellman, Andrei Rogachevskii*
Filming the Unfilmable
Casper Wrede's 'One Day in the Life of Ivan Denisovich'
Second, Revised and Expanded Edition
ISBN 978-3-8382-0044-6

95 *Eva Fuchslocher*
Vaterland, Sprache, Glaube
Orthodoxie und Nationenbildung am Beispiel Georgiens
Mit einem Vorwort von Christina von Braun
ISBN 978-3-89821-884-9

96 *Vladimir Kantor*
Das Westlertum und der Weg Russlands
Zur Entwicklung der russischen Literatur und Philosophie
Ediert von Dagmar Herrmann
Mit einem Beitrag von Nikolaus Lobkowicz
ISBN 978-3-8382-0102-3

97 *Kamran Musayev*
Die postsowjetische Transformation im Baltikum und Südkaukasus
Eine vergleichende Untersuchung der politischen Entwicklung Lettlands und Aserbaidschans 1985-2009
Mit einem Vorwort von Leonid Luks
Ediert von Sandro Henschel
ISBN 978-3-8382-0103-0

98 *Tatiana Zhurzhenko*
Borderlands into Bordered Lands
Geopolitics of Identity in Post-Soviet Ukraine
With a foreword by Dieter Segert
ISBN 978-3-8382-0042-2

99 *Кирилл Галушко, Лидия Смола (ред.)*
Пределы падения – варианты украинского будущего
Аналитико-прогностические исследования
ISBN 978-3-8382-0148-1

100 *Michael Minkenberg (ed.)*
Historical Legacies and the Radical Right in Post-Cold War Central and Eastern Europe
With an afterword by Sabrina P. Ramet
ISBN 978-3-8382-0124-5

101 *David-Emil Wickström*
Rocking St. Petersburg
Transcultural Flows and Identity Politics in the St. Petersburg Popular Music Scene
With a foreword by Yngvar B. Steinholt
Second, Revised and Expanded Edition
ISBN 978-3-8382-0100-9

102 *Eva Zabka*
Eine neue „Zeit der Wirren"?
Der spät- und postsowjetische Systemwandel 1985-2000 im Spiegel russischer gesellschaftspolitischer Diskurse
Mit einem Vorwort von Margareta Mommsen
ISBN 978-3-8382-0161-0

103 *Ulrike Ziemer*
Ethnic Belonging, Gender and Cultural Practices
Youth Identitites in Contemporary Russia
With a foreword by Anoop Nayak
ISBN 978-3-8382-0152-8

104 Ksenia Chepikova
‚Einiges Russland' - eine zweite KPdSU?
Aspekte der Identitätskonstruktion einer postsowjetischen „Partei der Macht"
Mit einem Vorwort von Torsten Oppelland
ISBN 978-3-8382-0311-9

105 Леонид Люкс
Западничество или евразийство? Демократия или идеократия?
Сборник статей об исторических дилеммах России
С предисловием Владимира Кантора
ISBN 978-3-8382-0211-2

106 Anna Dost
Das russische Verfassungsrecht auf dem Weg zum Föderalismus und zurück
Zum Konflikt von Rechtsnormen und -wirklichkeit in der Russländischen Föderation von 1991 bis 2009
Mit einem Vorwort von Alexander Blankenagel
ISBN 978-3-8382-0292-1

107 Philipp Herzog
Sozialistische Völkerfreundschaft, nationaler Widerstand oder harmloser Zeitvertreib?
Zur politischen Funktion der Volkskunst im sowjetischen Estland
Mit einem Vorwort von Andreas Kappeler
ISBN 978-3-8382-0216-7

108 Marlène Laruelle (ed.)
Russian Nationalism, Foreign Policy, and Identity Debates in Putin's Russia
New Ideological Patterns after the Orange Revolution
ISBN 978-3-8382-0325-6

109 Michail Logvinov
Russlands Kampf gegen den internationalen Terrorismus
Eine kritische Bestandsaufnahme des Bekämpfungsansatzes
Mit einem Geleitwort von Hans-Henning Schröder
und einem Vorwort von Eckhard Jesse
ISBN 978-3-8382-0329-4

110 John B. Dunlop
The Moscow Bombings of September 1999
Examinations of Russian Terrorist Attacks at the Onset of Vladimir Putin's Rule
Second, Revised and Expanded Edition
ISBN 978-3-8382-0388-1

111 Андрей А. Ковалёв
Свидетельство из-за кулис российской политики I
Можно ли делать добро из зла?
(Воспоминания и размышления о последних советских и первых послесоветских годах)
With a foreword by Peter Reddaway
ISBN 978-3-8382-0302-7

112 Андрей А. Ковалёв
Свидетельство из-за кулис российской политики II
Угроза для себя и окружающих
(Наблюдения и предостережения относительно происходящего после 2000 г.)
ISBN 978-3-8382-0303-4

113 Bernd Kappenberg
Zeichen setzen für Europa
Der Gebrauch europäischer lateinischer Sonderzeichen in der deutschen Öffentlichkeit
Mit einem Vorwort von Peter Schlobinski
ISBN 978-3-89821-749-1

114 Ivo Mijnssen
The Quest for an Ideal Youth in Putin's Russia I
Back to Our Future! History, Modernity, and Patriotism according to Nashi, 2005-2013
With a foreword by Jeronim Perović
Second, Revised and Expanded Edition
ISBN 978-3-8382-0368-3

115 Jussi Lassila
The Quest for an Ideal Youth in Putin's Russia II
The Search for Distinctive Conformism in the Political Communication of Nashi, 2005-2009
With a foreword by Kirill Postoutenko
Second, Revised and Expanded Edition
ISBN 978-3-8382-0415-4

116 Valerio Trabandt
Neue Nachbarn, gute Nachbarschaft?
Die EU als internationaler Akteur am Beispiel ihrer Demokratieförderung in Belarus und der Ukraine 2004-2009
Mit einem Vorwort von Jutta Joachim
ISBN 978-3-8382-0437-6

117 Fabian Pfeiffer
     Estlands Außen- und Sicherheitspolitik I
     Der estnische Atlantizismus nach der
     wiedererlangten Unabhängigkeit 1991-2004
     Mit einem Vorwort von Helmut Hubel
     ISBN 978-3-8382-0127-6

118 Jana Podßuweit
     Estlands Außen- und Sicherheitspolitik II
     Handlungsoptionen eines Kleinstaates im
     Rahmen seiner EU-Mitgliedschaft (2004-2008)
     Mit einem Vorwort von Helmut Hubel
     ISBN 978-3-8382-0440-6

119 Karin Pointner
     Estlands Außen- und Sicherheitspolitik III
     Eine gedächtnispolitische Analyse estnischer
     Entwicklungskooperation 2006-2010
     Mit einem Vorwort von Karin Liebhart
     ISBN 978-3-8382-0435-2

120 Ruslana Vovk
     Die Offenheit der ukrainischen
     Verfassung für das Völkerrecht und
     die europäische Integration
     Mit einem Vorwort von Alexander
     Blankenagel
     ISBN 978-3-8382-0481-9

121 Mykhaylo Banakh
     Die Relevanz der Zivilgesellschaft
     bei den postkommunistischen
     Transformationsprozessen in mittel-
     und osteuropäischen Ländern
     Das Beispiel der spät- und postsowjetischen
     Ukraine 1986-2009
     Mit einem Vorwort von Gerhard Simon
     ISBN 978-3-8382-0499-4

122 Michael Moser
     Language Policy and the Discourse on
     Languages in Ukraine under President
     Viktor Yanukovych (25 February
     2010–28 October 2012)
     ISBN 978-3-8382-0497-0 (Paperback edition)
     ISBN 978-3-8382-0507-6 (Hardcover edition)

123 Nicole Krome
     Russischer Netzwerkkapitalismus
     Restrukturierungsprozesse in der
     Russischen Föderation am Beispiel des
     Luftfahrtunternehmens "Aviastar"
     Mit einem Vorwort von Petra Stykow
     ISBN 978-3-8382-0534-2

124 David R. Marples
     'Our Glorious Past'
     Lukashenka's Belarus and
     the Great Patriotic War
     ISBN 978-3-8382-0574-8 (Paperback edition)
     ISBN 978-3-8382-0675-2 (Hardcover edition)

125 Ulf Walther
     Russlands "neuer Adel"
     Die Macht des Geheimdienstes von
     Gorbatschow bis Putin
     Mit einem Vorwort von Hans-Georg Wieck
     ISBN 978-3-8382-0584-7

126 Simon Geissbühler (Hrsg.)
     Kiew – Revolution 3.0
     Der Euromaidan 2013/14 und die
     Zukunftsperspektiven der Ukraine
     ISBN 978-3-8382-0581-6 (Paperback edition)
     ISBN 978-3-8382-0681-3 (Hardcover edition)

127 Andrey Makarychev
     Russia and the EU
     in a Multipolar World
     Discourses, Identities, Norms
     With a foreword by Klaus Segbers
     ISBN 978-3-8382-0629-5

128 Roland Scharff
     Kasachstan als postsowjetischer
     Wohlfahrtsstaat
     Die Transformation des sozialen
     Schutzsystems
     Mit einem Vorwort von Joachim Ahrens
     ISBN 978-3-8382-0622-6

129 Katja Grupp
     Bild Lücke Deutschland
     Kaliningrader Studierende sprechen über
     Deutschland
     Mit einem Vorwort von Martin Schulz
     ISBN 978-3-8382-0552-6

130 Konstantin Sheiko, Stephen Brown
     History as Therapy
     Alternative History and Nationalist
     Imaginings in Russia, 1991-2014
     ISBN 978-3-8382-0665-3

131 Elisa Kriza
     Alexander Solzhenitsyn: Cold War
     Icon, Gulag Author, Russian
     Nationalist?
     A Study of the Western Reception of his
     Literary Writings, Historical Interpretations,
     and Political Ideas
     With a foreword by Andrei Rogatchevski
     ISBN 978-3-8382-0589-2 (Paperback edition)
     ISBN 978-3-8382-0690-5 (Hardcover edition)

132 Serghei Golunov
The Elephant in the Room
Corruption and Cheating in Russian Universities
ISBN 978-3-8382-0570-0

133 Manja Hussner, Rainer Arnold (Hgg.)
Verfassungsgerichtsbarkeit in Zentralasien I
Sammlung von Verfassungstexten
ISBN 978-3-8382-0595-3

134 Nikolay Mitrokhin
Die "Russische Partei"
Die Bewegung der russischen Nationalisten in der UdSSR 1953-1985
Aus dem Russischen übertragen von einem Übersetzerteam unter der Leitung von Larisa Schippel
ISBN 978-3-8382-0024-8

135 Manja Hussner, Rainer Arnold (Hgg.)
Verfassungsgerichtsbarkeit in Zentralasien II
Sammlung von Verfassungstexten
ISBN 978-3-8382-0597-7

136 Manfred Zeller
Das sowjetische Fieber
Fußballfans im poststalinistischen Vielvölkerreich
Mit einem Vorwort von Nikolaus Katzer
ISBN 978-3-8382-0757-5

137 Kristin Schreiter
Stellung und Entwicklungspotential zivilgesellschaftlicher Gruppen in Russland
Menschenrechtsorganisationen im Vergleich
ISBN 978-3-8382-0673-8

138 David R. Marples, Frederick V. Mills (eds.)
Ukraine's Euromaidan
Analyses of a Civil Revolution
ISBN 978-3-8382-0660-8

139 Bernd Kappenberg
Setting Signs for Europe
Why Diacritics Matter for European Integration
With a foreword by Peter Schlobinski
ISBN 978-3-8382-0663-9

140 René Lenz
Internationalisierung, Kooperation und Transfer
Externe bildungspolitische Akteure in der Russischen Föderation
Mit einem Vorwort von Frank Ettrich
ISBN 978-3-8382-0751-3

141 Juri Plusnin, Yana Zausaeva, Natalia Zhidkevich, Artemy Pozanenko
Wandering Workers
Mores, Behavior, Way of Life, and Political Status of Domestic Russian Labor Migrants
Translated by Julia Kazantseva
ISBN 978-3-8382-0653-0

142 David J. Smith (eds.)
Latvia – A Work in Progress?
100 Years of State- and Nation-Building
ISBN 978-3-8382-0648-6

143 Инна Чувычкина (ред.)
Экспортные нефте- и газопроводы на постсоветском пространстве
Анализ трубопроводной политики в свете теории международных отношений
ISBN 978-3-8382-0822-0

144 Johann Zajaczkowski
Russland – eine pragmatische Großmacht?
Eine rollentheoretische Untersuchung russischer Außenpolitik am Beispiel der Zusammenarbeit mit den USA nach 9/11 und des Georgienkrieges von 2008
Mit einem Vorwort von Siegfried Schieder
ISBN 978-3-8382-0837-4

145 Boris Popivanov
Changing Images of the Left in Bulgaria
The Challenge of Post-Communism in the Early 21st Century
ISBN 978-3-8382-0667-7

146 Lenka Krátká
A History of the Czechoslovak Ocean Shipping Company 1948-1989
How a Small, Landlocked Country Ran Maritime Business During the Cold War
ISBN 978-3-8382-0666-0

147 Alexander Sergunin
Explaining Russian Foreign Policy Behavior
Theory and Practice
ISBN 978-3-8382-0752-0

148 *Darya Malyutina*
Migrant Friendships in
a Super-Diverse City
Russian-Speakers and their Social
Relationships in London in the 21st Century
With a foreword by Claire Dwyer
ISBN 978-3-8382-0652-3

149 *Alexander Sergunin, Valery Konyshev*
Russia in the Arctic
Hard or Soft Power?
ISBN 978-3-8382-0753-7

150 *John J. Maresca*
Helsinki Revisited
A Key U.S. Negotiator's Memoirs
on the Development of the CSCE into the
OSCE
With a foreword by Hafiz Pashayev
ISBN 978-3-8382-0852-7

151 *Jardar Østbø*
The New Third Rome
Readings of a Russian Nationalist Myth
With a foreword by Pål Kolstø
ISBN 978-3-8382-0870-1

152 *Simon Kordonsky*
Socio-Economic Foundations of the
Russian Post-Soviet Regime
The Resource-Based Economy and Estate-
Based Social Structure of Contemporary
Russia
With a foreword by Svetlana Barsukova
ISBN 978-3-8382-0775-9

153 *Duncan Leitch*
Assisting Reform in Post-Communist
Ukraine 2000–2012
The Illusions of Donors and the Disillusion of
Beneficiaries
With a foreword by Kataryna Wolczuk
ISBN 978-3-8382-0844-2

154 *Abel Polese*
Limits of a Post-Soviet State
How Informality Replaces, Renegotiates, and
Reshapes Governance in Contemporary
Ukraine
With a foreword by Colin Williams
ISBN 978-3-8382-0845-9

155 *Mikhail Suslov (ed.)*
Digital Orthodoxy in the Post-Soviet
World
The Russian Orthodox Church and Web 2.0
With a foreword by Father Cyril Hovorun
ISBN 978-3-8382-0871-8

156 *Leonid Luks*
Zwei „Sonderwege"? Russisch-
deutsche Parallelen und Kontraste
(1917-2014)
Vergleichende Essays
ISBN 978-3-8382-0823-7

157 *Vladimir V. Karacharovskiy, Ovsey I.
Shkaratan, Gordey A. Yastrebov*
Towards a New Russian Work Culture
Can Western Companies and Expatriates
Change Russian Society?
With a foreword by Elena N. Danilova
Translated by Julia Kazantseva
ISBN 978-3-8382-0902-9

158 *Edmund Griffiths*
Aleksandr Prokhanov and Post-Soviet
Esotericism
ISBN 978-3-8382-0903-6

159 *Timm Beichelt, Susann Worschech
(eds.)*
Transnational Ukraine?
Networks and Ties that Influence(d)
Contemporary Ukraine
ISBN 978-3-8382-0944-9

160 *Mieste Hotopp-Riecke*
Die Tataren der Krim zwischen
Assimilation und Selbstbehauptung
Der Aufbau des krimtatarischen
Bildungswesens nach Deportation und
Heimkehr (1990-2005)
Mit einem Vorwort von Swetlana
Czerwonnaja
ISBN 978-3-89821-940-2

161 *Olga Bertelsen (ed.)*
Revolution and War in
Contemporary Ukraine
The Challenge of Change
ISBN 978-3-8382-1016-2

162 *Natalya Ryabinska*
Ukraine's Post-Communist
Mass Media
Between Capture and Commercialization
With a foreword by Marta Dyczok
ISBN 978-3-8382-1011-7

163 Alexandra Cotofana,
     James M. Nyce (eds.)
     Religion and Magic in Socialist and Post-Socialist Contexts I
     Historic and Ethnographic Case Studies of Orthodoxy, Heterodoxy, and Alternative Spirituality
     With a foreword by Patrick L. Michelson
     ISBN 978-3-8382-0989-0

164 Nozima Akhrarkhodjaeva
     The Instrumentalisation of Mass Media in Electoral Authoritarian Regimes
     Evidence from Russia's Presidential Election Campaigns of 2000 and 2008
     ISBN 978-3-8382-1013-1

165 Yulia Krasheninnikova
     Informal Healthcare in Contemporary Russia
     Sociographic Essays on the Post-Soviet Infrastructure for Alternative Healing Practices
     ISBN 978-3-8382-0970-8

166 Peter Kaiser
     Das Schachbrett der Macht
     Die Handlungsspielräume eines sowjetischen Funktionärs unter Stalin am Beispiel des Generalsekretärs des Komsomol Aleksandr Kosarev (1929-1938)
     Mit einem Vorwort von Dietmar Neutatz
     ISBN 978-3-8382-1052-0

167 Oksana Kim
     The Effects and Implications of Kazakhstan's Adoption of International Financial Reporting Standards
     A Resource Dependence Perspective
     With a foreword by Svetlana Vlady
     ISBN 978-3-8382-0987-6

168 Anna Sanina
     Patriotic Education in Contemporary Russia
     Sociological Studies in the Making of the Post-Soviet Citizen
     With a foreword by Anna Oldfield
     ISBN 978-3-8382-0993-7

169 Rudolf Wolters
     Spezialist in Sibirien
     Faksimile der 1933 erschienenen ersten Ausgabe
     Mit einem Vorwort von Dmitrij Chmelnizki
     ISBN 978-3-8382-0515-1

170 Michal Vít,
     Magdalena M. Baran (eds.)
     Transregional versus National Perspectives on Contemporary Central European History
     Studies on the Building of Nation-States and Their Cooperation in the 20th and 21st Century
     With a foreword by Petr Vágner
     ISBN 978-3-8382-1015-5

171 Philip Gamaghelyan
     Conflict Resolution Beyond the International Relations Paradigm
     Evolving Designs as a Transformative Practice in Nagorno-Karabakh and Syria
     With a foreword by Susan Allen
     ISBN 978-3-8382-1057-5

172 Maria Shagina
     Joining a Prestigious Club
     Cooperation with Europarties and Its Impact on Party Development in Georgia, Moldova, and Ukraine 2004–2015
     With a foreword by Kataryna Wolczuk
     ISBN 978-3-8382-1084-1

173 Alexandra Cotofana,
     James M. Nyce (eds.)
     Religion and Magic in Socialist and Post-Socialist Contexts II
     Baltic, Eastern European, and Post-USSR Case Studies
     With a foreword by Anita Stasulane
     ISBN 978-3-8382-0990-6

174 Barbara Kunz
     Kind Words, Cruise Missiles, and Everything in Between
     The Use of Power Resources in U.S. Policies towards Poland, Ukraine, and Belarus 1989–2008
     With a foreword by William Hill
     ISBN 978-3-8382-1065-0

175 Eduard Klein
     Bildungskorruption in Russland und der Ukraine
     Eine komparative Analyse der Performanz staatlicher Antikorruptionsmaßnahmen im Hochschulsektor am Beispiel universitärer Aufnahmeprüfungen
     Mit einem Vorwort von Heiko Pleines
     ISBN 978-3-8382-0995-1

176 Markus Soldner
Politischer Kapitalismus im
postsowjetischen Russland
Die politische, wirtschaftliche und mediale
Transformation in den 1990er Jahren
Mit einem Vorwort von Wolfgang Ismayr
ISBN 978-3-8382-1222-7

177 Anton Oleinik
Building Ukraine from Within
A Sociological, Institutional, and Economic
Analysis of a Nation-State in the Making
ISBN 978-3-8382-1150-3

178 Peter Rollberg,
Marlene Laruelle (eds.)
Mass Media in the Post-Soviet World
Market Forces, State Actors, and Political
Manipulation in the Informational
Environment after Communism
ISBN 978-3-8382-1116-9

179 Mikhail Minakov
Development and Dystopia
Studies in Post-Soviet Ukraine and Eastern
Europe
With a foreword by Alexander Etkind
ISBN 978-3-8382-1112-1

180 Aijan Sharshenova
The European Union's Democracy
Promotion in Central Asia
A Study of Political Interests, Influence, and
Development in Kazakhstan and Kyrgyzstan
in 2007–2013
With a foreword by Gordon Crawford
ISBN 978-3-8382-1151-0

181 Andrey Makarychev,
Alexandra Yatsyk (eds.)
Boris Nemtsov and Russian Politics
Power and Resistance
With a foreword by Zhanna Nemtsova
ISBN 978-3-8382-1122-0

182 Sophie Falsini
The Euromaidan's Effect
on Civil Society
Why and How Ukrainian Social Capital
Increased after the Revolution of Dignity
With a foreword by Susann Worschech
ISBN 978-3-8382-1131-2

183 Andreas Umland (ed.)
Ukraine's Decentralization
Challenges and Implications of the Local
Governance Reform after the Euromaidan
Revolution
ISBN 978-3-8382-1162-6

184 Leonid Luks
A Fateful Triangle
Essays on Contemporary Russian, German
and Polish History
ISBN 978-3-8382-1143-5

185 John B. Dunlop
The February 2015 Assassination of
Boris Nemtsov and the Flawed Trial
of his Alleged Killers
An Exploration of Russia's "Crime of the 21st
Century"
With a foreword by Vladimir Kara-Murza
ISBN 978-3-8382-1188-6

186 Vasile Rotaru
Russia, the EU, and the Eastern
Partnership
Building Bridges or Digging Trenches?
ISBN 978-3-8382-1134-3

187 Marina Lebedeva
Russian Studies of International
Relations
From the Soviet Past to the Post-Cold-War
Present
With a foreword by Andrei P. Tsygankov
ISBN 978-3-8382-0851-0

ibidem.eu